Redemption

Stories of Hope, Resilience
and Life After Gangs

Redemption

Stories of Hope, Resilience and Life after Gangs

Anne Mahon

GREAT PLAINS
PUBLICATIONS

Great Plains Publications
233 Garfield Street
Winnipeg, MB R3G 2M1
www.greatplains.mb.ca

Great Plains Publications gratefully acknowledges the financial support provided for its publishing program by the Government of Canada through the Canada Book Fund; the Canada Council for the Arts; the Province of Manitoba through the Book Publishing Tax Credit and the Book Publisher Marketing Assistance Program; and the Manitoba Arts Council.

Design & Typography by Relish New Brand Experience
Printed in Canada by Friesens

LIBRARY AND ARCHIVES CANADA CATALOGUING IN PUBLICATION

Mahon, Anne, 1965-, author
     Redemption : stories of hope, resilience and life after gangs
/ Anne Mahon.

Includes bibliographical references and index.
ISBN 978-1-927855-81-2 (softcover)

     1. Ex-gang members--Canada--Biography. I. Title.

HV6439.C3M34 2017   364.106'6092271   C2017-902871-5

ENVIRONMENTAL BENEFITS STATEMENT

Great Plains Publications saved the following resources by printing the pages of this book on chlorine free paper made with 10% post-consumer waste.

TREES	WATER	ENERGY	SOLID WASTE	GREENHOUSE GASES
1	718	1	48	133
FULLY GROWN	GALLONS	MILLION BTUs	POUNDS	POUNDS

 Environmental impact estimates were made using the Environmental Paper Network Paper Calculator 3.2. For more information visit www.papercalculator.org.

Canada

FSC
www.fsc.org
MIX
Paper from
responsible sources
FSC® C016245

Each of us is more than the worst thing we've ever done.

BRYAN STEVENSON (FOUNDER OF EQUAL JUSTICE INITIATIVE),
FROM THE BOOK *JUST MERCY*

The tragedy of life is what dies inside a man while he lives.

BLAIR POPE
OFF THE WALL INMATE PUBLICATION
SASKATCHEWAN PENITENTIARY
JANUARY 1975, VOLUME II #1

The author is donating all proceeds from the sale of this book to support and mentorship for those who want to leave gangs, through the organization GAIN (Gang Action Interagency Network). Visit www.annemahon.ca for more information.

WARNING This book includes some language which may be offensive to the reader but has been included because it is authentic to the participant's voice.

Table of Contents

Foreword

We step out to the margins because it is the only way margins get erased. Look under your feet. Suddenly, we are moving from being separate and superior, to connected and compassionate. We are tentative in locating ourselves at the edges of things because we fear folks will accuse us of wasting our time. But the prophet Jeremiah writes: "For in this place of which you say, 'it is a waste,' there will be heard again the voice of mirth and the voice of gladness…the voices of those who sing."

Anne Mahon, in this fine and sensitive collection, has made those voices heard. She has chosen in *Redemption: Stories of Hope, Resilience and Life After Gangs* to be an enlightened witness, who through her kindness, tenderness and focused, attentive love has returned people to themselves. In this book, she has embodied what James Baldwin called "us achieving ourselves." And these voices come through loud and clear.

For thirty years I've worked with gang members in Los Angeles and have been privileged to be reached by them. My life has been altered and my heart reshaped. And the day won't ever come when I have more courage, or am more noble or am closer to God than the thousands of men and women I've been honoured to know. But no one goes to the margins to rescue anyone or to feel superior. The gift in standing at the edges is not to save the world but to savour it. What we receive is the gift of awe, an ability to stand in awe at what the poor have to carry, rather than in judgment at how they carry it.

Anne Mahon shows us through these clear voices the possibility of our exquisite mutuality. That if we imagine a circle of compassion, and then imagine no one standing outside of that circle, our "standing with" dismantles the barriers that divide. Only then, in this kinship, can we obliterate the illusion that we are separate. This fine book helps us stand against forgetting that we belong to each other. No "Us" and "Them," only "Us."

Anyone who believes in God, believes in a God of second chances. We are heartened to journey with those featured in this book as they come to terms with and do the hard work of transformation. We feel edified to witness people inhabiting the truth of who they are: exactly what God had in mind when God made them. Every story here asserts this: it is the privilege of a lifetime for each one of them to be who they are.

So, we don't go to the margins to rescue anyone. Saving lives is for the coast guard. We wander to the edges...and go figure...we all find rescue there. Every one of us, returned to ourselves. "Oh nobly born," the Buddhists put it, "do not forget who you are."

Redemption: Stories of Hope, Resilience and Life After Gangs is an invitation to our own nobility, found in the exquisite mutuality of kinship. We don't just "observe" these lives here in this volume, but feel, palpably, "Us achieving ourselves."

And before too long, we cease to care if anyone accuses us of wasting our time. "For in this place, of which you say, it is a waste... there will be heard again, the voice of mirth and the voice of gladness...the voices of those who sing." We hear you.

GREG BOYLE, S.J.
FOUNDER OF HOMEBOY INDUSTRIES
AUTHOR OF *TATTOOS ON THE HEART*

Introduction

A book can be a catalyst for another book's creation. The first time I read Father Greg Boyle's book, *Tattoos on the Heart*, it was 2011 and it had just been published. Reading his tender depiction of tough Los Angeles gang members leaving their gangs and transforming their lives was memorable. During the summer of 2013, after the release of my first book, *The Lucky Ones: African Refugees' Stories of Extraordinary Courage*, I had been asking myself what was next for me and whether my first book was a one-off life experience.

My answer was that I wanted to write another. Like my first book, my next would be about a disempowered community of people and focus on hope and transformation. I am an extremely curious person who wants to connect with people on a deep level and bear witness to them, expanding my world and growing in the process. I considered a few different topics, but they didn't feel right.

Then in the fall of 2013, I was serendipitously reminded of Father Greg's book while listening to a speech at an event I was invited to for a completely unrelated reason. I reread his book immediately. A few days later, I was once again asking myself what the topic for my next book could be. The idea floated up effortlessly: a book about Winnipeg gang members who had left their gang and rebuilt their lives. I instantly knew it was the right answer.

I was curious about the kind of lives people live before they join gangs, what being in a gang is really like, and most importantly, how someone entrenched in that violent, criminal world can get out. My challenges would be trying to figure out how to find participants, gain their trust and convince them to share their stories with me, while being an outsider to the gang world. I knew that in writing these stories I would be far out of my upper middle-class comfort zone, but I liked the idea of that. I began to research the topic and community right away.

Like many Canadians, I knew nothing about the realities of crime, gangs and the lifestyle associated with them. My hometown of Winnipeg, however, seemed seriously threatened. A 2014 Winnipeg Police Service report described Winnipeg as "Canada's Aboriginal street-gang capital." The inner city and the storied North End, built by a determined working class, have become neighbourhoods that make many people afraid. Headlines repeatedly document drive-by shootings gone wrong, drugs and prostitutes on too many street corners, and innocent victims of stray bullets. Not surprisingly, accurate gang stats are hard to come by. Winnipeg's Gang Action Interagency Network (GAIN) estimates that in 2014 there were approximately thirty different gangs in Winnipeg and 1,500 active youth gang members, with fifty-eight percent being Indigenous.

SO, ON A SNOWY WINTER DAY in December 2013, a friend of a friend introduced me to P, who had once been the leader of a well-known Winnipeg Indigenous street gang. This new friend knew I would value meeting P. His story was one of power, violence, addiction, prison and, more recently, a new-found Christian faith and a sincere desire to live differently by severing himself from his gang ties. P and his family had moved to a small town outside Winnipeg. P knew he had a reputation that preceded him, so one of the first things he did when he moved to this town was to announce his presence to the local RCMP in order to be agreeable. Shortly after, there was a break-in on his street, a few doors down, and he felt obliged to go right to the RCMP office to declare his innocence.

I met P along with his wife and two young children, at their small, humble, sparsely furnished home. My friend came along to introduce us and help us feel comfortable. P was huge: loomingly tall, muscular, broad-shouldered and imposing. He had tons of tattoos and looked tough. He would have made me nervous under different circumstances, but he had an easy smile I found surprisingly friendly, and his kids were crawling all over him. He offered me a Coke and seemed to genuinely want to talk about his life.

P's current life underlined the enormous cost of leaving gang life behind. His new reality, as he described it to me, was one of a humble return to poverty after the money from crime—and the partying and purchasing it brought—dried up, isolation after separating himself from his old gang members and his entire family who were entwined together, loneliness and fear of discrimination because he was both an outsider in his new small town and racially distinct, fears that his former enemies or gang members would find him (as much as he was trying hard to keep his new location anonymous), and struggles in finding work.

As I listened to him, I was struck by an unexpected parallel—other than his criminal past, P's life and hardships were essentially similar to what I had heard in the refugees' stories I'd documented in my first book. I knew that refugees resettling in Canada face many overwhelming struggles and insurmountable obstacles: difficulties finding meaningful employment, crime-infested, low-rent neighbourhoods, isolation and loneliness while trying to develop new friendships, lack of education, and possible discrimination and judgment. But naïvely I didn't expect someone born locally to be dealing with the same circumstances. I had not had much contact with the locally disempowered and poor. Meeting P reinforced for me that there are many people born and raised in our community, and in Canada, living highly

> His new reality, as he described it to me, was one of a humble return to poverty after the money from crime—and the partying and purchasing it brought—dried up...

marginalized lives. Although P eventually decided not to participate in this book, he contributed to it in a significant way. On that day, he graciously shared the hard truths of his life, and he opened a door for me into a foreign world right here in our province.

Writing this book, I have learned about the darkness of addiction and the violent, chilling worlds of drug dealing and prison life, which go hand in hand with gang activity. Any drug user, even a casual one, is only one step removed from the machine of gang economics and potential violence.

Any drug user, even a casual one, is only one step removed from the machine of gang economics and potential violence.

THE NINE PARTICIPANTS in this book trusted me and generously shared their stories. At times, this felt like a miracle, but at other times it felt completely natural. This book took one year to research and two years to write. During the early phase of research, I reconnected with a local social worker named Mitch Bourbonniere, who I had originally met thirty years earlier through my husband. Mitch specializes in working with gang members who want to leave gang life behind, as well as youth who are on the fringes of gangs and at risk of getting fully drawn in. I remember vividly something Mitch said to me during an early conversation about this future book. He told me I'd need someone to take me into *the jungle* and that he'd be the one.

I met with thirty-five or forty people during that research year, read books, observed workshops for newly ex-gang members that Mitch was facilitating, and asked a lot of questions. When I was ready to interview participants, I had a number of potential people suggested to me and had already been introduced to a few of them. A crucial part of developing trust and getting to know each participant was us being introduced to each other by someone we both already knew and trusted. This created a chain of trust. Although these people who introduced us were not present during the interviews, they had enabled a prior meeting where we got to know each other. There were six different people who did this: friends, co-workers, or people at organizations who provide support services to the participants. Mitch, for example, was one. In some cases, there were a number of people the participants and I knew mutually. I had even coincidentally met two of the participants in my daily life, before they were suggested as possible narrators.

Interviews took place in a private spot in a community space so I felt comfortable. So many people had expressed concern for my safety, but I have not felt afraid. I interviewed each participant at least two or three times (and sometimes up to six), taping our conversations. Once those interviews were transcribed, I diligently wrote from their exact words. Participants' safety has always been a concern for me. What if they divulged personal details that could anger former rivals or once-gang members and create a desire to settle an old disagreement? Each narrator and I have carefully reread their story together so they have approved exactly what is written. At times, we have consciously worded sentences to keep certain details to a minimum. Specific gang names are never mentioned. Each participant has assured me multiple times they are comfortable with what they have shared.

These are stories of rejection, neglect, low self-esteem, violence, abuse, addiction, and regret. But they are also stories full of candid and surprising insights on forgiveness, self-awareness, humility, hope, joy, and trust.

What underlies these personal stories is a tough combination of poverty, family dysfunction, and early exposure to violence. Also, it is important to acknowledge that many of the five Indigenous participants and their families have a history of intergenerational trauma from the impact of colonization, residential schools and other horrific policies that led to stripping Canada's Indigenous of their culture and family life. All these debilitating factors have something in common: they are out of a child's control. As vulnerable children, most participants were left to survive, doing the best they could do, frequently with limited resources and support. These are stories of rejection, neglect, low self-esteem, violence, abuse, addiction, and regret. But they are also stories full of candid and surprising insights on forgiveness, self-awareness, humility, hope, joy, and trust. Demonstrating, perhaps, that those who have seen the darker sides of life are particularly adept at then recognizing life's contrasting goodness.

So, what then is needed to help prevent youth from joining gangs or to assist those who want to leave? Mitch Bourbonniere claims that the biggest need is for positive mentors—quality people who spend time with the ex-gang members and offer support. Troubles often start as early as age nine, ten, or eleven. All the participants in this book understand that and have expressed strong desires to put their lives to good use for others by helping prevent youth from joining gangs. As well, the presence of a positive focus to help former gang members feel good about themselves and to encourage them to stay away from that lifestyle cannot be underestimated. They must have something to go to that makes them feel accepted and valued—employment from a social enterprise business model or the opportunity to educate others by giving talks about gang life, for example.

So, can people change? That is one of the fundamental questions that comes from this book. These participants deserve our open-mindedness as we witness their stories. In conversation, Anonymous, a participant in this book, said, "If we don't tap into the humanity of each story, then we are only looking at the surface and missing the opportunity to connect with the participants. Then we risk sitting in judgment." And, as Father Greg Boyle asks in his foreword, "Can we stand in awe at what these people have faced, instead of standing in judgment?"

I have come to care deeply about each of the participants. We've had enlightening conversations and shared our humanity. I've learned a lot. I miss being with the participants now that the book is completed. At the time that this book is going to print, I find myself out of contact with two of the participants. I've agonized over this, trying everything I could to reach them. One story remains in the book, because it's strong and is the only female story, but the other story was cut because there were some further questions about it that couldn't be verified. Another participant, Chris, experienced a significant personal setback earlier this year. He says he is back on track and hopeful for his future. He is a resilient person. That participant's challenges, together with my inability to make contact with the two others, brought

So, can people change? That is one of the fundamental questions that comes from this book.

me to think even more about the complexity of redemption. Father Greg said to me, "It's not about success, but fidelity." Redemption is possible, but for many, it is challenging and fragile. These insights only make me respect the participants even more. The daily fight for transformation and redemption lives on.

ANNE MAHON
WINNIPEG, AUGUST 2017

CHRIS

It was August 3, 2007 and I was in Headingley jail, lying on my bunk. Suddenly I could feel something in my chest. It felt like I couldn't breathe right, couldn't really move. After we were locked up, I told the guy in the cell beside me, "If you hear me faintly kicking the wall, call the guards and tell them to take me to the medical, man."

He's like, "Why? What's up bro?"
I said, "Fuck, I feel like I'm dying."
He said, "Just go to medical."
I said, "I ain't going to roll out, I ain't no bitch. But something doesn't feel good man. I feel like I'm going to die."

The next morning the guards pulled me out and told me my mom had died that night. I call her my mom, but she's my grandmother. Growing up, she was the only person that I feel ever loved me; with her I knew that I had a home, and I belonged. Her name was Katherine Courchene. She was born on Valentine's Day, February 14, 1948.

So I called home and there was no answer. Next, I called my uncle. When he answered, I said, "What happened? Is Mom dead?" He couldn't talk so he gave the phone to my auntie. I said, "Is my mom dead?"

She said, "Yeah, she died last night." Then I lost it. I blacked out. I don't know what happened after that.

I remember having meetings with the guards later and they said, "You can't go to the funeral. You got this escaping lawful custody charge. You sawed off your handcuffs and you escaped."

I was like, "Yeah, but I'm not going to run away from my mom's funeral, man. If you guys don't let me go, I don't know what I'm going to do here. I really don't give a fuck. I'll fuck this whole place up, I swear to God."

The next day, they said, "Okay, we're going to let you go, but we're going to keep the keys here. You're going to be shackled to your waist and to your ankles. At no time will your handcuffs come off."

I said, "Okay, yeah. That's all I'm asking for. I'm not going to run away."

I went. I was a pallbearer, and fuck, I had to shuffle, pulling my mom's casket. I don't know man. I was so mad at myself. I had never told Mom that I was full-fledged gang banging, but she knew. She could see my colours and the people I was with. She'd say, "Chris, when are you going to get your life together? I didn't raise you to be like this. I didn't teach you to act like that."

I said, "I know Mom."

She said, "When you get out, why don't you go to school, graduate, become something? You're smart. You always have been."

Then I said, "I know, Mom. I promise you when I get out this time, I'll change. I'll go to school. I'll graduate. Just watch."

WE WERE BORN IN WINNIPEG IN 1982, me and my twin sister, Krystal. But we were taken from our biological mother because she was doing time for seventeen robberies. My granny and grandpa legally adopted me from birth and raised me for the first eleven years of my life. That was awesome. My father took custody of my sister Krystal. Years later, he would tell me that he had wanted us both, but he could afford to take only one. My grandpa, he was the chief and counsel on my reserve. I grew up on Fort Alexander, Sagkeeng First Nation. My grandmother was a stay-at-home mom. She spent a lot of time with me. It was the greatest time of my life.

There's no one else that compares to my mom. She was a good listener. She hung on every word I said. We'd go into town to Powerview, and we'd go to Tasty Treats. It was a small place where they sold food. We used to get their mushroom caps and some ice cream. We'd just sit there and talk about everything: about what we wanted to do in life and how we were going to achieve it. She used to talk about how she wanted to graduate from high school and go to college or university and then get a job somewhere. At first, she wanted to be a health care aide or a nurse. She turned out to be a liaison officer at Stony Mountain Penitentiary. That was cool. From my mom, I learned to be assertive, not passive; to take no shit from no one; to talk from the heart when I had something to say; to tell the truth. And, that word is bond, family is everything and no matter where you come from, you are somebody and you can do something.

My grandmother and grandfather got divorced in '93 when I was eleven years old. Their marriage was bad and there were a lot of problems, especially with my grandfather and other women. My grandmother found a new man in her life, Bob. I was mad at him, so I acted out and sometimes wouldn't go to school. Today, I love him and hug him. I appreciate him giving her happiness and love. When the time came to decide who I would live with, my grandmother said I should go with my grandfather. She didn't want to take me to court and have me sit on a bench and decide. She thought there would be more opportunities for me and better schools in Winnipeg. She wasn't aware of the gangs and violence.

So I moved to Winnipeg with my grandfather. We went to live with my biological mother, Suzie. She was more like a sister. I never had love for her like I did for my mom. I understood that she wasn't like a real parent. I'd already heard stories about her. My granny used to say my biological mother had some problems, but she was trying to work through them. She was shooting up, she was drinking, she was sniffing and she was hooking. She was partying all the time. She even got my grandpa on Talwin and Ritalin. When you mix those two together, they make synthetic heroin. Suzie wasn't a good person.

It was residential schools that got her fucked up. That was her hurt. Those schools fucked up my grandparents too, because they always drank even though they were educated. When they were drunk, they'd cry

> Those schools fucked up my grandparents too, because they always drank even though they were educated.

and feel their pain. They'd be talking in their language but I'd get the gist of it. I'd know how they were treated, how they couldn't even speak their own language there. I remember thinking at those times, *All that residential school crap has had its ripple effect and I don't want to be a victim of that.* My whole life had already been affected by them being in residential school, and I didn't want to take on that handicap; I swore I would *never* let it be my handicap. Seeing my family members all fucked up because of what happened in those schools made me want to break the cycle of drinking and violence. What I didn't know then, but realize now, is that I was already living the cycle: the drinking, the violence, the gangs. It took me some time to try to do better.

I left behind my childhood when I got to the city. We couldn't just go to the store and buy food or clothes or presents. No more Christmases after that. Whatever I needed, whatever I wanted, I had to take. My biological mother said, "This is not like back home. You're not living with Granny and Grandpa anymore. Over here you got to grow up and get stuff on your own." I thought, *Okay. Well, if that's the way it is, that's the way it is.*

My first month in Winnipeg, I was already shoplifting to get groceries for myself. Otherwise I couldn't eat. There'd be nothing in the fridge. My biological mother would say, "You're eleven years old; you can get away with anything right now. You could get away with murder, but when you're twelve, you're going to the Youth Centre if you get caught." She schooled me on the justice system. She taught me never to rat, not even on myself. She said, "Don't bother giving the cops any statements, not even on yourself." She said, "That's their job. Let them find out." She took me down Main Street and showed me all the bars and introduced me to the bar owners. I started hustling at those bars—Walkmans, clothes, anything. I even started doing garages: break and enters. Car stereos were a big thing for me because I could pull them out fast. I'd go in there with my flat head screwdriver and, *bang, bang, bang*, I'd pull it out and go sell it at the bar. I was probably doing ten a day. I would make more than enough money. I'd just say, "Here, just take it, $10 or whatever."

I left behind my childhood when I got to the city.

I went to school at first because I wanted to get to know people. I grew up in *Little Chicago, the D*, The Lord Selkirk Developments off Dufferin Avenue. I went to Wellington Elementary when I first got here. Grade 6. There were already gangs—eight or nine different gangs. Fuck, there were lots, man, lots. People were talking about them. Then I went to Niji Mahkwa Aboriginal School and RB Russell High School. I kept going off and on until Grade 9 or 10.

I'd heard stories about the city before I came. My automatic impression was that everyone was a gangster, sold drugs, carried straps and did dirt. And everyone was. You couldn't even go to the other side of the bridges, Arlington or Salter, without having to change your shirt so you could change your colours; otherwise, you'd get done in. The North End was one gang, south of the bridges were a few others. In those days, we used to watch the bridges. Anybody that came over wearing another colour, we'd roll on them, roll hard. We'd fuck the shit right out of them or blast them. I had my first gun at age eleven. I was shooting at people, cars, houses, sometimes shooting at the air. At the time, I was still thinking, *If you shoot at a wall of*

a house, it's going to get stuck in the wall. I didn't realize what I was doing. It didn't even dawn on me that a bullet could go right through a wall and kill someone. I was just a kid. Those were real bad times.

I'd see the gangsters on the streets. They would have gold chains, gold rings, nice clothes, everyone hanging around them. That's what I wanted, so that's what I started working towards. First, I was just rolling with my bros from school. We were doing break-ins—cars and houses—buying weed then breaking them in half and hustling them at the Merchants Hotel. I was trying to get my name up, trying to get people to recognize me. I just wanted people to fear me and not to fuck with me. If no one fucked with me, then I wouldn't have no problems. My dream was to own part of the city one day, like a mayor or something, own the streets with the drug trade. That had been my dream since I moved into the city, because those guys had money and they weren't starving. Everyone respected them and feared them. That's what I wanted.

At age thirteen, even before I joined my first gang, I had my first charge—theft under $5,000 and possession of weapons dangerous to the public peace. I went to Manitoba

Youth Centre. The first legit gang I joined was the big north-side gang. I was fourteen. I was never initiated in or beaten in because my biological mother was a G-girl and all the head gangsters partied with her. One guy made me a G (that's a capital G with two vertical lines through it like the money symbol). He promised me that I'd get my patch when I did my time in Stony—but I never got it.

I was taking so much from my community then: fighting my own kind, making my own people suffer. I didn't even realize that. To me, the people I was hurting weren't like somebody's kid or dad or loved one. I just ruined their lives. I just thought of them as motherfuckers with different colours who were against me.

Once I was eighteen and no longer considered a youth, I got upgraded to the Remand Centre when I was charged, and then, you usually get sent to Headingley. That was awesome, because I finally made it to adult corrections. You could smoke and everyone was there. The gangs were running the jails.

I stuck with that first gang until I was twenty-two or twenty-three. Then I dropped my colours and left the gang because they made me promises that they didn't keep. I did so many missions for people, but when I got locked up, I wasn't getting no help from them. All of a sudden, nobody was sending me money, no one was remembering me. I was getting tired of that. I thought, *I'm building everyone's rep up. What the hell do these other guys do? They just sit there and collect and hustle weed or coke, while I'm out there making the moves, doing the dirt.* I'm like, *Fuck it, I'll just do it myself. I don't have to go through any council.* And some of my bros were turning into crackheads and cokeheads. What happened to the G-code, where you just drink beer and smoke weed? We used to make fun of cokeheads, crackheads and pill junkies because they were fucked. Then my own bros started. And guys were turning into skinners (rapists), getting caught up in banging underage bitches. My OGs were either fucked up on drugs or in prison, and the strikers (next level down) were now in charge. They didn't know me or care about me. I thought, *Fuck these guys.* I'd be getting into trouble because our people were getting fucked up on the streets. I was defending myself. We were rolling (killing) each other—our own people. It was getting ugly. Guys were doing things I didn't agree with.

So me and a couple of other dudes started another gang while we were in Headingley. We were all waiting for sentencing for federal offences and knew we were going to go away for a long time. I was looking at eight years. I had met one of those guys when I was eighteen and he was fifteen. We had always represented together. So we recruited ex-gang guys from my first gang. We didn't want a gang with initiations or ranks, no shit like that. I said, "Come to my side, man. We won't punch you out. We won't give you fifty shots to the face and then call you *bro* after." We wanted to make a big gang because we knew we were all going to the Pen (Stony) once we were sentenced, and it was run by the gangs. We needed numbers. We'd find out what guys were in for, and if they were looking at a lot of time like we were, we'd recruit them. We started recruiting a bunch of murderers. So that's how we came up with our name. Right off the hop, we started beefing with my old gang.

The Crown came to my lawyer and wanted to make a deal: if I'd plead guilty to armed robbery, escaping lawful custody and disguised with intent (wearing a disguise) then they'd lessen another of my armed robbery charges to theft under $5,000 because

they'd found no weapon. I was supposed to have eight years at Stony, but my lawyer blew the first case out of the water. I didn't even find out until the night before the trial. I found his home number and called him up, wondering what was going on with my case. He couldn't believe no one had told me. He said, "You're getting out tomorrow, I made a deal." He found a precedent in a case in Texas that got me off my armed robbery charge because of my wording during the robbery. The Crown couldn't really pin it on me because it was like I'd tricked the cashier at the store into giving me the money instead of implying robbery. I had said to the cashier, *Don't be a heat bag* (someone who's showing the money everywhere). My lawyer said I wasn't actually robbing; I was drunk and laughing. This all felt too good to be true. I had stayed in jail for two years already and got double time for that.

I got out of Headingley on October 3, 2007. When I was being released, I didn't want to leave jail. I cried. Two guards were like, "Okay, roll up for release." I had tears coming down my face.

I said, "Yeah, okay, give me fifteen minutes. I'm just playing a card game."

The other inmates couldn't believe it: "What the are you doing, man?" they'd said. "If I was you, I'd be running to the door right now."

I said, "Why would I want to leave when I got all my brothers here?"

Then the two guards came back twenty minutes later and asked me again to roll up. I said, "Come back after." I was talking to one of my brothers who I'd started the gang with.

He said, "You got to do it, bro. Don't worry. We'll get out soon." Then I gave away my canteen and Walkman, passed them around to my homies.

I said, "Okay, well, I'll fucking go out there and I'll do this for us, man." I was the only one getting out. Everyone else was looking at life sentences or double digits. I felt loneliness. I just wanted to take them all with me. I didn't want to leave unless we all left.

As soon as I got out, I started hustling to support my bros inside. I only supported my homies, the ones on my block, so that was fifteen or sixteen. The gang was recruiting other guys, but some of them I knew from prior and I didn't know why they were being recruited. But I trusted my bros because when I was in jail, they did anything for me. They did dirt inside for me; they were ready to die for me. That was the kind of love I needed that I wasn't getting from my old gang. That's what I wanted, what I needed at the time.

One month after I got out, my son, Ambruce, was born. I had got out for a bit before, but fucked up and breached right away. I was drunk; I wasn't at home, so I got taken back in. I was out only a few days and that's when my girlfriend at the time (who is now my old lady) and I made Ambruce. I think it was a blessing, man.

The minute I held him that first time, it made me think, *What am I going to do? Who the fuck is going to be there for this little guy?* Right away I thought, *This is me, this is mine.* I started relating back to my mom and what she taught me, thinking that she had really loved me. She cared about me when nobody else did. I wanted to be there for my son because I never had a father. I didn't even have a mother. I just had my grandparents. I didn't want my kid to grow up like that. All my friends, their dads were all gone. I thought, *I can't do that to him.*

But I loved my bros too. I kept hustling after I had Ambruce. I was still representing. I didn't want to tell them my plans because they did so much for me. I kept hustling and sending money. I tried to keep my distance from Ambruce, so he wouldn't get taken away by Winnipeg Child and Family Services (CFS). I let his mother take care of him. I would support them and see them every day, bringing groceries and chillin' with them, but I didn't live with them.

I started thinking more and more about family and that I should be doing good. I remembered promising my mom I'd change my life. That's what helped. I couldn't imagine telling her that I didn't do it, again. And my girlfriend said if I went back to jail, she wouldn't bring Ambruce to see me.

Being kidnapped by another gang is what changed everything for me. They pretended it was a drug deal—they had a wad of money to buy. I got into their van and they drove off. It went bad. I thought I was going to die that day. But I escaped out the door of the van at a red light. One guy had me by the hood of my sweatshirt and started stabbing, but I got free of the shirt and ran. I was like, *I got to be in my son's life. I don't give a shit about nothing. Fuck all these guys. I have to do this.*

I'm ready to die for him. I don't give a fuck about nobody else. If they come after me... I'll die for my kid. At least he'll know I died for him. That was maybe six months after he was born. So I put down the drugs and the colours, went back to work and went to school. I didn't really come into his life permanently until then.

After that, I started getting word from the Pen, Headingley, Brandon, that people were calling me a rat, hating on me because I turned my back on them. I said, "I don't give a fuck. You guys know where I am, where I live. You know what I'm about. If you really want to take it down that road, I'm there man." I was willing to fight for my life and for my future with my son.

When my buddy, the one I started the gang with, got out, it was all good. People tried to talk shit about me, but he went down to their houses, kicked the doors open and punched them out. He was okay with me leaving because we were brothers since we first met, when we scrapped it out in the developments. (That's how I met a lot of my bros. We'd be at a party and somebody'd give me "the look."

I was willing to fight for my life and for my future with my son.

ON JUNE 8, 2008, I found my first real job with BUILD (Building Urban Industries for Local Development). My probation officer had heard about BUILD. It's part of an Aboriginal social enterprise that accepts people with backgrounds like mine, where we receive training, job experience and a supportive environment. It helps us go from being unemployable to being an asset in the labour market. While at BUILD, I took a parenting course, a budgeting course, workplace safety course, first aid and CPR. I even got my driver's licence through their drivers' licensing program. This social enterprise group is made up of non-profit organizations that got together to work on problems in the inner city. And the solutions are employment, mental health support and job opportunities. That's what BUILD brings to the table. The only profit is in making the community stronger.

Then we'd just scrap it out. Whether I won or lost, afterwards we'd all drink and it'd be good.) My brotha's in Stony right now, doing life. I call him *brotha* because he's more than just a *bro*; he's like family. His story would have been mine, if I hadn't changed my life around.

Life ain't so hard if you got somebody behind you. Shaun Loney formerly at BUILD and my current boss, Lucas Stewart, are those guys. They're my hype-men. Without that kind of support, I don't know... The opportunity to work meant everything to me. Because I thought, *Who's going to give me a job?*

Who's going to trust me? But it was weird. I'm Aboriginal, coming from the ghetto, ex-con, ex-gangster from the north side, good for nothing, just straight from the gutter, straight from the dirt and these two well-respected men backed me in every way they could. And they're white.

I became a construction supervisor for Manitoba Green Retrofit (MGR) in the fall of 2013. MGR is a sister company to BUILD. We specialize in retrofitting low-income housing. We make everything look brand new so the next tenants can have somewhere decent to call home. We change lighting, do basement and wall insulation, change older furnaces to energy-efficient ones and install low-flush toilets.

I've surprised a lot of people I used to know from the 'hood. Especially when they see me driving. They're all like, "Chris, you got a car now?"

And I say, "Yes, I do." They ask if I'm hustling or something, and I say, "It's a whole different type of hustle now." They're surprised because we all grew up together and we were all about the same thing—making money and building our names up. Now I'm back in the same 'hood, but it's like I'm on the other side of a big fence and we're talking through it. If you want to be a gangster you can't come through. I'm working for a living and changing the community with every house we turn over, and every job we take. It's all about helping the community. When people who knew me from my past see what I'm doing, it gets them thinking that maybe there's something they can do too, to change their lives and their communities. I have people I grew up with and we were in bad situations and some of us are still stuck there. But they see people like me, people who got a chance to work and make a difference. They're thinking, *If Chris can do it, and he comes from where I came from, then I can do it too.*

I got people who look up to me and who are changing their lives because I'm changing mine. I don't know—it's just fucking weird, and awesome, and fortunate, and a blessing. To have this chance, to have people like Shaun and Lucas believe in me. I never thought I'd see a day like that. They helped me save my life. They gave me one to save.

Anyone can come up to me, someone that comes from the gutter, that comes from the struggle, and I'll break my back trying to help them. I will give them that chance too. I'll take them places they never thought they could be. I'll help make them the people they always wanted to be. I'm part of something that's greater than myself. Fixing up those houses no one wants to live in, I'm helping take care of people who no one else wants to help. I feel good about helping.

When I got my first paycheque from BUILD, I though, *Man, I could make this in one chop, one drug deal*. I was living off $700 every two weeks for a family of three. And I started to have anxiety attacks. It's easier to be a gangster and not give a fuck. You feel carefree as long as you're breathing. I was working, not selling drugs no more, I had a son. And I could barely afford rent, then there were the other expenses like diapers and clothes... But I had promised not to go back to hustling or being a gangster. I had made that promise to my mom, to myself and to my son. So I thought, *I got to go to school.*

After my six-months training course was up, BUILD gave me a certificate so that I could get a job with a construction company. When Shaun asked me what I wanted to do, I said, "Well, your construction supervisor here has a grade 8 education and he became a red-seal carpenter and he's Aboriginal. His kids grew up white. That's the way I want to be." Growing up white meant like in the movies—the three-bedroom house with the lawn; the white fence and a cherry tree in the front; the mother and father both home being there for the kids; and the kids going to good schools. It would be a healthy environment, actual family stuff. And I wanted to become a red-seal carpenter because that would make me certified across Canada. Shaun told me my best bet would be to go to school, because I was still young. So I said, "That's what I want to do, go back to school and become a red-seal carpenter."

Shaun said, "You don't want to go and get a job?"

And I said, "I don't want to work, I want to get a higher education so I can get paid more. I want to work my way up and maybe I can even become a boss here." They said that if this was really what I wanted to do, they would try to help me get schooling and

But I had promised not to go back to hustling or being a gangster. I had made that promise to my mom, to myself and to my son. So I thought, *I got to go to school.*

I should pursue it. They told me I could do it. How could these guys see so much in me when I couldn't see that myself? They gave me the confidence to be the man I am today. They've shown me how easy it can be to set a goal, take hold of it and make it happen. I never knew it could be this easy. But that's what it feels like when these guys are telling me what I am capable of.

So I went back to high school and finished my grade 12 as a mature student. They took me to the Aboriginal Centre and then RB Russell School. I felt more comfortable at RB Russell because that's where I had gone before when I tried to go to school. I lived close by and my cousins were going to that school too. I had friends and family to give me support. It was hard at times; English and computers were tough, but math came pretty easy to me. I made out okay financially because I had employment insurance from my time at BUILD and I got support from my band and council.

After I graduated, I gave Shaun the idea of apprenticing Level I carpenters because then they'd know more than the basics. It took me two-and-a-half years to complete my Level I apprenticeship and become a lead hand. When I graduated from high school and also my Level I carpentry, I dedicated my diploma to my mom. I said, "This is for my mom, Katherine. See, I told you I could do it. I didn't lie this time."

In 2010, the John Howard Society flew me to Ottawa and I spoke about Bill C-10 (now Bill C-31) on behalf of 700,000 ex-cons to the members of Parliament. The Conservatives had record suspensions, instead of pardons. Now I am ready to take the next steps to move on to my second apprentice level, but I can't do it with a criminal record. I feel that the proposed legislation paints everyone with the same brush. I think that the pardon should be meant for people who clearly have demonstrated, without a doubt, that they have reformed and that they have only a very small chance of re-offending. All these guys were in business suits and ties. They got cameras following them around. They said, "Wow, this guy is an everyday Aboriginal from the ghetto and he really changed his life around." I felt respected. I felt like I was given a chance to talk. I was speaking and somebody was actually listening and taking note. A pardon one day would mean a clean slate, sort of like being baptized—my sins would be washed away. I could move on with my life.

THE JOY I FEEL TODAY is nothing I can describe. I can't even put it into words. I'd have to make up new words for joy, greatness, love. Every day I open my eyes is a blessing. Back in the dark days, I didn't even want to open my eyes. My daughter, Sabrina Katherine, was born in 2010. I am happiest when I am with my kids and my old lady. We go out, we play, we stay home; we'll just be together. To be with my kids, to talk with them, to hold them, to kiss them, to love them—that's the best feeling ever. To sit there, eating some toast, talking about our day; that's what means everything to me.

> Every day I open my eyes is a blessing. Back in the dark days, I didn't even want to open my eyes.

Every day, my son tells me he loves me and, every day, I tell him I love him. We tell each other when we wake up, before we go to bed and even throughout the whole day: "I love you, dad."

"I love you, son." I say, "Who's the best daddy?"

"You are."

"Who's the coolest?"

"You are."

I say, "Why do you love me, son?"

He says, "Because you take us places and buy me stuff and spend time with me."

I say, "That's it?"

He's like, "Oh, oh, and you're the handsomest!"

I say, "There we go, my boy!"

I tell my son the truth about my gang life. I'll never lie to him. He will be the only one that will know my deepest, darkest secrets.

He knows that I've been to jail. He says, "Daddy, you used to be a bad guy?"

"Yup"

"You're a good guy now, eh dad?"

I say, "Yup."

He says, "You're the best dad eh?!"

MY BIOLOGICAL MOTHER PASSED AWAY IN 2008, nine months after I got out of prison. My twin sister, Krystal, committed suicide on October 3, 2011. It was hard for her when our biological mother died. She loved her and missed her and wanted to be with her. Without our mother, my sister would feel just pain, a constant pain in her heart.

When I was a kid, my mom took us to church. I used to go to Sunday school and

I got my first communion and all that. We were Catholic. I don't care about church, but I believe in Jesus. I love him. I believe he's real. I also believe in my Aboriginal culture. I don't see much difference between the two, other than how we speak to God. Religions don't bug me because I see everybody looking up and they're all praying to someone. It's all the same energy, regardless of whether they believe in Jesus or something else. I told my son, "You got to love Jesus more than you love Daddy, more than you love Mommy, more than you love Sabrina."

He's like, "Okay."

I said, "You have to." Because then he can go to heaven, even though I can't. At least he can go there. I've turned my life around, but I don't know if I can do that many rights to make up for all the wrongs that I've done.

But don't judge me because of who I was, because that's not me today and it never will be again. The man I am today is just as good as any other man out there without a criminal record, who's not a gangster. I'm just as good as anybody else. If my mom could see me now, she'd probably say, "Yee hoo! See my boy, I told you you could do it."

I was introduced to Chris by Shaun Loney who hired him at BUILD. Shaun has a passion and infectious hope for his work of employing those generally considered unemployable. When I met Chris, he immediately committed to being in the book and to being identifiable. He told me he has no fear about living his life now. It strikes me that Chris is a man who keeps his promises—to his mom; to his bros in prison, supporting fifteen or sixteen guys for some time; to his family; and to me.

But Chris also reminds me that redemption and change are fragile. Recently Chris shared with me that he'd just gone through some dark times. He said, "I got blinded by addiction and the money," dealing and using again after nine years clean. He graduated from rehab this summer. He said, "I now feel like I'm back on track and back to reality. There's going to be some tough days and slips, but you don't have to give up easily."

Thank you to Dave Kattenburg of www.greenplanetmonitor.net for sharing content from his October 2013 interview with Chris for his podcast entitled "The Power of Social Enterprise."

JUSTIN

My anger comes from my mother and my good heart comes from my father. That's the thing about me—I've always, always had a good heart. Maybe that's what led me to the gangs. I was stupid and naïve enough to think that the gang members were *my boys* and I wanted to help them.

I grew up in The Maples in Winnipeg, an area people considered middle class. I come from an Asian family. My parents were immigrants from the Philippines, but my older sister and I were born here in Canada. My mom was the homemaker of the family. She had a few odd jobs for pay, like the one in a sewing factory, but she didn't work very often. My dad was really the only one working and he didn't get paid much. He made enough to pay the mortgage and groceries. I have a sister, two years older than me. As I look at it now, we were a pretty low-income family.

My early years were spent playing, having fun and feeling free. Our family used to go camping when I was young. There weren't too many responsibilities or stresses for me. I was just happy. Things started to change around grade 4 when I was eight or nine and many of the other kids were playing organized sports. The guys playing soccer were really good, and a couple of guys took karate—these were the popular kids. My dad said he'd put me in karate, but that didn't end up happening. I don't think he could afford to. I was a sensitive kid and I wanted to fit in with the other kids playing sports. It started to really bother me—I wanted to be part of that group. I always wanted to have friends, a lot of friends. I wanted to be liked.

Around the same time, things started to change with my mom too. There was a lot of abuse from her. When my dad disciplined us, it was only once in a while. He would give us a beating, but I knew that I had done something wrong when my dad hit me. But with my mom, there were times when we just didn't know what we'd done wrong. One time, my sister dropped a desk drawer on her toe and cut it open. You'd think our mother would have comforted her, but instead she viciously beat her—pulled her hair and scratched her. I turned away, didn't do or say nothing, but she beat me too. If one got a beating, the other got a beating. But for what? I didn't know what made my mom that way. She had a lot of heat in her.

But now I understand a bit better why my mom was an angry person. It was the life she'd lived. I started to dig around and I talked to my grandma (my mom's mom). My mom was born when her mom was young and it was too hard to take care of her, so she gave my mom away. My grandma's sister raised her. And who knows what relationship my mom and dad had. They each slept in their own beds.

My aunt (my mom's sister) and her family lived next door to our house. While I was growing up, it was always my mom, her sister (my auntie), my grandma, my sister and then my cousin—they did everything together and left me at home a lot. (My cousin was gay and came out when he was fifteen. He was always very feminine.) They'd go to the States on weekends or go shopping and they'd never take me. My dad would be tired from work so he napped a lot on the weekends. My mom said I didn't listen and I ran around too much. I believe now that I had ADHD when I was a kid. I'm on medication for it now. But in my mom's eyes back then, I was a bad kid. Now I think, what did I do that was so bad? Running around a mall? Not listening? Wanting to play all the time? I was just being a kid. Being left alone made me feel like I didn't have nobody else. That was a big hurt for me.

All the girls, my grandpa and my cousin, they'd be in my uncle's station wagon, with him driving. Once in a while my grandpa would tell them straight, "Why are you guys leaving Justin at home all the time?" I remember this one time, they were getting ready to leave and I was crying. Someone put a Bruce Lee movie on for me, but I was still upset. My grandpa grabbed me and put me in the back of the station wagon. He shouted at my mom, "Why the fuck do you keep leaving him at home?" The group in the car gave each other looks; I knew they didn't want me to come. My grandpa was there for me. Even years later, when I was locked up at the Youth Detention Centre in Tuxedo, he'd ride his bike from The Maples just to come and visit me.

My dad was always a man for letting things go. Anytime something angered me, he'd just say, *Don't worry.* My dad helped his family out a lot. I had an uncle who was always Mr. Showboat. He owed a lot of money and my dad helped him pay it back. My dad would also help my sister out by picking up my niece at things and driving her home. He'd always be bringing food to my sister too. (I guess I'm like my dad because, over the years, whenever I've had money, I've always given some to my friends or my family. I've given my sister a lot—she's a single parent—and every time my mom or my dad asked, I'd give them money too.)

I was really angry as a kid. At school, I got into trouble as long back as I can remember. I couldn't really concentrate. I think it was the ADHD, but back then I don't think teachers knew what it was I had. They just labelled me a bad kid. I was always messing around, being annoying. I was usually one of the last ones on the speed math tests we used to do. On my report cards, I'd get S for "satisfactory" or NS for "not satisfactory." I rarely got G for "good" and never VG for "very good," but I don't remember my parents bitching at me for my marks. I remember the one time I did get Gs on my report card—that was in grade 3. I got all Gs and Ss. It wasn't the best, but it was still good.

I used to get in physical fights with kids in the class too. I remember this one bully in grade 4. He was picking on kids and punching them in their faces. I liked to help other people in any way I could be of assistance. (Maybe it was part of the wanting-attention thing, you know.) So I thought, *Screw this. I'll go fight him.* He really gave it to me and beat me up. I was one of those kids that pushes instead of punches. But he punched me like in a real fight. I had a bleeding nose, I felt like crap and I was embarrassed. I sat at home and thought about how I had to fight him again and do better. The next week I built up the courage, tapped him on the shoulder, and when he turned around, I did to him what he had done to me. I really wailed on him and made him cry. I learned how to fight from that guy.

School wasn't going good and I never got attention from my family, so being labelled as a bad kid was the only attention I ever got, and that's what I loved—being bad. It was cool. By the end of grade 6, I was recruited to be part of a crew. It was an Asian-based gang and our name was about being brothers. The guys who recruited me were older, grades 9 or 10. That's how gang members find their little gang members: they pick eleven- or twelve-year-olds with some dysfunction in their lives and they recruit them. When they recruited me, I felt like money, like gold. I felt as though I was finally accepted somewhere. I had a few friends who told me not to join, but I told them not to worry. I joined anyways.

> School wasn't going good and I never got attention from my family, so being labelled as a bad kid was the only attention I ever got, and that's what I loved—being bad.

I should have been depending on my family instead of the gang, but I wanted to be accepted by these guys. We hung out at the basketball court in The Maples. There were maybe thirty of us. We'd get into fights—nothing big, just fistfights. We smoked some pot, but it wasn't like the serious drugs I'd get into later in my life. That gang only lasted a year. It was a little pansy gang. It was nothing.

By then, I wasn't going to school much. I couldn't sit there. I couldn't learn. I'd just get there and want to get out and hang with the boys. They were all skipping school too. Sometime during that year, I was skipping so much that I didn't even finish grade 7. I'd been given a lot of chances from the principal of Ken Seaford School, Mr. McKinley. He was the only principal I knew who'd give me a chance, but I'd screw it up.

Things weren't good at home either. I think I was twelve the last time my parents ever laid hands on me. I had had a teacher in an earlier grade tell me that my mom and dad had no right to hit me. I started thinking about that. I started to rebel back and tell them straight,

"You can't touch me." When my mom tried to hit me, I'd push her back. I also started to run away from home. I'd go to friends' houses, but then the next day, their parents would take me right back home. My parents were getting worried, I could tell. They used to ask me, "Why are you doing this?"

Then I started hanging out with another group of guys. They weren't a gang; they were independents. We just hung out and smoked weed. They were older too, maybe in grade 11, and had driver licences. I think I was thirteen. We started stealing clothes. We were at Polo Park Mall and I wanted to be the cool kid. I grabbed a pair of jeans from a store, put them in my jacket, and just walked off. My friends didn't even know. Then when we got to the car, I pulled out the jeans and everyone was like, "What the hell?!" I felt like wow. I had wanted some new clothes, seeing we never got anything we wanted when we were kids, and I wanted to put on a show for these guys. So I started stealing more... and more... and more. That became a trend. Some of the guys I hung around with even started stealing laptops and crazy, high-end stuff.

Then we moved on; we started jumping guys. We'd drive around and jump people on the street for their jackets. We'd park the car a few blocks away, then plan everything out and watch for a guy. We'd jump out of the bushes, circle him, start beating him up and steal his jacket, or his skateboard and other stuff. We did it because we wanted things and money. We'd go buy some weed or some junk food from 7-Eleven. But we also wanted the power.

I got charged for the jumpings (robberies) and got locked up. The cops caught the plate number of the guy who drove us around. He wrote a statement on my friend, and then my friend wrote one on me. The cops picked me up, charged me, and put me in the Youth Detention Centre. I was thirteen. I was scared when I was getting locked up, but I also felt cool again. It just fueled the fire inside me even more. I got out on bail on that first robbery charge, and the judge gave me probation. But I went right back to the jumpings. The next time I got charged, it was because we beat a guy up really badly. Something happened with the guy's spleen and he was hospitalized for a while. I didn't even hit him. This other guy hit him with a bat and stomped on him. I was just standing there looking. I took the rap and never ratted out that guy. So my next charge was aggravated assault. That's when I did my first stint, six months in the Youth Detention Centre. Open custody.

With open custody, you sign a form for your day pass and go to school outside. They gave us bus tickets to ride the bus to school. (Later on, that would be taken away because a bunch of kids were going on leaves and stealing cars. They got into a high-speed chase and killed someone.) I went to school but that didn't last long. First, I went back to Ken Seaford School. I was maybe in grade 9 then; I don't know for sure. The first day I went back to school from the Youth Centre I was with this Aboriginal dude from the Centre—he was older than me. We didn't even make it to school. His apartment was close by, so we went there instead. We just hung out and smoked cigarettes. We came back to the Youth Centre at the end of the day and we thought everything was good. But the Centre's staff found out and I was made to stay in my room there for a week, for skipping school. They didn't send me back to Ken Seaford. Next, they sent me to Edmund Partridge School on Main Street. I was given more bus tickets, but this time I went to school because I felt I had to. They put me in "the rubber room"—it was a portable on the school grounds, but in the back. It was where all the bad kids went. We weren't even allowed inside the school. It was crazy. One of my good friends today, KC, was there along with his brother. KC never got into the gangs as deep as I did. He was just with a little gang of local boys back in the day. I lasted maybe a couple of months there, only until my time at the Detention Centre expired. Then I dropped out right away.

THE YOUTH DETENTION CENTRE is where I made good connections with guys who I'd join up with later on. It's the school of hard knocks, and it's not a very good place to be. They're building a monster there because people are meeting each other and making plans. Some of us guys talked about being in a bigger crew together, some of the guys would become some of the biggest drug dealers in the city and some would also later become my enemies. Guys on the outside were bringing me things—money, clothes— while I was inside. When I was out, they'd treat me so good: I'd go to eat in restaurants and they'd buy me mad bottles (lots of booze) when we partied. Those guys were making so much money, I thought they were ballin'. I also got into stealing cars with a guy I met in the Detention Centre. I grew up too fast being in there.

By the time I got out, my parents didn't have any control over me anymore. I was maybe fourteen. They couldn't do nothing. They tried to get so many different people involved. My parents had a good friend who was in the RCMP. He was always trying to help me, talk to me, but it just didn't work. I was running away from home constantly. One day, my sister saw me on the bus. She was crying and she gave me some money. I guess it was stressful for her too. I was running away because my parents didn't accept me. But it was my choice to run away, right? I could have done something different, maybe talked to my parents. But our family was built not to talk about things, especially things inside ourselves.

Then I joined the next gang that formed. It would eventually become a big organized Aboriginal street gang. This group took gangs to a different level. A Filipino guy, who grew up with guys from that crew, came to The Maples to recruit for the gang. He was

making an Asian-based chapter. I didn't last long in it. I quickly caught this guy's drift—he had us stealing money and cars, but we had to give it all to him. He gave us rags like nothing. (He gave us bandanas with the colours of the gang without us having to do any initiation, and later, he was even patching guys over without knowing them.) The Asian part of the gang quickly broke up.

I stayed under the radar and out of the Detention Centre for a couple of years. My dad moved me to Vancouver to live with my uncles, but that didn't work. Instead, I hooked up with my cousins and their friends. It was still drugs and gangs. The gangs there were more sophisticated than in Winnipeg. They were on a whole different level. I came back to Winnipeg because my uncles couldn't handle me. It's a good thing I left there because I would have become out of control.

When I came back to Winnipeg, I started dealing weed for my friend, but that didn't last long. I ended up smoking everything he gave me. He was pissed off at me. I asked him to give me another batch so I could make it up to him, but he said no. Then I started driving around with an older friend who was running crack. I took a bunch of money that wasn't mine and spent it. It was like 1,000 bucks. But nobody did nothing to me. I had a lot of respect from being in the Youth Centre, doing stupid stuff and hurting people. I was this type of guy—little, but violent. If you messed around with me, you were going to get it: either you'd get stabbed or I'd pipe you out with something. I could really hurt people. In the gang life, I knew how to put fear in people. That's another thing that probably fuelled me to be who I was.

Then when I was sixteen, I hooked up with some friends, kids that weren't even bad; they were just school friends from the neighbourhood. One day, we were walking around and I had this BB gun. I remember it was wintertime and I had a big jacket on. All of a sudden, I looked at this gas station and told my friends to come with me. I put my shirt over my face and told the guys to do the same. They wanted to know why, but I told them to just come with me. We robbed the gas station and got a wad of money. We started robbing convenience stores and gas stations all over the city. It was BB guns and meat cleavers. We probably robbed ten or fifteen in the span of a week.

In the gang life, I knew how to put fear in people. That's another thing that probably fuelled me to be who I was.

We were trying to be smart, dividing into two different groups and going to different parts of the city, but then we got caught. We had robbed a Subway Restaurant in Charleswood and the cops saw us driving down Roblin Blvd. I don't know what they knew, but they did a U-turn and pulled our minivan over. We tried to be casual about it, but the others were just schoolboys, goody-goods that I had pulled into this mess. After we were arrested, most of them wrote statements. They got off, but I got three years. I got the maximum because I had an extensive record for assaults and robberies. I had no way out. I started doing my time in the Youth Centre.

I wasn't good in the Youth Centre. I was fighting and causing shit, so I got transferred to the Agassiz Youth Centre in Portage la Prairie, a town close to Winnipeg. (I had already turned eighteen.) I lasted one week in there. It was a weird place with a peer-group thing going on. Instead of the counsellors or administration working with the detainees, the youth inmates counsel each other. On my first day, we sat in a circle and the others introduced themselves. We stated our charges.

I was with guys that were in there for rape. In jail, they're called skinners. Rape is something that you just don't do. It's very wrong. In the Youth Centre, I had been locked up with this guy that was there for sexually assaulting some kids. Almost every day, he'd get a beating from me or someone else. So my eyes kinda lit up when I heard that there were skinners there at Agassiz. (I've changed my view on rapists since then. I've worked in programs with kids that had sexual assault charges and I've come to realize that, unless he's a predator, a rapist is like any other human being that needs to do the work to turn things around, especially if he's a guy who's sincere.)

When this one guy at Agassiz told us he was a skinner, I said, "What the fuck?"

Another guy in the group said to me, "Check yourself." I guess it meant check, see what you're doing here, stop and think. I thought, *What? This guy's a skinner*!

So I said to him, "Fuck you."

After they had to tell me to check myself a couple more times, someone said, "Group, steady out." Then these kids started calling me out saying, "Do you recognize what you're doing here?"

I said, "Oh my God, are you serious? I'm already eighteen." I was the oldest one there. These were just kids. I told the staff I wanted to sign a waiver and get out of there; I wanted to go to an adult facility. I told them that if they didn't move me I was going to hit someone. They didn't budge on moving me to Headingley so *Boom*, I hit someone. The whole group tackled me and restrained me. It was the guys in there who did that, not the staff. After that, they put me in the quiet room and left me there in my underwear. At night, they gave me back my mattress and a blanket. I repeatedly told the staff I wanted to go to Headingley. After a week, they finally agreed I could be transferred, so I went to court and signed the waiver.

When I went to Headingley, I wasn't in a gang. I was just alone. I was nervous, but one of my old gang buddies was there and we reconnected. I was constantly getting into fights. Lost some, won some. I was still skinny and little, but I could throw my own. I helped out my buddy in there a couple of times when he had beefs with guys. I was sent to Brandon Correctional for a while too because of my fighting.

While I was in Brandon, my grandpa died. It was 1999. I was allowed to go to the funeral. They gave me an escort and shackles. I got to wear my own clothes: dress pants, dress shoes, and a polo. I didn't cry. I guess I was out of tears. I was happy to see my family, but I *loved* seeing my good childhood friends from school. I was always happy with my friends. They were like my family should have been for me.

Shortly after the funeral, I was transferred back to Headingley. When charged as a youth under the Youth Act, you have the right to apply for early release. I applied, but I thought I wasn't going to get it because of being bad and doing all that fighting. One of the guards came to support me in court, which was a big surprise. The judge saw that I hadn't been put on probation earlier when I was released from doing my maximum youth time, which is usually supposed to happen. That was a technicality. So he released me five months early and I did the rest of my time on probation. I was very happy to be out. I went back to my mom and dad's house. I stayed maybe six months. I remember partying and celebrating my twenty-first birthday there. Things with my parents were okay. They didn't have control over me; they let me do whatever I wanted so they could keep me home and safe.

ALL MY BUDDIES WERE INVOLVED in selling drugs: working for people, taking orders on the phones, driving around, doing deliveries. Money was there. I drove around with them to different places while they did their deliveries. I started hanging out with these twin brothers who were really heavily involved with the drug game. They were moving a lot of stuff, mostly crack, through the West End of Winnipeg. They started to make some noise and attract police attention. There was this puppet crew for a biker gang that was trying to take over the whole city including the West End, where the twins were big competition. A bunch of my friends were aligned with these twins. So pretty soon, we started to regroup and fight the biker gang. We were in a turf war, but I didn't consider our group a gang. To me, it was just a bunch of West

> I was happy to see my family, but I *loved* seeing my good childhood friend from school. I was always happy with my friends. They were like my family should have been for me.

End boys who had grown up together and had started to make some money. But I guess anytime the police see a group like ours, they label them a gang. I was part of that group. That's when things started to get serious.

I was basically seen as the muscle, doing collections and muscling people—doing dirt is what that's called. That's how I made my money. I was political. I'd come in and show face, warning other guys to get off our guys. I advocated to make sure things were okay between this crew and that crew. I wasn't dumb. I made sure people were getting along for the most part and that our crew wasn't making too many enemies, that we weren't doing too many stupid things like robbing other gang members or fighting over a girl. Getting along would benefit everybody because people would get more drugs that weren't diluted. Then everybody could make money. But there were a lot of stupid things that were done anyway and, unfortunately, we did make a lot of enemies. I was an easy-going guy, a good talker, a salesman. But if the other guys gave us no choice, there would be consequences. I always, always, always had my hand at my waist. The gun was always cocked. Just pull it out and *Boom*. I was always ready.

Eventually the crew got greedy. Everybody does. The twins started depending on their guys hustling to make more money. They taxed them. The twins wanted to kill a buddy of mine really bad because he lost a lot of their money. My buddy moved to Vancouver and went into hiding. The crew couldn't get to him, so they got to his older brother who lived here and had a wife and kids. They visited their house every other day and beat up the brother in front of his kids and wife. This brother was also in the drug game, but not with this crew. Things changed for me then. It's a rule that you don't involve kids or family. So the next year, 2002, I left the twins' crew and joined a new one.

It's a funny story, how I became friends with B, the leader. It was summertime and he had a nice car. We were cruising around in his Mustang convertible: B, his brother, and me. B said, "Hey Ho, you have to get this guy named Justin for me." (Back then, even though everyone knew me by my street name, Jose, B's brother had given me the nickname Ho. It came from a line in a Jay Z song. The nickname isn't about screwing around with girls or anything.)

I said, "Justin. Why?"

B says, "He's this kid from The Maples. He tried to jack one of my buddies."

Three weeks before, I had one of their guys, a full patch member, in my van and I was going to take his drugs and money, but he got away. I didn't know at the time that he was friends with B.

I said to B, "You're sure you want to go after this guy? I know him."

"Yeah," he says. "We need to get him."

I always had this little gun on me; it was a 25. I pulled it out and put it to his neck while he was driving. I said, "I'm him." I cocked the hammer back and said, "Pull over."

B says, "No, let's just talk. Let's talk." So we talked. The guy I had planned to jack was this little Osborne Village kid in B's crew who made lots of money; he had a lot of crystal-meth people locked down around the Osborne Village area. B and I talked about the situation and ended up laughing about it. Later, he made me shake the guy's hand. B and I got closer after that.

B, the leader, had maybe thirty guys on his side of the gang. He had recruited white kids who dealt crystal meth in Osborne Village. I led the Asian side. We had, easily, 150 guys. Although the majority were Asians, there were also Blacks and Aboriginals. That crew became big. A lot of people thought our crew was aligned with a major biker gang, but we weren't.

The twins gave me trouble when I left and joined B's gang, but it backfired. When I came into B's gang, I became a loose cannon. We were raging wars on a lot of crews, but especially the twins' crew. That's how I got known. Houses were getting shot up, people being shot. I have friends that are now doing time for murder. The twins aligned with another well-known crew of brothers. That led to a turf war. But for me, it wasn't even a turf war, it was personal. I had had enough of the twins going after my buddy's brother and family. So I told my buddy that was hiding in Vancouver that he had to come back to Winnipeg and fight this war, or he wouldn't be my friend. He came back and he stood by my side. This all went on for a year or two.

Our gang started to get in the limelight then and our heads started to get really big with all the power, money, drug turf. We tried to take over the central area in the North End, around Dufferin and Salter, over the Arlington Bridge. We were trying to get in there and guns were blazing. That was the turf of the gang founded by the bunch of brothers. They stood their ground. I respect them for that. You can't lie down; that shows weakness. Later on, a lot of those guys—old-school guys—would become my friends. It's funny how a lot of enemies become friends, later on, in jail.

IN LATE 2004, I WENT TO JAIL AGAIN. I went in for kidnapping; that's what they say. I had been with some guys from another Asian crew who were looking for two guys who owed them some money. I thought they were going to beat them up. When they spotted them in a restaurant, we all went in and instead, they kidnapped them. These guys were stupid, because they grabbed the two guys right in front of witnesses in the restaurant. It was all over the news. I got out on bail six months later and then the charges were dropped in March 2006. I was in the Remand Centre first. There was a lot of shit going on in there, a lot of people getting muscled and beaten up. The staff blamed our crew, so they put some of us in the hole—solitary confinement. I spent five of my six months in solitary. That was at the end of 2004 and the beginning of 2005. I know, because that's when my daughter was born.

KEITH LEVIT

I had met my girlfriend in 2003; today, she's my wife. We met in the bars and she just started hanging around. At first, she wanted to be with me because I was a bad boy, but then she saw something more in me, maybe that there was a heart there too.

The staff at the Remand Centre said I could have an escorted visit to see my daughter at the hospital when she was born, but then they didn't let me do that. I don't know why. I held my anger in at first. Then they promised me an open visit with my daughter and my wife, but when that didn't happen either, I flipped out. There were three of us in the hole at that time. After getting our thirty minutes outside of solitary, we covered the camera pods (where the guards watched us from their office) with newspaper, threw stuff around, and made threats with broomsticks in the common area. We refused to be locked up for about six hours. So the swat team, who were guards trained on how to raid a room, had to come in. They took us to the hole in Headingley.

I did get a few visits with my daughter while I was in Headingley. The first time I held her, I was shocked to have this little baby in my arms. I know I was happy and felt some joy, but at that time hustling and gangs were the only way of life I knew, so I continued on with that.

I SPENT MY ENTIRE SIX MONTHS in Headingley in the hole. I tried not to think much about my wife and daughter. That would just cause a lot of stress. When you're in jail, you've got to focus your mind and keep face, not show any signs of being upset. You can get beat up for roughing it, for showing your emotions. If you show that you're stressing, then others feel that negative energy and get stressed too. No one wants to see it, because nobody wants to go through that themselves.

When you're locked in the hole, there's nothing to do for the twenty-three-and-a-half hours a day. So we used to talk back and forth a lot from our cells to pass the time. There were five or six rooms on two levels, so maybe ten or twelve guys. At times, it was helpful to have the other guys to talk to, especially if I had some of my friends in the hole. But it could also be annoying. Some guys are so obnoxious, just banging on their cell doors, making noise, and yelling every single day. You tell them to be quiet, but they don't listen. So when one of those guys would get out for his thirty minutes (we'd go two at a time), we'd tell the other guy going with him for the break to beat him up. That fighter would get more time in the hole, but it was worth it.

Sometime in 2005, after I was back out of jail, our gang started having a lot of problems with our leader, B. He was giving his own guys food (drugs) that was garbage, diluted down. Guys weren't liking that. My Asian friends always had the good stuff and so some of the other guys in B's crew were going to them for their drugs instead. There was tension between me and B. Then B was shot dead in his hometown of Thompson in a turf war. I became the president, the boss. At the time, I liked being the boss, but it was also a pretty heavy responsibility and had its headaches. You have to learn how to control your guys—that's hard. For example, if they touch another gang member they have to pay $5-10,000.

By 2007, I started to think more about getting out of the gang. There was way too much going on. We were in the limelight too much and the police gang unit started breathing down our necks. You couldn't take a piss without them knowing. Some of our guys had been charged with murder. The gang was falling apart. There comes a time and a point in life where you've got to go low key. There was this one biker gang guy who I respected a lot, and he kept telling me, "Ho, you gotta duck once in a while." He told me I was causing a lot of heat on myself and not to be stupid. It was good advice and he was right,

but I didn't listen. The cops dismantled our gang because of the violence, the shootings and murders. By that point, I wanted to get out. I was thinking about my daughter and I felt conflicted. I started off by staying away from gang members and trying to get a job. I worked in a labour job, but it didn't last long. A month later, I was charged with possession of a firearm—I got caught with a gun in my car—and went back to jail. I believe I did six months then.

I had developed a serious drug addiction: morphine, pills, OxyContin, Percocet, cocaine. I had been addicted for four or five years. I needed to get rescued. That's a term that gang guys use when you are becoming too addicted and you need to go to jail and clean up. It's our inside joke. So going back to jail for the firearm charge, I got rescued. I got off the pills, the morphine and cocaine. There aren't any resources or help in jail for getting off drug addiction, but somehow it wasn't so bad. Maybe my brain automatically switched off the addictions because it knew I wasn't going to be getting anything to help my body fight through it.

During those six months in jail, I started to think—*Is it worth it, all the violence and the responsibilities of being the boss and keeping gang members in line?* The answer was *No*. I could see that guys I thought were my friends really weren't. There was money disappearing and backstabbing going on. I knew this for a long time, but I had just ignored it. I was sick of all the shit. So when I got out, I left the gang. Nobody gave me a hard time. I had gained respect on the streets. But my problems still weren't over: when I got out I started drinking and doing cocaine again—a lot of cocaine and even some crack.

One night, I was drinking and doing lines of coke with my brother-in-law and I got really delusional, to the point where I smashed him against his front window, grabbed a piece of the broken glass, and stabbed him. I remember running outside and falling to the ground. My limbs went weak. I don't know what happened, but when I woke up, I was in an ambulance and breathing hard. They brought me to emergency. The staff never said it was an overdose. I don't know what it was.

I was on a hospital bed, breathing hard, and I'd lost my speech. The doctors were jabbing something in my chest. I could see them, but they were fading away. There was this light and it was becoming brighter and

brighter. I was sick of my life and just wished I could be gone from this world. I remember telling God to take my life. I kept repeating, *I don't want to be here anymore.* But while I was saying that, I came back and could feel someone pinching my foot. Later, the staff told me I had almost died. When I came back, I was unhappy. I wanted to go; I wanted to die. But there was a reason I didn't go. I know that now.

I stayed in the hospital a month. At first, I couldn't walk. I tried to get up but my legs couldn't work. The hospital aides had to put this toilet seat beside me and help me get on it. I tried to wipe myself but I couldn't do it. The aide had to wipe me. It was so embarrassing that I started to cry. I was very sick while I was there. I had pneumonia and my kidneys stopped working. A specialist told me my kidneys were dead and so I was put on dialysis. But three weeks later, the specialist said my kidneys were okay. It was a miracle. I believe it was God who restored me. Once I got out of the hospital, that was it, I never did drugs again.

I see now there have been a lot of times I could have died. I've had bullets flying past my head so close I could hear the *shwoop* sound. I was also in a really bad car accident in 2007, before my time in the hospital. I was driving so fast on the highway that I ended up going sideways. I had my foot on the brakes, but my hands were not on the steering wheel. If I had continued to go sideways, I would have hit a post that would have crushed me. Instead, all of a sudden, the car spun a quarter turn, so I was travelling in a different direction—backwards. The back of the car hit the post. My seat broke and I flew all the way to the back window and injured my neck. But I walked out of the car. I don't believe it's a fluke that I lived. I've always believed in God—I was raised Catholic—but I didn't have real faith, didn't see the real power of it till later, after I started healing and helping.

I see now there have been a lot of times I could have died. I've had bullets flying past my head so close I could hear the *shwoop* sound.

AFTER I GOT OUT OF THE HOSPITAL, I worked odd jobs. I was a shipper-receiver, then did labour and masonry. Right before I took the masonry job, I ran into a buddy who was once a gang member and had a criminal record. He told me he was working with kids that had behavioural problems. That appealed to me right away. During my times in the Youth Detention Centre, I used to think about working there some day. That was something I really wanted to do. I asked my friend how he got into that job. He told me to call Kevin Bruce, a guy who worked at this place called Eagle's Nest that had programming for Aboriginal youth. My buddy gave me Kevin's card.

Three days after I started the masonry job, I quit. Masonry is a hard job: lifting bricks, carrying pails of concrete, and I wasn't in good shape back then, but also, I kept wondering if I could have a chance to work with kids. Right away, I called that name on the card I'd been given. When I spoke to Kevin on the phone, I knew his voice right away. I said, "KC?"

He knew my voice too. "Justin? What the hell?" We had been in the portables at Edmund Partridge School together when we were thirteen. Now he's a social worker and has kids. Back then, I knew him as KC, but now he uses his real name, Kevin.

I said, "I've gotten out of the lifestyle, but I need some help. I want to follow your path."

He told me to come down to Eagle's Nest and talk about a program he was running.

It was a program that's mainly for First Nations youth who are at risk—guys who are fifteen to thirty years old and have dropped out of school. It's a place where they have access to a lot of resources and can build life skills like first aid, CPR, suicide prevention training, and food-handlers training. My parents and wife supported me. They knew this was something I really wanted to do. My wife has been in the helping field for fifteen years. She knew that even when I was entrenched with the gangs, that I wanted to get out. She knew how much I wanted to do this program because it didn't matter that I had a criminal record. It was a chance for me to get my foot in the door to work with kids. It was 2008. I took the program and it was very helpful.

In the beginning, the younger participants looked at me like I was just any other participant. But when I called them out on stuff, they'd call me a rat and say I was on the staff side. I told them, "I'm not here to F-around. I'm here to make something of my life." I was open to learning about the spiritual and traditional side of things. We learned about Aboriginal culture. I respected it and started to smudge and to pray for people. I also started to help my peers in the class. I could relate to a lot of them. I shared my life, told them things I had gone through. I did two phases of the program, each three months long. There was a spark in my soul again and I was trying to become whole.

Things started to happen for me, just like a miracle. I went to CDI College and took a course for an addiction community service worker. I had never graduated from high school, but I went as a mature student and I graduated from that program. Eagle's Nest let me take their program while I was at CDI, as long as I wasn't skipping. Participants at Eagle's Nest are given an incentive to attend—fifty dollars a week, so about $600 for three months. Even though I was broke and the only income I had was that fifty bucks a week, I didn't take it. Instead, I saved it and gave it back to the staff to use for the next group of youth that came in, as prizes for good attendance, participation, and good behaviour: $300 for first place, $200 for second, and $100 for third place. Why didn't I take that money when I needed it? To me, Jesus did not take money while talking about the word of God and his way of life. I would go on to work for Eagle's Nest, running this program from 2013 to 2015 until things there changed and I became burnt out.

Around this time, I also met my good friend, Mitch Bourbonniere. He came to Eagle's Nest to do a medicine-wheel teaching and give a gang-awareness talk with guys who'd gotten out of that life. I went to Mitch afterwards and told him I wanted to speak about my gang life too. He gave me that opportunity. Mitch has helped me a lot and been like a second father to me.

Then I got to tell my story at a big conference. Police and probation officers were there. I was so nervous. When I was speaking, I mentioned my former gang's name. Afterwards a man named Floyd Wiebe pulled me aside to speak to me. He was co-chair of GAIN (Gang Action Interagency Network). He told me his son, TJ, had been murdered in 2003. Floyd started a foundation to honour his son and to get youth talking about drugs and gangs. Floyd told me that the day before his son was murdered, TJ had been pistol-whipped by some guys in my gang because of a drug-related incident. We both shed some tears. I was not directly involved, but I told him I was sorry on behalf of the gang.

From there, Floyd and I became close. We had this idea about creating a gang-awareness drama to take to schools so younger kids could learn about gangs before they get involved. If kids learn early, then when they go to junior high or high school, they are more informed. Floyd passed away unexpectedly in December 2015. We had lunch and talked more about this idea just one week before he died. Even though Floyd has passed away, it is still my dream to put this awareness drama together.

My father died five years ago in 2012 of cancer. My dad hadn't told me he loved me since I was a little kid, when I was maybe three. To this day, my family doesn't say I love you to each other. But my dad used to hint at it, especially when I was down and out or high on drugs. I knew my dad loved me, he just didn't know how to say it. I had never told my dad I loved him either. I finally said it to him on his last day, but by then he was unresponsive. He wasn't dead, but his spirit was gone. I don't think he heard me say it. It was too late. Sometimes I catch myself feeling like I don't want to say it to my daughter, because of how I grew up, but I say I love you anyways.

IN 2015, I APPLIED FOR A JOB as an educational assistant (EA). When I was a young kid, there were no supports at school, no EAs. I thought it would be a job where I could really help young people. I had a principal for a while when I was at Maples Collegiate; he just didn't like bad kids. Today, that principal is the superintendent of a North End Winnipeg school division. When I applied for the EA job, I went to see him to try and talk to him about the job. He told me, "I don't give chances to guys like you." I didn't get the job. That superintendent is the same person who takes EAs meant for specific students (often CFS kids) and instead uses those EAs for the entire classroom. That's scamming the money. If kids with FAS (Fetal Alcohol Syndrome) or autism can get the support they need, it can really make a difference.

I know about this because my wife and I have a number of foster kids who live with us. We have two right now. They're good kids who have been with us three years. The very first foster kid we took in was kicked out of a group home where I worked briefly in 2013 before getting the job at Eagle's Nest. We had him for about a year, but it was very, very difficult. He'd been in fifteen to twenty homes.

Being in a group home is a lot like going to jail because you've got rules to follow and kids are coming and leaving which makes for different dynamics. You've got to keep your head up with a bunch of guys acting tough; you gotta hold your own ground. He couldn't tell me I was wrong because I'd been through that kind of life. We could relate. We clicked, but still, having him live with us was too hard. He brought gang members home to our house. I had to call the police and he had to leave. Now I can understand what my parents went through.

In 2016, the CFS agency that my wife works for approached me about running a specialized group foster home. My cousin and I run the home out of a second house we own. Four teenage boys live there together. They have supervision 24/7. It's a different kind of group home—we have less policies so we make it more of a brotherly home environment. Sometimes it is very challenging, but at the same time, it can be rewarding. I also run a program for a CFS agency that gives kids in care (ages fifteen to twenty-one) support, resources, and learning opportunities before they leave care. It's a lot like the Eagle's Nest program I used to run. It's called Youth Of A New Day. Running this program is a part-time job. My life is pretty busy with this program, the group home, and my other work as a contractor building a new home for resale and doing personal training for kickboxing.

FORGIVENESS... it's a big word. It takes courage to forgive. A lot of people have so much pride and anger, it makes it hard for them. But if you can't let go of things, you continue to carry that burden inside you.

I remember I was sitting at my mom's house watching TV when we heard there was that Columbine High School shooting in Colorado. This was when I was taking the program at Eagle's Nest. My family thought the shooter should die. That would have been me too, before, but that's when I knew my soul was starting to open up. I said to my family, "How could you guys wish death upon someone? Sure, killing a bunch of people is wrong, and it angers you, but wishing death upon someone is just about as bad as murder." I know that *not* wishing death upon others is one of the rules of the Creator, or God.

My family said, "You'd forgive this guy?" That's when I started to realize that we have to forgive everything. I used to resent my mom so much for all that I went through. I used to yell at her and make her cry. But after my dad died, I started to say to myself, *Let go of things, it is what it is.* Since then, I've tried not to yell at her anymore. I've gone from trying to change my mom, to trying to accept her as she is. I try to show her a way to change, through my own change. She is starting to learn too. I still have some anger towards my family, those feelings still come out sometimes, but I am working on forgiveness. I am not perfect; there is still a part of me that needs to let go more. But I think that me and my mom have a better relationship now. My mom moved in to live with us in May of 2016. Things are going good.

When a person does you wrong, if you don't let it go, then you are always thinking about that person and those negative thoughts go down to your heart and hurt you even

> It takes courage to forgive. A lot of people have so much pride and anger, it makes it hard for them. But if you can't let go of things, you continue to carry that burden inside you.

more. Why let that be inside of you? Why not just forgive the person, and *Boom*, it's gone. It's our God, our Creator, who created forgiveness. But then there's forgiving myself —I have never really given myself a chance to do that. I'm sorry to the victims for what I have caused them. Maybe forgiving myself is another thing that I've got to work on.

I AM PROUD OF MY WIFE AND DAUGHTER. They gave me hope, strength, and they've helped me see that I was still young and there was room for change. My wife is straightforward, compassionate, and a caring, loving mother. She took a lot of bullshit from me for many, many years. Over time, she started to understand that I couldn't change with the snap of a finger; I had serious issues and shouldn't be judged just because of the way I acted. She had to look deeper than that and see why. She's changed my life. My wife made me feel like I was worth something and that there was hope. A lot of my life I thought there was nothing I could do to change because a life of crime was the only thing I knew.

You just gotta find that place where your soul can find that spark. Sometimes, when I was trying to lead a better life, there was still that little part of me that wanted to get sucked back in, especially when things didn't go my way for a bit. Sometimes I'm still tempted to go back to partying. Then weakness kicks in. It's the demons. You gotta stay positive and be around positive people. About four or five years ago, I got into kickboxing. Today, it's a big factor in my life. Kickboxing and working out are my self-care because it's a good way to work off stress. It's also become a lifestyle for me, a focus so I stay healthy and fit. My daughter works out there too, sometimes. My teacher, Brian at Ultimate Muay Thai, is always there for me. He is another positive person in my life. And you ain't gonna find hope if you are not with people who are going to encourage you. That's the big step, to get away from the people that give you no hope.

Today, the things that give me hope are my family, kickboxing, my dad's spirit, my culture and traditions, and having something to believe in: a higher power—that's huge for me. When I was struggling and weak, I would pray and let that higher power into my life, let it take control. You have to believe in it. It's something very powerful. I'd pray, *Don't hold me back, pull me forward.*

I believe there is a voice of a higher power that is trying to talk to me and give me wisdom. I usually don't talk to anybody about this because I think people would think I was crazy. But I've heard a voice in my head before, telling me things that are helpful, things I haven't thought of myself and have never been taught. Then later, I've had someone, like an Aboriginal elder, surprisingly say the same thing to me. Or, I'll be wondering something and a few days later in a conversation with someone, I will be given the answer I needed without them even knowing the question. I believe there are no coincidences.

Today, I know that the reason I'm here is to help kids. I wish I could take back the pain I've caused victims, but I will never take back the life I've lived. I believe that I walked a suffering life to get that experience, so that I could be here today to make changes and to help others make changes too. I believe that was the walk of life that God put me through, just like Jesus suffered on the cross. To learn about real life, you've got to suffer. Now, I can tell people, "Hey, I've been there; I know what it's like." I want to do anything to give back to others and to better myself. I believe that's one of the missions that God is giving me. It's been said that Jesus hung out with criminals and helped them get out of that life. It's the same thing for me. Giving to others is also helping me to heal my soul from the things that I've been through. I notice that as I help people more and more, things just keep getting better and better for me personally.

Interviewing Justin was an especially visceral experience for me. I had a strong intuitive sense of how tough he was when he was younger, but I could also feel his sincerity and his generous heart. That reminded me of the wide spectrum of humanity. When we first met to talk over tea about the book, Justin became committed to the project in only a few minutes. Participants were given an honorarium for their time, but Justin refused to take his. Instead, he insisted that I find someone who needed it more, someone who was going to school and trying to make good choices.

REGINA

I come from a well-known gang family. Growing up in that kind of family, you are just automatically *there*. It's not that you want to be in a gang; it just runs in the family and is always a part of your life. My father was in a street gang in his youth, fifty years ago when they were first getting started. I have seven brothers and four sisters, and my two older brothers hung out with a bunch of guys who lived in the same 'hood.

Their group was big and, seeing this was in the inner city, the cops eventually labelled them a gang and gave them a name. Although others see them as a gang, my brothers still don't think of themselves that way; they think of themselves as family. But the gang just kind of went down the line and my younger brothers started getting involved. Almost all my brothers are still in that gang today. It's basically like a family business.

My parents were alcoholics, and I had to babysit and cook and clean all the time. I grew up fast. My dad was physically abusing my mom. I'd stick up for my mom and then my dad would physically abuse me too. I ran away from home when I was twelve. My parents couldn't find me for two weeks; I didn't want to be found. But eventually when they did, my dad gave me a good lickin'. I decided that'd be the last time my dad would hit me.

So I called Child and Family Services (CFS) because I wanted to get away from my home life, and I placed myself in their care. First, I was in a foster placement on a farm outside the city with a woman who was running the farm by herself and was really looking for a worker. I was given a weekend visit with my grandparents and so I ran away. Then I was in five different group homes. I felt frustrated, hurt, unwanted—any bad word you can think of.

When I was fourteen and still in CFS care, I joined a gang, a girl gang. Strictly all girls. (They're very rare.) We started by hanging out with some guys in a gang, but no girls are ever really *in* their gangs, so we made our own and gave ourselves a name. I still went to school while I hung out with gang members and partied on the weekends, but I didn't care about schoolwork or anything. By the time I was fifteen, I decided that my life was going down this wrong road anyway, so what was the point of turning back?

I was in that girl gang from age fourteen to seventeen. I didn't create the gang; I just joined it. But I was one of the main members.

> By the time I was fifteen, I decided that my life was going down this wrong road anyway, so what was the point of turning back?

There were, I think, five of us who were hanging out all the time. It was the power; it was the money; it was the partying. But most of all, it was the respect. Once I was part of a gang, I gained a lot of respect from a lot of people. That was the big thing.

The leader used to say, "You're the muscle. I need you." I was the type that didn't put up with anybody. If she told me to go punch out a girl because she didn't like her, I would do it. I didn't care about hurting anybody. I knocked out girls' teeth; I blacked out girls' eyes; I smashed their heads into curbs; I stomped on their heads. I did everything.

We started recruiting girls, and these girls recruited more girls, and eventually we started running drugs. Then the idea of prostitution came up. Our leader wanted to traffic off some girls and these girls wanted to do it for us. I didn't agree with that, but there's nothing you can say when your leader decides something. You can't say it's wrong; you just kind of go along with it. I never communicated with any of those girls because I didn't want to put myself in a legal predicament. I've never collected any money from them either. I knew that having young girls out there on the streets selling themselves to give money to somebody else was crazy. I knew that in the pit of my stomach. I hated it. But like I said, at that time I couldn't tell my leader what to do. I would have gotten hurt for even saying anything.

I got pregnant when I was sixteen and had my baby when I was seventeen. While I was pregnant, I decided that gang life wasn't for me. I was going to leave—well, try to leave. I knew it would be hard to quit, especially when I was living right in the 'hood where all my gang members lived, but I was doing it for my baby.

The leader had a very big mouth, but I never saw her fight. She always had someone doing that for her. Even though I knew there would be serious consequences— like getting stabbed or shot—I phoned her up one day and told her, "You know what, I'm having a baby so I'm leaving the gang. I don't care what you say. Do what you gotta do, but I'm leaving. I choose my baby."

The leader shouted, "You're a fucking bitch. What the fuck do you think you're doing? Do you think you're going to run around this 'hood acting like you're fucking solid? I'm going to show you solid."

I said, "You know what? *Whatever*. Do what you gotta do. As long as I protect my baby, my baby's going to be okay."

She said, "Your baby ain't going to be okay. I'm going to kick you so fucking hard in the stomach that your baby's going to come out your mouth."

I said, "You know what, nobody's going to threaten my baby. You had better fucking hope to God I don't catch you first, because if I do, I'm going to fucking kill you for saying that about my baby."

The next day, the leader came to school with a baseball bat, looking for me. It just happened that I was sick so I wasn't at school. A lot of the girls phoned me and said, "Holy fuck, she's fucking going to fuck you up *herself*. She came to school looking for you. She came with a bat. She ain't playing."

A few days later, she came to school with a baseball bat again. She wanted to hurt me really bad. The first swing she took was at my stomach. Lucky thing, I moved back. Somebody caught the bat, pulled it from her hands, and threw it. I went running after the bat, took it, and hit her right across the face with it. I broke her cheekbone and knocked out a couple of her teeth. I shouted, "Nobody messes with me. I don't give a fuck. You guys want to fuck with me? This is what's going to happen to you, because I'm not playing."

Nobody wanted to mess with me after that. A lot of the girls didn't say anything to me; they respected that I was becoming a mother and wanted to change my life for my child. But very quickly, some of the girls left that gang and wanted to start hanging out with me. It wasn't supposed to be like that. It was supposed to be a friendship, but in a way, I guess we were still a gang. We got into trouble with the law: we were charged with assault causing bodily harm. After that, we all had a no-contact court order, so we couldn't see each other anymore. A couple of girls left the city. Eventually we all went our own ways.

I HAD MY FIRST BABY, A BOY, IN 1995. I was living back at home with my parents then. My parents were still drinking hard and so one day, CFS came to apprehend all of us kids from our parents. CFS said I had two hours to get my baby out of the home and find a safe place for him. So I called the baby's other grandparents and they came and took him. But then they decided they wanted to keep him. I didn't want to lose my baby. CFS told me I had two weeks to find independent housing with proper space and beds for my baby and me. I had amazing help from my CFS support worker. She had a good friend at Manitoba Housing who found me a place to live, and another friend who was moving away and gave me some furniture including a bed, a crib, and lots of great baby stuff. So CFS gave me my baby back. I knew then that I would *never* let my child be in someone else's care again.

At eighteen, I was suffering from being broke all the time and so I moved back in with my parents. They had got treatment and stopped drinking. My father never went back to drinking, but my mom couldn't do it. I gave birth to my daughter in 1997. I had quit high school and the only reason I ended up going back a few years later was because of a fight I had. After I had my second child, my boyfriend cheated on me with one of my close friends. She stopped being my friend because she wanted my boyfriend. She didn't like that he kept coming over, being there for my kids, bringing McDonald's and stuff like that. So one night, she came to my house because she wanted to fight me. I was getting ready to go out with some of my friends. In front of everyone, she said, "Look at you, Regina, you have nothing going for yourself. You're stuck on welfare with two kids and nothing to show for it." She said, "I'm in school, my kids are in daycare, and I have your boyfriend." We ended up fighting in the middle of the busy streets of Broadway and Young. It was nine at night, but still daylight. There was a bike close by and I flipped her on top of it, and her back got badly hurt on a pedal. That was the end of that.

But I felt really crappy. It bothered me that this girl looked at me that way. I wanted to do something. So I did. Shortly after that, early one morning, I asked my mom if she could watch the kids for me. She said, "Yeah, but where are you going at this time of the morning?"

I said, "I'm going back to school. I registered the other day and my first day's today."

She said, "Really? Oh my God, if you're going back to school, I'll watch the kids whenever you want. I'll be here and take care of them as long as you go to school."

I only needed a few credits to get my grade 12 diploma. I started doing this work placement at a neighbourhood community centre for one of the credits I needed. Eventually they told me I was doing well and working really good with the kids. They offered me a job there if I graduated. I was really motivated, so I finished my grade 12 and took the job. I really thought I was going to turn my life around there.

I worked at the centre for a number of years, but I got caught back up in the lifestyle while I was there. My downfall was seeing my gang friends hanging out there, while I was working. Eventually my hours started getting cut because funding was being decreased and some programs were ending, so I wasn't making the money I wanted to make anymore. I had moved out of my parents' house and got my own place in The Maples. I was running out of things (diapers, food), but I didn't want to ask my parents for anything. I was too proud to ask for help. I hated being broke. I thought, *What can I do now?*

By then it was 2006. I had had my third child, and then six months later, my mom passed away of kidney failure. I'm one of the oldest of the twelve kids. It was hard to see my family struggle after my mom died. She was the one who held our family together, making sure that everyone was taken care of and that we took care of each other too. My dad was lost without her. They'd been married for thirty-something years. I was basically the only one living outside my home at that time. I would cook lunch and supper for my family and deliver it to them every single day. My dad didn't know how to cook or clean because my mom had done everything. Alls he knew how to do was work. But eventually, he lost his job at the slaughterhouse because he couldn't function after my mom's death. Then he lost the house. After that, I just couldn't see my family struggle anymore. I gave up everything I had worked hard for, threw it all away, and went back to the life of drug dealing. Things would have been different if my mom hadn't passed away.

I had only $200. I knew my brothers were in the drug trade so I asked one of them, "Can you give me one of the deals that you give your homies? Can I get a ten bag for the same price?"

My brother said, "What are you going to do with it?"

I said, "I'm going to flip it."

He said, "Get out of here!"

I said, "No, for real. I'm going to flip it."

I bought $100 in groceries and gave him the other $100. I made $200 off that. So when I made that $200, I flipped it into $400, then into $800, and just kept going from there. I started my business by talking to random custies (crackheads) I knew, and I handed out the number for my business cell to them. I decided that I didn't want to do this all by myself, so eventually I started bringing girls in to work for me. First, I had two girls working. One would stay up all night and the other would work all day. It worked out perfect. Alls I had to do was go get the drugs and bring them back and give them the cell phone to work the calls.

I started wanting to deal even more. I've never been a person to do drugs or alcohol. No, my addiction was money. It felt good. That's it. After a while, I had so much money, I just gave it away. I'd buy things for my family and give gifts to friends—groceries, or furniture. As long as my little brothers and sisters had shoes on their feet, clothes on their backs, and food in the fridge, I didn't care. I started making a name for myself; everybody in the neighbourhood started to notice me. Including the cops. I wasn't ever flashy, but I had new cars, new furniture, and my girls and I always had lots of new clothes and jewelry. (Now, my daughter tells me that she wondered why we had so many nice things back then.)

My husband at the time had drug debts he couldn't pay to his dealers, so I agreed to pay them off if the dealers left us alone. Then I contacted the same guys to ask them to start supplying me. After that, I didn't bother with my brothers because I didn't need them to hook me up with their connects anymore. I eventually started dealing with higher drug lords who were running the business because I started dealing in *birds*, that's a large amount of crack cocaine—twenty-three-and-a-half ounces. Today, just one bird costs anywhere from $2,000 to $2,200.

When I got to buying a bird, I turned that into two birds, then five. When I started dealing with the big guys, I'd buy five at a time and then they'd throw me five more for free. I started flipping them. Eventually I was sitting on fifty birds. I used to have a phone that I only used for selling birds. The girls would break up a bird into 200 to 240 pieces of crack cocaine at twenty dollars each and sell it on another phone, all in less than a day. If I was selling a full bird, I made about $1,500. But if we were breaking it up, that was worth a lot more, like three or four grand.

The drugs were never in my house. My kids never knew what I was doing. They never asked any questions because I still had my legit job at the community centre too. By then, I managed about ten girls. They were the only ones I trusted. I always felt safe. I never carried a weapon to protect myself. I never had a reason to because I never dealt with anybody I didn't trust. I had to know the person. Those girls were friends and employees. Alls it was about with us was making money. I always told these girls "Take care of your kids and your families. This is why we're making money. We're not doing this just to go get drunk or whatever. We're doing this to take care of our children." I knew how wrong selling the drugs was, but I didn't care enough to stop. I was committed. My name alone carried a lot—a lot of trust from a lot of people.

The big guys who sold me the drugs started getting caught and going to jail. The

> I always told these girls "Take care of your kids and your families. This is why we're making this money. We're not doing this just to go get drunk or whatever. We're doing this to take care of our children."

cops were asking questions about me. They even stopped my little sister at the community centre and asked her questions too. But my sister was young; she didn't understand what they wanted to know. She always thought that I did only legit work.

At one point, all my brothers were locked up. Their phones were drying up, which means their business was dying out because they didn't have no *food* (a slang term for drugs). So I took all the guys working for my brothers and started supplying them with drugs too. I told them, "All the money that's running off these phones goes to help my brothers survive in jail." I told the guys, "Don't mess this up."

Eventually my girls and the guys from my brothers' gang all started getting together. The girls were never actually *in* the gang. Ever. We'd *represent* all the time—who and where we came from. I wouldn't have called us a *gang*, but because my brothers are all gang members, that was enough to have us girls listed as being part of their gang. I didn't think of us as part of their gang though, because it was all guys and there were no females in any of these gangs. I figured that what I was doing was just business, but the police listed us as gang members because of my family. And we're *never* going to get off that gang list. I'm never going to have a good name. Ever. It's really sad to say, but it's just the way it is, no matter what I'm doing today and how much I try to change my life.

IN 2007, I HAD MY FOURTH BABY. Around then, I also took custody of my niece because my sister got caught selling drugs for me. She ended up going to jail for two years, so I took care of her baby. My partner (boyfriend) and I had these two little babies who were six weeks apart in age, as well as my older three kids to take care of. It was difficult, but we managed. I stopped running all the drugs and started staying home. I sold my phone, which is like selling your business. For the next year, we just did the family thing and lived off the money I already had from that business.

In February of 2008, the cops raided our house. Earlier that day, I had told my partner, "We need to do something; we're low on funds. We can't just sit around here like this." He said he was going to go back to drug dealing with his gang members and he left. I thought, *Well, I'm going to get back on my phone again.* So I got a new phone and then called my girls and met with them. We started handing out the number, telling people I was back in business. Not even an hour later, my phone was banging with people calling and I got rid of a lot of *food*. People were happy I was back. The girls kept working the phone and I went home. I had no money on me.

My partner came in and said he had made just over $900. We were sitting there talking about how things were going to get better. Some of my brothers were with us. Not even twenty minutes later, the cops kicked the door in. They dragged us into separate rooms. A cop held a gun to my face and said, "Where are all the drugs?"

I said, "There are no drugs. You're coming to an empty house."

He said, "Don't fucking play games with me. Where are the drugs?"

I said, "How stupid do you think I'd be to bring drugs into my house? You guys pulled me over two days ago and you never found nothing on me. What do you think, that I'm fucking dumb? There's no drugs here."

All of a sudden, one of them came out of a room with a bird: twenty-three-and-a-half ounces of crack cocaine. Then another cop came running in from outside, saying he found ten pieces of crack on the ground outside my bedroom window. Then they found the money that my partner had. We also had $150 sitting on a dresser that was from his mother, for our baby. They confiscated that money along with the $900. I knew exactly how much was there because I had counted it before they busted through the door. Later, when I saw a copy of the police report, there was no mention of the confiscated money, just the drugs.

I found out that my partner had brought the drugs into the house, but he hadn't planned to stay long. He said he had them in the bathroom in the pocket of his jeans. We ended up going to the police station, but they didn't want nothing to do with my boyfriend. They didn't care that he was a gang member and this was his third drug arrest. They didn't care that my brothers had been in the house too. They wanted me. I told the cops what they wanted to hear.

I told my partner that I made a deal with the cops—I'd promised to confess that every-thing was mine if they didn't charge him. My partner was so mad. He said he'd have gone to jail; he didn't give a fuck.

But I told him, "I don't care. They didn't want you or my brothers. They were threatening me, telling me that if I didn't take these charges, they would arrest you, my brothers, my sister, and the kids would go to CFS." Just the thought of losing my kids was enough for me to give up everything. Because I'd had that brief experience of giving my first baby to his grandparents and then almost losing him, I thought, *Why risk all that?* The cops wanted me to go to jail, but I didn't have any prior charges, just that first youth probation charge from when I was sixteen, but no criminal record as an adult. So they had to let me go on a promise to appear, trusting I'd show up in court. It was my first arrest.

I took the blame for the drugs because I wanted to keep my children, but because of the nature of the charges, CFS came to see me the very next day. They had decided to keep my file open and do pop-in visits rather than remove the kids from my care. After three months of these random visits, the CFS caseworker said they were closing my file because every time they came to see me, the kids were well dressed and well cared for and were eating fruit and some kind of vegetables. They said they didn't usually see kids eating healthy food like that. They said there were no signs of abuse or neglect.

Shortly after the raid, I went to see my old boss at the community centre and I said to him, "I've been charged with possession for the purpose of trafficking. It's a lot of drugs, enough to get me a couple of years in jail. I'm on the verge of losing my kids, my house, and everything I have. I'm going to lose it all, and you know how I feel about my kids." I said, "I need to start work because if I continue selling drugs, I'm going to lose everything. I'll say *fuck my life* after that. I'm not messing around with you. It's either I get back into working and stay away from dealing drugs, or go all out and continue doing what I've been doing." I was desperate to go legit. For real.

He said, "If you are serious about this and really want to get your life straight, then you need to start with yourself. I can help you with a job, but you need to want to change. I can't do that for you."

I told him, "I wouldn't be here begging you for a job if I wasn't serious. You know me; you've seen me grow up from the age of thirteen. You know everything about me. You think I would come here and beg you for a job if I didn't want to change? I would rather say f-you and walk away." That's when he told me he could help me out with a couple of hours a week.

That boss says now that I'm a hard worker and that he always knew I had potential. He knew I had something to offer all the young kids there, especially the girls who wanted to run around with gangs and hang out with the boys. I had my street experience and he knew all about that. If it wasn't for my boss, I wouldn't be where I am today. He had given me plenty of chances and I had messed them up, but that day he took another chance on me.

So I went back to work at the community centre instead of dealing. It was hard to walk away from that life when I had so much respect and trust and knew basically the whole city. Years before, I used to sell drugs to all the moms of the kids I met at the centre. I messed up a lot of lives and ruined families, and I hate the fact that I did that to people. I feel guilty for it. Even though I did all that, those parents of the children I worked with didn't hold it against me. They let me move forward. They told me they were glad I was out of all that and said that they were doing good too.

> So I went back to work at the community centre instead of dealing. It was hard to walk away from that life when I had so much respect and trust and knew basically the whole city.

A year later, when I was sentenced, the court attorney wanted me to get twenty-four to thirty-six months in jail, but because I was working and didn't have any cause (trouble within that year) and I was obeying my PTA (promise to appear in court), they didn't send me to jail. The judge agreed to two years less a day on house arrest. The only reason I got the house arrest was that I was holding down a legit job. The house arrest was from November 2009 to November 2011.

I could only be inside my house or at work. I had four hours a week to get groceries or whatever I needed. I didn't have a monitor—those are just used for car thieves. I had to call a probation officer as soon as I got to work and as soon as I got home. I was not allowed to make stops or eat out. Five of my girls who are still my friends today moved in and did the whole two years with me. Being on house arrest took away my personal freedom and my freedom to raise my children outside my house. My girlfriends did a lot to help me during those two years. They took my kids places and did errands for me.

IN THE BEGINNING OF 2011, I started work for a restorative justice agency where many of my clients are young girls who come in for counselling after getting an assault or theft charge. The executive director knew about my history and that I was on house arrest because she and my community centre boss were good friends. In the beginning, not many other people I worked with knew that I was on house arrest. They figured I was just a regular person. But then people started finding out and they were very surprised. But everyone accepted who I was and what I had done. They said, "It's your past and you're trying to make it better." It was easier to move forward with these people because nobody was looking down on me. Everybody here is understanding and supportive. If you are having a hard time, you can always sit down with somebody and talk about what's going on. It's an awesome place to work.

I am a community justice worker and have my own caseload, working with clients one-on-one and helping first-time offenders and people dealing with outstanding charges. Some people walk in off the street and others are direct referrals from the Crown. I help them develop a plan for themselves, maybe to manage their anger or to get counselling. Clients who deal with their charges here, outside the court system, are giving back to the community. That's what restorative justice is.

I can relate to a lot of my clients. I work with mostly young females who are struggling with identity and who want to find a place for themselves. They'll say they're in a gang. But then I say, "No you're not. There are no female gang members. You're an *associate* of these gangs. An associate is just there, taking up a spot. That's it. You're never going to be *in* the gang. You can represent all you want, but in reality, you're not going to be a member. A member gets a patch and respect from everybody." These girls are just wannabees who want to be known for something. Then I tell them I come from a family of gang members and that I know first-hand what gangs are like. I'll say, "Well, let me tell you a little secret. I know there are no girls in that gang because my brothers run that gang." I tell them, "You don't want to be in a gang anyway. You don't want to do any of that. I've lived a hard life, and I'm still living a hard life trying to stay out of it."

A lot of girls that come through our agency have attitudes and think they're cool.

They say they don't want to be there, don't care about anything. They sometimes think their charges are a joke. I always tell them, "I don't take you seriously."

And they're like, "What do you mean?"

I say, "I can tell you're not the person who you're trying to be. I think you're hiding behind something. And all those friends that you think are your friends, aren't. Where are the people you got into trouble with right now? They don't have a charge. You do. Are they here to help support you with whatever you're going through?"

They always say "No."

Then I say, "You need to think about stuff like that. Don't worry about what other people think about you, or how you're going to look in someone else's eyes, because you're the only one that has to worry about you." Most of girls lighten up after that.

A lot of girls will say that I don't know what they are going through, and I'll laugh and say, "Yeah, I do know. Maybe I don't know exactly, because I'm never going to know about how you or anybody else is feeling *exactly*, but I do know how it felt when I was going through something similar, and trust me, it wasn't a good feeling. As soon as I tell them about my time in CFS and that I came from a family that once abused alcohol, they know I understand. And then I tell them that my first long-term relationship (ten years) was with a guy who abused me. He broke my nose and my ribs, tried to light me on fire, and tried to run me over with a car. I've been raising kids by myself since seventeen. When they find out my background, they are always surprised.

They'll say to me, "That's crazy. When I first met you, I thought you were born in the suburbs." They just can't believe I was once in a gang. They say, "You don't even look like you'd be mean. You're so nice and you're funny." But they usually open up to me right away because they know I can relate.

I say to my clients, "It's up to you if you want to take my advice, but I'm really hoping that you're going to take something out of what I say."

They need programs and guidance, depending on what their home lives are like. There are a lot of good programs they can attend. My old community centre has tons of programs. I ran a girls group there for a long time. We did lots of things the girls really liked: crafts, workshops, outings, traditional teachings.

We even invited successful young Aboriginal women to talk with them. They could be themselves instead of having to try and put on this show and act like they were hard, or solid, and could handle all this. It gave the girls hope. MERC (Magnus Eliason Recreation Centre) and Teen Challenge have programs too. There is everything these girls could possibly want out there. They've just got to ask for help or be guided by the right person.

A lot of young girls seeking attention and turning to assault or theft are in CFS care. They just want some respect. Nobody pays attention to them or pats them on the back for their good behaviour. Instead, these girls just hear about what they do wrong and how shitty their attitudes are. Instead, we need to ask, *Why are you like that? What's bugging you? What happened today?* Deep down, most girls want to talk about whatever is hurting them. If they don't, they start hardening up. They build a wall and the feelings get stuck. The more they keep that stuff in and get good at it, the more they get solid. They shut their feelings down because they don't want to hurt. Then eventually they don't care anymore; they stop crying inside and become careless and heartless. That's a bad thing. They'll end up like I did—not caring and not giving a crap about who they're hurting or who's hurting them. I know. I was once like them.

I've seen so many girls change and turn their lives around. Girls who wanted to be gang members but now have good, legit jobs and are taking care of their families. All because they just needed a little positive attention. I tell them they can do anything they want. I always get girls who come back wanting to see me and keep in contact with me after they've finished their programs. I think they see me as a hopeful person.

When I was younger, I thought that a big benefit of being in a gang was the respect I got, the street cred I built up. But I feel way more respected now. I have five children and this good job. The respect I feel today is the respect of knowing that I'm doing something good for myself, for my children, for the future of other young girls like my clients,

> ... we need to ask, *Why are you like that? What's bugging you? What happened today?* Deep down, most girls want to talk about whatever is hurting them.

and for anybody who comes across my path. Being able to share my knowledge of the streets is a gift that I have gained, and I know girls that have been impacted in a positive way by my life. That makes me feel good.

IN FEBRUARY 2013, MY PARTNER and the father of my fourth child was murdered in a gang-related crime. A few months later, in April, I went to a gang-awareness workshop. It was about preventing young people from joining gangs. I thought it would be a great idea to go there and see what people thought, especially with me having firsthand experience.

The discussion was about needing more programming and support. All these people want to try to help, but honest to God, they're never going to stop gangs from happening. Ever. They're always going to be there. I often tell people that gangs run things just like a business: developing a strategic plan, answering questions like, *What can we do better? How is this affecting us?* Gangs are never going to change, but people can.

Anyway, at first things went along fine at the workshop, but then a woman who was a facilitator said, "I think it's very hard for someone to change once they're hardened by the gang life. Take a look at the incident that just happened a few months ago where that guy was shot inside Johnny G's restaurant. Apparently, this guy left behind a child and her mother. He didn't care."

I interrupted and said, "Whoa, did you get this from the newspaper?" I said, "You guys don't know anything about gang members. All you know is what crime they're in jail for. Everybody looks down on them. Nobody gives them a pat on the back for something good they've done."

She said, "Getting a little offended, are we?"

I said, "Actually, yes, I am. You don't know anything about these gang members, or their lives, or how they've grown up. All you know is what you read in the paper. For your information, the man that you're talking about was more than a gang member; he was my partner and the father of my daughter. He was the best dad; he took good care of his kids. Did you know he was going to school? He was getting eighties and nineties. He didn't wait for anyone to tell him that he needed to go back to school. He took it upon himself. It takes a big person to do that. So don't sit there and talk about his life when you knew nothing about him."

Then I burst into tears and said, "If you really want to help someone, then don't ask them, *So what did you do to become a gang member?* People feel intimidated when you ask them that question. They'll feel like they just want to shut down because their first thought will be that they are being looked at differently. I wouldn't want to share any of my life with someone who's going to sit there and judge me. What's the point of sharing my life with you? Instead, you need to ask them, *What are you good at?*" Then I got up and walked out of there. I wanted to stay longer, but honestly my anger just took over. I was so hurt.

I take these words, *What are you good at?*, and use them with my clients. It's important to be known for your talents or for something good you've done. If you have someone pointing a finger at you and talking about everything bad you've done, then who cares, right? If you're being acknowledged just for something you regret, you're going to hold it inside as long as you can. You're not going to sit there and tell people you regret doing it. That's why I find a lot of men and women re-offend. If half the people in jails were credited for the good things they've done, I bet they wouldn't re-offend. Some re-offend because they don't know how to change, or they're too scared to change or make different choices. Then they do what they know best and that leads to re-incarceration or something even worse.

I HAVE ALWAYS TAKEN PRIDE in being a very strong, independent woman. I've tried to never depend on anyone else. Everything I've done, everything I have, everything my kids have is because of me. It took me swallowing my pride to ask for help and for what I wanted back in 2008 when I asked my old boss for that job. It was a challenge, trust me. Living on minimum wage and working at a community centre wasn't ideal after having had so much money before.

When I was younger, I did a lot of things that hurt a lot of families and destroyed homes. I didn't care about it at the time, but as I got older I did feel crappy. What I did was definitely wrong, and some of these feelings of regret are never going to go away. They can eat me up inside and they'll likely always be there. But I've made amends and I'm not going to listen to someone tell me how shitty a person I am, when I already know that what I did was wrong. Each day, I try to remember that after I did all that, I now give back to the community and do what I can to try and make up for all the bad things I've done. I can't keep living in my past life when I'm trying to move forward.

Today, I'm way different than I was. Now, I'm more humble. I'm more at peace with myself than a few years ago. That's from working at a great organization that specializes in restorative justice. I've learned a lot about myself. I've learned to respect myself, to respect others, and to respect my children. My children are my biggest priority, but most important is my own life. If I can't take care of myself, I can't take care of others.

Some people say they are going to change, but they fall back into the same trends. I've seen it plenty of times. I've done it too. But some people do change. Not everybody is the same. It depends on whether people really want to change, whether they really love or care enough about something or someone to leave everything behind, forgive themselves, and more forward. For me it was my kids.

My kids would say that I'm a great mother, a caring mother, and that I care about others too. I'm happiest when I'm with them and we're lying on my bed and talking. My oldest son has moved out now, but the other four are with me. My kids are not involved in gangs. They are involved in things like sports and choir. My kids have been isolated, in a way. They never play outside, never sleep over anywhere. I never let them walk anywhere; I always drive them. They tease me. They ask me, all the time, about being in a gang. But I usually say, "I don't want to talk about that right now." But they do know about my background.

> I'm more at peace with myself than a few years ago. That's from working at a great organization that specializes in restorative justice.

I have an unusual tattoo that really represents who I am. It is two fairies, one holding two handguns and the other holding a sawed-off shotgun. I picked the fairies because I am the nicest person you'll ever meet, but the guns are because if you cross me, I'm the meanest person you'll ever meet.

Even to this day, there are neighbourhoods I can't walk in. I can drive through them, because who's going to stop a moving car, but if I was parked and someone saw me, they'd definitely attack my car. They don't care. I once had my car window smashed. My kids were in the backseat; glass went in their hair and their mouths. I've had plenty of phone calls from guys saying they're going to come and shoot up my house. That's just from being who I am and having a long history of family involved in gangs. There is a gang agreement that no women or children are to be targeted, but I even had a call from a guy saying they were coming to rush my house and I was fucking dead, and they *didn't give a fuck* if my kids were there. I made a call to my brothers and to my partner's gang and I had thirty guys in my house, everybody blocking windows with shotguns and the kids in the laundry room in the basement. Shit gets real then.

After my house arrest, one of my brothers told me I was done. It was for my safety and because I'm a mom. He didn't want me to do any more time. He told everyone to not associate with me, not tell me what was going on, and not ask me for anything. It was an order. So I pulled myself away from the gangs. In general, I no longer hang out with any gang members, but I still see my brothers and my dad; they are family. I was offered money from the RCMP recently to give up my brothers. I told the RCMP I would never turn my back on them. Ever. If people can't understand that, then that's too bad for them. That's my family and my kids' family. Everything we do—family gatherings and stuff—we do in our homes. We don't really communicate with each other outside family gatherings. I don't party with them or hang out with them. Our family situation is a little different, so I don't bring anybody else around. It's just family. I have a lot of respect for my brothers and they respect me and my work. Our close family relationship is not a big deal. We were taught by our mother to support each other. Our mom raised us to be a very close family.

WHAT GIVES ME HOPE? Helping these young girls and my children and their education.

> There is a gang agreement that no women or children are to be targeted, but I even had a call from a guy saying they were coming to rush my house and I was fucking dead, and they *didn't give a fuck* if my kids were there.

I have hope for the best for others and for things to change. But dreams? No. I don't have dreams for the future. It's too hard to wish for something that might never happen. I'm really just living day-to-day.

The former executive director at Regina's employer introduced me to her. I was extremely moved while listening to Regina talk about her exchanges and connections with her young, female clients there. Regina has transformed her life experiences on the streets and knowledge of gangs into information to benefit others. She has a university degree from the streets, hard fought and irreplaceable. Regina and her story make me think of Canada's missing and murdered Indigenous women. Her shared wisdom has most certainly helped to save the lives of some of the young Indigenous women.

The organization that sponsored the workshop Regina spoke of is the same one that will be receiving the author proceeds from this book. Regina originally wasn't sure about participating in this book for that very understandable reason. I am grateful to her for her openness, her ability to forgive and her generosity in deciding to share her story.

At the time of publication, Regina is no longer working at her employer and I have been unable to contact her.

RYAN

I am an ex-drug dealer, an ex-addict, and an ex-gang-affiliated person. I made money off other people's misery, and then I made my own. You can't be a drug dealer and not be around gangs because the drugs all come from somebody who's connected; there's always an affiliation somewhere down the line.

When I was doing drugs and hanging around with the gang, they offered me a patch and wanted me to get the gang tattoo. But I didn't do it. I knew I didn't have the parts, the balls. To be a proper leader, you have to be clean and sober and to really represent. But I loved the drugs more than I loved the gang—more than I loved anything back then. If I had gotten the tattoo, I'd have been committing to the gang, saying *I will live this life for the rest of my life*. That's how I saw it. I took gang commitment very seriously.

But, when I looked around the room full of gang members, I realized that pretty much everybody sitting there was a drug addict, including me. How could we form something that was going to stay solid? It would take just one guy making a mistake to disband the whole thing. I knew I couldn't serve the gang in a way that would make it work.

I was twenty-six or twenty-seven and had a gang mentality, but I was also immature because I had stunted my emotional development due to drugs and alcohol. However, I also knew that one day I was going to have to grow up. My parents didn't teach me to be a drug dealer. My parents didn't teach me to be a junkie. I chose that. I also knew that there was something else out there, and I wasn't going to serve the gang my whole life.

A lot of my ex-friends are still part of gangs, or now incarcerated or dead. There was probably something greater than myself watching over me, because there have been several situations where I should have ended up dead. And although I've never been charged, I've come close. One time, there was a big police sweep with a gang I was hanging out with and I just missed it. So I didn't go to prison, but during those days I was already *in* prison—a living hell because of my addictions.

I WAS BORN IN GRANDE PRAIRIE, ALBERTA but my mom was from Winnipeg, so two weeks after I was born, my mom, my dad and I moved back to Winnipeg. My journey there began in East Kildonan. I remember living in an apartment and both my parents were in my life. When I was five, we moved to St. Vital. I would call my life then middle class. We weren't rich, but my brothers and I played hockey and other sports. I also remember my dad being gone a lot because he was a long-haul truck driver. And when he was home, he liked to go out and see his friends.

Even though my dad wasn't home much, I think my mom did a great job raising me and my two younger brothers, Rory and Jared. I remember my brothers and me being very loving and close growing up. My mom had her parents and her siblings in Winnipeg, and we spent a lot of time with them. My uncles, Mark and Dan, were really solid for me and in my life a lot, and I was close with my Auntie Pat (my mom's sister). She passed away when I was thirteen.

Sunday suppers were always at my grandma and grandpa's house. My grandma would cook and my grandpa and I would play baseball in the front yard. It was always a good family setting. I did miss my dad, but times were still good because I had my grandpa. My grandfather would watch the hockey games on TV with us. He would take me to my hockey games and baseball and soccer, because my mom had three kids and my dad was always gone. My grandfather did great, but now I would say it was my dad that I needed.

When I was four or five, we also had these great neighbours, Ben and Mary, who I used to spend a lot of time with. They had no children and Ben treated me like his son. He played catch with me after dinner and would take me up in his plane or they'd take me to their cabin. Ben probably saw the disconnect I had with my dad. He was a really important man in my life, but then he got leukemia. I didn't understand why he got sick and why I couldn't go over to his house, or why he was in the hospital. My mom would sit down and try to talk to me about it, but I just didn't understand. When I was seven, he passed away. He was around forty-five. I took it really hard. Ben had a very strong impact on my life.

Around the same time, we also had a woman next door that I called "neighbour." She affected my life too—but in a different way. She used to buy me Slurpees and treats, but then I would go over to her house and she would touch me inappropriately. I didn't feel comfortable with that and I knew it was probably not right, so after she did this a few times I talked to my mom about it. My mom didn't want me to go over there anymore. Those times with "neighbour" affected the way I thought about women— I became afraid of them.

One of my closest friends, Mike, lived across the street; but there was a lot of abuse in that home. I had never seen abuse until I saw it there. My mom and dad had never fought like that. When I would go over for sleepovers, Mike and I had to stay secluded in his room because we could hear his mom getting beaten up pretty badly. I really couldn't understand it. I remember even wetting the bed at times, because I was scared. I could have gone home, but I was also scared of having to tell why and getting Mike's family in trouble. So instead I just stayed in Mike's room.

My mom felt strongly about raising us boys in the Catholic religion. She wanted to give us a good education in a Catholic school, so my parents sent us to St. Emile's. It was a private Catholic school and they had to pay, which they probably couldn't even afford. My parents also probably wanted to keep us sheltered from the realities of life. The school didn't appeal to me though. St. Emile's was run by nuns back then, and they were strict. The principal was strict too.

In grade 1, I had my first incident there. I pushed a kid in the sandbox and got sand in his eyes. I don't remember why we disagreed, but I do remember being angry. I definitely had anger issues. By grade 2 or 3, I was already fighting. By grade 4 or 5, I was in the principal's office regularly and I was even suspended sometimes. In grade 7, my desk was placed right beside the teacher's because I kept getting into trouble. I knew then that I didn't care for authority figures.

I felt disconnected in school. There were two sets of guys in my class and I'd jump around between the two groups. I wanted to be friends with everybody. I could easily be coerced into doing things for other guys—fighting, teasing, bullying. That was pretty sad now that I think about it.

THREE DRAMATIC INCIDENTS changed my life when I was ten or eleven. They all happened close together: *bang, bang, bang.* They created a disconnect inside me and with my family.

First my parents' marriage broke up and my dad moved out of the house. My dad was an alcoholic. I knew something was off because my dad would be out late at night at the bar, and when he'd come home, he really didn't want to spend time with his family. My mom didn't want that and then there was abuse—verbal, and sometimes it would get physical. My mom probably wanted her husband at home, but he was a long-haul truck driver and had to be away for long stretches; that's how he provided for us. Then when he got home, he'd feel like he needed a release because he'd been on the road for so long. My mom didn't work when we were young, but when my dad left, she had to go out and get a job. That was a bit of a game changer.

There was so much hurt and pain in me. I became the abuser in my family. I started where my dad left off.

Money got tight after the split. And that's when my anger issues were taken to another level. There was so much hurt and pain in me. I became the abuser in my family. I started where my dad left off. I beat the shit out of my brothers. I thought it would toughen them up, but now I can see I was actually harming them. During that time, it also became even more important to me to fit in with friends. I wanted to hang out with certain individuals. I would later pay a big price for that.

Right after my parents split, there was a second dramatic incident. I was violated. It was a Friday, a school in-service day. I was still going to St. Emile and in grade 6. There was this guy who lived down the street from our house. I think he was in grade 12, and he had an in-service that day too. He and his friends had been nice to me. I'd been to his house before and hung out with those older guys several times. They used to have campfires in the wooded area close by our houses and sit around smoking. I thought it was cool to hang out and smoke. On that in-service day, I went down the street and knocked on his door, planning to go and hang out with him again. I was probably looking for something, maybe to feel a sense of belonging and to fit in with older guys. That Friday was supposed to be a day like any other day. There were a few guys there and no parents around.

They were in the basement smoking weed and cigarettes and drinking alcohol. They gave me some Kahlua. Then they took me into a bedroom in the basement... I used to say I was abused, but really I was raped—by each of them. I didn't know how to express what happened to me.

Afterwards, I went for a walk and then I went home. But I didn't want to walk past the house again, so I cut through our neighbour's yard and then got to my mom's. I didn't tell my mom anything. I didn't try to tell anybody anything. I didn't talk about it until I was, like, thirty. I couldn't. The guys that did it warned me not to say anything, but also, I felt it made me different from other people and I felt ashamed about it for so long. It really screwed me up. Also, for a long time I had a hard time identifying my sexuality, and it made me shy towards girls. I have always been very careful how I treat a woman because I knew what it felt like to be pushed around.

After that day, I didn't go back to that guy's house again, but I'd see him regularly around the neighbourhood. And I still went to hang out in that wooded area where older kids were smoking. I had a friend that would go there, and we'd go together with his sister. That neighbour guy wasn't always there, and only once or twice did I see any of the other guys from that day. After that Friday, there were a few other times in the wooded area that some of those guys took advantage of me, but never in the same way as on that Friday.

I had tried some weed before this. We were young kids in the neighbourhood, experimenting. Someone would bring the weed along, it would just appear. But after that violation, I branched out from marijuana and alcohol to acid and LSD, and then came mushrooms. Even during those early years, I was already a heavy user. Starting those drugs was the third terrible incident in my life. This was the beginning of my years of drug addiction.

I had a paper route at that time and I would do odd jobs for my grandpa—cutting the lawn or painting—so I always had money for my drugs. Working hard was something my grandpa instilled in me. But even back then, I started cutting corners, like dumping the flyers in the bush or collecting paper route money early. Then, when I was fifteen, I started selling marijuana to keep my habit going, to put clothes on my back and to buy certain things I wanted that my mom couldn't afford.

I was doing all the shit my mom didn't want me to do; I was an out-of-control drug addict hanging out with the wrong people. As I got older, I didn't try to hide anything. I'd be too crazy and so I was floating around from house to house like a nomad, burning bridges with both my parents and playing the blame game. I'd be in and out of my mom's house, my dad's. (My dad didn't come to a lot of his visitation days, but he had let me live with him for a while.) Then I'd call my grandma and grandpa and ask to live there for a while. My grandfather figured out what I was doing. He pulled me aside and asked me where I got my gold bracelets and big gold necklaces. How could I afford them? My family tried to get me help. I had a counselor at the Addiction Foundation of Manitoba (AFM) who I liked. When I was fifteen and in my first drug treatment centre, I had to tell my grandfather that I had tried cocaine. It tore him up. It tore up my whole family. Every single time, I'd go back to my mom and say, "It's going to be different." But it never was. I dropped out of high school when I was in grade 10.

A lot of things changed when my grandma passed away. We had always had a good family setting and we lost that when she died. One Christmas she couldn't get off the couch and then six months later she was gone. Cancer. I had helped to take care of my grandma. I was over at their place a lot. She was so sick, I had to feed her. She died in 2000 when I was nineteen.

I did well selling drugs until around then. I always had money. I could do pretty much whatever I wanted. But before my grandma passed away, I had started dabbling in cocaine and really getting into smoking crack. It was bad. I was snorting so much cocaine that my brother was trying to slow me down by hiding ounces on me. I got into my first drug debt with the wrong people. That's when my family was first put in danger because I brought my brothers into that life and they both started working for me. I went into hiding, trying to detox and put my youngest brother, Jared, who was then fifteen or sixteen, in the position of taking care of the business I had developed. We needed to keep on getting money from it to pay off my drug debt to my supplier and his boss. Eventually, Jared would do five years inside Stony for dealing.

I had been Jared's hero. I had a big screen TV and everybody was driving me around, bringing me to bars. We'd be getting VIP in certain bars. The owners would know who we were and who we were with. I was living a reckless lifestyle, but I always had money in my pocket and I liked to glam. I was down with people that you didn't mess with. They were making a name for themselves and there was an excitement to being around them. There was an empowerment there too, and it helped me feel that I belonged, that I was accepted.

I was hiding a lot of things and hurting my family. Look at the trauma I had pulled my brothers and my mom through, the craziness—and look at what I was dealing with myself, the pain inside from my abuse and from not being able to tell anybody. I was afraid I'd be judged, or they'd think I was gay. I started to think about killing myself. There were two close calls. I had wondered about committing suicide even before the drug debt. I had a gun in my mom's house and one time I thought about blowing my head off, but I broke down and didn't do it. Then another time, I had been up for three days from the coke and was in my basement with an extension cord tied to the ceiling and a note written to my family. I wanted to end my life, so I didn't put them through any more misery. But I was also thinking about the pain my mom and brothers and grandfather would go through if I did end my life. Then I remembered that counselor I had at AFM and called her. She couldn't help me at the time because I was now an adult and needed adult services, but she told me where I could go. She knew that I was going through a really hard time.

Finally, I paid off my debt and then my family gave me a chunk of money to move to Calgary and try to make my life better there. I was going to try and stay sober. I went with some of the same people I had been partying with in Winnipeg. I even had a legit job for a while at an auto parts store. Things were halfway good for a while. We didn't know where to get coke or crack. I was clean for a bit, but once we found the crack, I just started up again. The money from my job was just never like what I made from dealing, so I went back to dealing too. I stayed there four years.

Calgary became a different demon for me. It wasn't just a little operation; it was really on another level. We had bigger things going on out there and I was in the middle of it. It got pretty serious. First, I got stabbed with a big hunting knife. I was in our house and a friend started demanding drugs from my buddy and me. I told him not to fuck around with us; I didn't think he'd do anything, but he pushed my buddy aside and came at me. He ended up slicing me twice on my right arm by my wrist. It was slit down to the bone. I was lucky though. He would have got me in the gut and tore me open if I hadn't blocked

him with my arm and moved. The guys there broke us up and took the other guy out of the house. I was so fucked up, I went right back to dealing. I never even went to the ER. My friend cleaned up my wounds every day until the cut was better.

Another time my brother got kidnapped and held at gunpoint by our bosses. They were looking for a lot of missing crack. The only way my brother got out was because my buddy helped him. I couldn't see him for a week and a half because he was so beaten up. If that was what was happening to my brother, imagine what was taking place to other people who were trying to mess with us. It was not good. Then it all started to fold because one of the guys got deported. My brothers left for Winnipeg, but I stayed.

I had working-class friends—really good friends out there who were legit. They didn't like what they were seeing in my life. By then, I was sleeping on a friend's couch and all I wanted to do was get high, so this one guy tried to help me. He called my dad and got me a bus ticket back to Winnipeg.

When I got to Winnipeg, I detoxed at my dad's for a bit, but then I got back into the drugs pretty quick. I stayed only about three weeks and then left for Ontario. My brother Rory had gotten me a legit job at a fishing resort. I thought if I was in the bush that would help me stay clean. But I still had the same mentality and so nothing changed. I ended up leaving town because a friend was trying to help me get clean and took me to my grandfather's house, but I left and went to Kenora and started dealing out of there. I stayed about three years.

I had tried several treatment centres out there, but every time I'd start cleaning myself up I'd get a proposal to start selling dope again. I wasn't really a nine-to-five kind of guy at that time (I was about twenty-eight), so I'd start dealing and then get back into drugs myself. I had a good friend and eventually she pushed me to go back to Winnipeg because she thought it would be better for me. So I left Kenora for Winnipeg, but once I got back there it was more of the same thing.

Throughout all this time, I was never charged with anything. I never would have made it in prison, because being a drug addict in there I'd have been paying for my drugs and I would have had no money in prison to support my habit. Automatically, the prison staff would have put me on a gang range because of my brothers' involvement. (Either you're going to click up with a gang in jail, or you're going to get hurt.)

Altogether, I think I tried rehab at least twenty times. As time went on, I was homeless and couch surfing at friends. I had nothing I could call my own except for my clothes. I'd stay up all night, walk the streets, smoke crack, and then return to a friend's couch to sleep a bit and do it all over again. I was making just enough money doing under-the-table jobs to keep my drug habit going. Probably one of the things that truly saved my life was being so broke at that time and not really having a home. Otherwise I might have died a crackhead.

While I was in treatment in 2011, I was in the same centre as a woman I had met briefly a few years before. We had made some connection, but lost touch. When I saw her again, we began spending time together. We were both sober at the time. We'd walk around for hours and hours and just talk. We were both really wounded and had faced a lot of

> I had tried several treatment centres out there, but every time I'd start cleaning myself up I'd get a proposal to start selling dope again.

the same traumas. We decided to try to be together, but it was for all the wrong reasons. I could see her pain and I wanted to make the pain better for her. I loved her and cared deeply for her, so I moved in with her and her two kids from another relationship. But then after eight months, I started using drugs and alcohol again and that added to her pain. She was trying to be a good mom, but she was slipping and sliding with her addictions as well.

While we were together we conceived our first son, Gavin, who was born in 2013. But we were in an abusive relationship: emotionally, physically, and mentally. It wasn't just me and it wasn't just her. We were both unhealthy for each other. My son's mom had me arrested three separate times on false accusations of harming her. CFS came to our home each of those three times. A number of times CFS asked me, "Are you stable enough to watch your kid?" But CFS saw my wife was drinking again and told me they thought I was the better parent, so when we split I had Gavin with me.

We reconciled for a short period of time in 2014 and our second son, Julian, was born in 2015. I was sober and she claimed to be, but it wasn't really the case. She was unhealthy, so I walked away. We had only engaged two times together and because of the lifestyle she was leading, I didn't feel sure Julian was mine, so I asked for a DNA test. When Julian was first born, I wasn't getting to see him much. I only got him for one weekend. Then, Julian and Gavin were apprehended from their mother by CFS. That's when Gavin came to live with me full time. Through the DNA, the courts finally confirmed I was Julian's father. That's when I went on parental leave and took Julian out of care to live with me full time.

SHORTLY AFTER MY FIRST SON'S BIRTH IN 2013, I started my final journey to recovery. It was October 12, 2013. I had just gotten my last paycheque from a job I was doing then—working at an oil company in the distribution and bulk packaging area. I was starting parental leave to take care of Gavin who was only three months old.

That night in October, me and my dad were going out to the Jets game and my mom was looking after my son. She could see how antsy I was and she knew I was up to something. She asked me to please not drink and not do anything stupid. I told her I wouldn't, but in the back of my mind I was already playing out the night—how I was going to get drunk and get high. I had been straight for three weeks, so I felt I had to make up for that and get in three weeks' worth of partying. When I was fully in addiction, I'd be spending $100, maybe $200 a day on drugs. So after I'd been off for a while, I'd go on a big bang, making up for all the lost time. I had gone to different bank machines earlier that day taking money out of my account so I had a wad of cash on me, probably $1,500. Enough for a good night. But in my mind, I was still planning to be home by 10 pm.

My dad came to pick me up at my mom's house, but we left to go back to my dad's for drinks there first, and then we took a cab to the game. I was drinking at the game and my dad kept telling me to slow down, but once I started, I couldn't stop. After the game, we went back to my dad's place. My mom had called there and I told her I'd be home. She said, "Gavin's here waiting for you." My dad was trying to get me to stay there, but I wanted to go out, so I did go back out and I smoked crack cocaine. The person I was with asked me about my family and my life. He said, "You don't look like you come from a

bad area." And I didn't. I had put myself in bad areas. I remember that while I was getting high, I was feeling like I just wanted to be able to go home and be with my son. But I was too high and just kept taking more drugs. The high was terrible though because I knew I had walked out on someone who needed me—my son. I knew he couldn't be with his mom at that point; I had to be the stable parent. I had a job to do taking care of my son. If Gavin didn't have me, he would have no one.

I still had a pocket full of money and a twelve pack of beer. I started pounding back the beers, and then the guy I was getting high with told me he couldn't get me any more crack. Thank God. I probably could have kept going for days, but he was sick of hearing me talk about what a shitty person I was because I wasn't with my son. The guy told me, "Just go. Go home." I actually got a cab and went back to my mom's. It was 10 am the next morning.

When I came through the door, my mom said, "I'm not watching your son anymore." She put Gavin in my arms and I held him. But I was jonesing on crack cocaine. I knew I was really fucked up and I couldn't take care of him then. I begged my mom to please watch

Gavin and so she did. She told me to go into the next room and sleep. But she came into the bedroom and said to me, "Before you go to sleep I want you to remember this—if you ever do this again, I will call CFS on you and you will never see your son again."

I put my face in the pillow and I've never prayed so hard in all my life, because I knew how serious my drug addiction was and I knew my mom was serious too. I prayed to my ancestors: my grandma, my aunt Pat, and to this older Turkish man I once knew who really believed in me. (He had once told me I was a good worker.) I believe they were watching over me. I also prayed to whatever else is bigger than me—God. I knew I really needed help because I would have done anything for crack cocaine. But I also knew then that my addiction would take my son from me, because it had taken everything else from me already. But God heard me that day because, for once, I wanted something other than to be a selfish addict. It wasn't about me anymore. It was about my boy.

For the next couple of days my mom watched my son while I went through bad times withdrawing, crazy head. I kept thinking about all the trauma I had put my family through, all the problems with my ex and her family. My newborn son was in the middle of it all.

When my mom put Gavin in my arms that day, I knew I was broken. My dad hadn't been there for me and I didn't want to be like him anymore. I didn't want my child to be part of the child welfare system. I knew how serious my drug addiction was. But that was my last use. I never went back to drugs or alcohol ever again. October 13, 2013 is my sobriety date. Every other time I had decided to get clean, I ended up back in the lifestyle in some form. I had the best of intentions. I was going to make money to buy a home, but that never happened. Instead, I'd ended up strung out and a junkie again. This time I was living for my son. If I were to pick up drugs today, my kids would never see me again. Either I'd kill myself because of the pain I'd be going through having let them down, or I'd overdose. Today, I'm clean and I'm useful to people again.

OF COURSE, IN THE BEGINNING, all I could think of was the drugs and I was terrified of everything. For starters, I was coming off a relapse. Also, I thought everyone was after me; CFS was calling and the cops were watching me. My mental health wasn't good. Plus, I didn't know how to deal with other people because I'd spent so much time smoking crack by myself. I didn't know how to interact with the world, let alone with people who actually cared for me and wanted the best for me. The only thing I knew was Gavin. My mom made me take care of my son. He came to my AA meetings and he came with me when I went for counselling. I was a single parent on the bus pushing a stroller, but it was my son who saved me. While Gavin was sleeping, I'd be doing a million other things: talking to lawyers, talking with CFS, making sure that if Gavin's mom wanted access she called Winnipeg Child Access Agency (I was calling them many times a day), making sure my employment insurance was going to be coming in since I didn't have much money. Then I'd be wondering if the cops were going to come and arrest me again for some crap story that was made up about me and CFS would be on me saying I might never see my son again. My mom wasn't easy on me either. And I was also trying to stay sober. It was a lot.

But I also had so much support. At first, I couldn't really be left alone much. I went to the twelve-step program and had my sponsor. He was working with me on a daily basis. In those first six months, I also had two wraparound services working with me: Assertive Community Treatment (ACT), through a research project called At Home/Chez Soi, which looks at poverty, homelessness, and mental health issues (because I was essentially homeless and couch surfing at that time); and Tamarack Recovery Centre. A wrap-around service has many people working together to give those who are addicted what they need: psychiatrist, social workers, family support workers, a psychologist, crisis workers, a nurse, and several community-service workers. They blanket the person, blocking him from the crap that can come from the system. They advocate. It was a godsend that I had two organizations supporting me this way because, generally, people in Winnipeg who can access one wrap-around service are lucky. I also voluntarily took courses through Child and Family All Nations Coordinated Response Network (ANCR) and from the Addictions Foundation of Manitoba (AFM). When I was taking those courses, I was learning about what was really going on with me underneath everything. A few years before,

I had told someone at Tamarack about my sexual abuse, but opening up about it was a long process so I was now working on my issues, facing them with a counsellor.

When I became part of the ACT program, I was assessed. I didn't even know that I had mental health issues up until then. They said I had depression and anxiety. So I had two demons right there: mental health issues and an addiction. They say you have to treat the addiction before you can treat the mental health. Once I started dealing with my addiction I slowly started to stabilize. I didn't have a hope before that.

During the early months after my sobriety, I didn't want nothing to do with nobody other than those people helping me. My baby son was my best friend then, and he will always be my best friend. All I did was go to AA meetings or counselling for support and then go back home. I didn't even own a cell phone for six months. Everything related to Gavin, and when it didn't relate to Gavin, it related to my recovery. I also had to decide to stop talking to anybody who was affiliated with the lifestyle. At times, that even meant my brothers. My one brother was incarcerated and my other brother was only around sometimes.

At around the eight-month mark of my sobriety, a counsellor asked me if I had had any past involvement with gangs. At that time, I had talked only about my drug dealing and affiliations, and I was still hanging on to that story. I had denied having any involvement with gangs, but finally admitted that I had. That counsellor gave me the name of a guy who works with youth and adults who've been involved. I took help from everyone else, so I called him too. His name is Mitch Bourbonniere.

When we met, Mitch asked me to go help him recycle scrap metal. So there I was with this biker-looking guy helping him carry old metal, and he's asking me questions about my life and my affiliations. He knew all the guys I knew. I received help from Mitch's Action Therapy Program. It's also a wrap-around service that supports families and youth. The focus is on "lateral empathy" (youth helping others) and connection to Aboriginal communities and traditions.

Mitch has been guiding me ever since. He took me to my first sweat lodge and to other ceremonies. Mitch is amazing. I see the way he conducts himself, and the way he will help anybody. But he will not work harder for you than you are going to work for yourself. He's put me in contact with so many other people that have helped me, like a psychiatrist and others in the community. He introduced me to Larry Morrissette, executive director of Ogijiita Pimatiswin Kinamatwin (OPK), an organization that supports marginalized and at-risk Indigenous youth, as well as men coming out of gang life. Larry also founded Children of the Earth School. He worked very hard to help make the inner-city neigbourhoods of Winnipeg safe. Larry and OPK really helped get the CFS system off my back, because I wasn't doing anything wrong. Larry is the one who helped me get my passport, helped me get my criminal record and child abuse registry checks. He paid for all that because I was a single father and I didn't always have extra money for those kinds of things.

In October of 2016, Larry died suddenly. It was a shock and pretty emotional for me. (His daughter let me know—I was one of the first to find out. I had just been talking with Larry that day.) Larry was full of love and compassion. He helped my family so much and many other families. His loss is a huge hit for the community. He believed in me—a

seventeen-year crack addict with some known ties to a street gang. He never judged me. I always respected him. Larry was humble and a man of very few words, but he fought for what he believed in. He was also a jokester and could be very stern. I was a pallbearer at his funeral. That was a huge honour. I feel his presence almost everywhere because when I'm in the inner city, I know that Larry walked down the same streets. Now he is my ancestor, so I am able to speak to him through spirit.

Some of Larry's closest friends are elders who have become my friends too: Chickadee Richard, Vern Dano, David Blacksmith, Eric Courchene, Wilford Buck, and Mike Calder. I listen very closely to those elders because they're in touch with spirit very deeply. I also have a social worker, Jamie, who is a friend, mentor, and spiritual helper. She is always the one to tell me the truth. She's like a rock when I'm losing it.

Mitch also introduced me to the Bear Clan and the Mama Bear Clan. These are two North End community groups that patrol the streets to bring safety and create awareness about local violence. The bear is a protector, and so we protect our community and

KEITH LEVIT

But the two guys who really helped me the most are Mitch, who is like my dad, and my recovery sponsor, Kevin Madden. He's got twenty-six years of sobriety. I want to honour them. These are men I can hug and tell them, "I love you."

Without Mitch's Action Therapy Program, Larry Morrissette and OPK, Tamarack Recovery, Bear Clan and Mama Bear Clan, I would not be where I am today. It took a lot of people working with me. Many still do. I talk to Mitch every day. Every day. Without all those supports as well as my mom, I would be screwed. I would still be a drug addict. They all saved my life. But as much as all those people were my supports, I had to show up. They didn't do the work. I had to do the work. They didn't get their asses up and go to the meetings, I did.

MITCH INTRODUCED ME to Aboriginal spirituality and ceremony. At the time, I was almost certain I had some Metis ancestry. My mom told me that my grandmother was adopted and her birth name was Bourbonniere (the same as Mitch's, and he is Metis). I started to go to ceremonies: Sun dances and sweat lodges. At a sun dance, a community will

the streets. These groups are role modelling for the community and showing people that change is possible. I walk for the women and children, but I also walk for those elders I just mentioned, as well as elders like Stella Blackbird and Gladys Marinko. I'm not perfect, but I try to carry that respect into my everyday life as well. Now I wear the Bear Clan patch because I believe in it, and I have committed to never going back to drugs and alcohol. The patch gets taken away if you do. The Bear Clan lets me give back to the community that I helped fuck up.

come together for four days to pray for healing and some people will make a sacrifice for others. The first time I sun-danced, the main reasons I did it were for my children and my babies' mom. They weren't old enough or strong enough to be able to sun-dance, so I did it for them. I sacrificed myself and prayed for their needs. I also attend sweat lodges at least once a month. I went to one recently because I was having a problem and wanted to sweat about it and to speak to my elders, my grandmothers and grandfathers, about what I should do. I knew they would give me the answers. Answers come to me while I'm sitting in ceremony. I really put my faith in the Creator.

Those sun dances and sweat lodges and living by the seven sacred teachings have helped me to stay grounded enough to continue sobriety and break the chain for my children. When I'm having hard days in my regular life, I think back to that sun dance and how hard I fought during it. I smudge a lot too. That's using smoke from sage, tobacco, cedar, and bear root to cleanse and purify the body, the mind, or even a space. It's my medicine. Smudging is also something I've brought into my kids' lives. It's something I do with them, especially if we're having a hard time or if I feel there's negative energy. Gavin knows how to smudge. Julian and Gavin have their spirit names. They both have rattles and medicine bags. I've received so much from the Indigenous community. They have helped me and my family heal. It's by far one of the greatest gifts I've ever received.

I FOUND OUT IN THE FALL OF 2016 that I have no Aboriginal descent in me at all. I went to the Metis registry at St. Boniface Historical Society to look up my genealogy. Finally, the Society said they couldn't find any link. I wasn't upset, though, because Aboriginal spirituality is the path I've chosen and I would hope that nobody shames me or guilts me on it even though I'm white. Everything that I do is with Indigenous people; everyone I work with is Indigenous and my children are Indigenous (because their mom is). The Indigenous way of life is all my children see now and know. My understanding of the twelve-step program is to become spiritually connected. So Aboriginal spirituality is what I practise.

Today I am going to school at the University of Manitoba and I have my own place and my own vehicle. I am taking the

Applied Counselling Certificate Program (ACCP). After that, I want to get my Bachelor of Social Work. I also volunteer with Mitch's Action Therapy Program, giving back and helping youth, just like the program once helped me. I want to be part of the solution. I never used to talk about my sexual abuse because I didn't think that other people would have gone through something like that. But almost any person that has come out of the drug life or the gang life has probably been affected by trauma in some way. That trauma could be sexual abuse, or it might be another serious trauma like a parent committing suicide or passing away, severe fighting in the home, or even a kid being left alone while the mom or dad goes out partying. There are so many different forms of trauma.

My goal is to help youth and be a strong role model for them. I'm telling my story because I want to help make a difference. I want them to hear that it's not impossible to get out of the gang crowd and to kick an addiction. The youth need to know that there is a way out. I want to join Mitch's Action Therapy Consulting. Mitch is my mentor. Today, everybody I associate with works with youth.

If I were to give advice to a person who has had some kind of serious trauma, I'd say to find someone that they trust, whether it's a therapist, or whoever, and just start talking about it. The more they can get it out, the more they are going to heal. Every time I speak about my own rape, or other traumatic things, I heal a bit more. I tried to sober up several times but the rape was the one thing that I could never speak about. Then when I did speak about it, it was still another five years before I could live in my own skin. Now I truly believe that only because I keep talking about it, can I keep on letting go of a little bit... and a little bit more. Now I don't care who finds out, because it's part of my story. I guess I've matured; I want to get it out and live again.

I am carrying around literally twenty-plus years of drug addiction, gang affiliations, and trauma that will probably remain into my late, late, late life in some shape or form. I am going to have character defects there (like I might be ultra-sensitive), but I'm going to turn the negatives into positives. I still get very angry about a lot of things. (Just because I sobered up, doesn't mean I don't get angry.) But I know how to control it better. I have a conscience now. I'll talk about my problems rather than stuffing them down, because otherwise I'd just become a ticking time bomb. That's the truth.

I just wish my kids and me could have their mother as part of our lives. I still love that woman to death, but addiction is a very sick thing. I don't blame her; she has trauma and things she needs to work on. But right now, there's a boundary that I have to put up from addiction and manipulation, for my kids' sake.

When I think back now, I wish I had listened to the teachings that my grandfather and my mom and dad had given me. My life would have been so different, but back then I was egotistical and thought I could do things my own way. My grandfather was "an elder" to me, still is. We talk regularly. He's ninety-three and he still bowls and golfs sometimes. He is a great man. I think I gave my grandpa one of the greatest gifts I could ever have given him. I did an article about OPK for the French newspaper, *La Liberté*, that he reads. There was a photo of me and my boys, and he could see that I'm clean now.

Even though I don't say it to her, my mom is the one who saved me. I've backed away

KEITH LEVIT

from her a bit because now I've got my own apartment and need my space. My mom has had three drug-addicted, gang-influenced boys and she's been there for us no matter what. My mom has been going through all this madness since I was eleven or twelve. That's like twenty years almost... and that's just with me. She's cared for my brother while he was living with her on parole and had cancer. My mom has opened up her home and helped me raise my sons. Now she's opening up her home to my other brother and helping him to get well, leave the lifestyle, and look after his son. Even though I don't say it, I know my mom is super strong and now that I think about it, my mom's the biggest survivor I know. She's who has kept us all together. My mom has carried the weight of me and my brothers on her shoulders, thinking about what she felt she had done that was wrong. But it's nothing that my mom did wrong. My mom didn't raise us in any way to be the way we were. I brought that into the home. It was my own decision. I have to take responsibility. I think my mom gets her strength from her mom. She didn't want this life for us. She's grandma now to my kids, like my grandma was to me.

My relationship with my dad is decent. He'll come by and visit the boys here and there. We talk every now and then. My dad helped me set up my boys' bunk beds. My dad gave me a good work ethic. But everybody has issues they are dealing with and I've learned that just because I'm dealing with mine, doesn't mean everyone else is dealing with theirs. I have caused some of that pain,

but maybe some of it was also there before I was even born.

I don't put too much bearing on my childhood family. I have a different kind of family now. I've got the support of so many people, as I've said. But my two biggest supports on my road to recovery are my sons, Gavin and Julian. I had to fight very hard through the systems for custody of both of these boys and everything positive I have been doing has been for the sake of my two beautiful, gorgeous boys.

My old life taught me not to trust anybody. My trust was ruined when I was eleven and it affected everything. But at some point, you have to trust others; there's always somebody out there that's willing to help. I also have to trust myself, trust that I'm going to make the right decisions, because, you know what? I'm sober, I've changed my life, and I don't have anything to hide. I'm 100 percent legit.

When I was planning my first interview with Ryan, I wanted to find a location convenient to his home, so he wouldn't have far to go and could easily pick up his kids at daycare afterwards. People at a neighbourhood community space close by kindly allowed us to borrow a room. During the interview, I was shocked and horrified when Ryan told me that, out the window, in the room we were sitting, he could see the house where he had been raped all those years ago. When I expressed concern about that to Ryan, he told me that for years he had walked past that house every day to pick up his family's mail at the community mailbox. That day, he said, being in the room and seeing the house was okay, that this was part of his healing journey and he felt it would help him. He said, "Over the years, I have pushed so much trash down inside me, but over time, more keeps getting revealed to me. It's a reminder that I have to keep moving forward." Today, he continues to be in therapy. He says, "I really had to fight for my children, so that's why I put a lot of work into myself. I want to be the best dad my boys can have and to make right decisions that are based on my children. Today, my whole life revolves around my boys." I was, and am, amazed at Ryan's courage, openness, and positive approach to his healing.

I am also amazed at Ryan's conscientious thoughtfulness and deep sense of gratitude for the support he has received. This was especially evident on the day Ryan was photographed for this story. Ryan brought two vests with him to wear in the photos. His Bear Clan Patrol vest honours his friend and the founding father of the Clan, Larry Morrissette, in addition to bringing awareness to all missing and murdered Indigenous women and girls and their families (because Bear Clan's mission is to make neighbourhood streets safe). The second vest is for the Mama Bear Clan Patrol and honours his mentor, Mitch Bourbonniere, and the women of the North Point Douglas neighbourhood who are showing that love and compassion can bring communities together. In the photos, Ryan's sons are wearing bright coloured cloths around their necks. These are Ryan's sun dance prayer ties. They are filled with Ryan's family's prayers for his next Sun Dance ceremony.

GARRY

We had a normal life in the beginning. I was born in the early '60s and my sister, Kathy, was born three years after me. My early memories are actually of fun times, like the day my dad bought a brand new 1966 Mustang. I was four years old and I remember the smell, the feel, and the look of that car. Years later, I would fix it up and own it. I went to a local school for grades 1 and 2. We lived in the country, just outside Winnipeg on Bird's Hill Road. Back then that area wasn't developed very much. There was a field out back of our house and we had a big garden. It was nice. My dad would park his truck out back and work on it.

But my dad was tired all the time from being on the road as a long-haul truck driver. He was eating a lot of speed and he wasn't consistently stable. One minute he'd be flying high, and the next morning I'd pity the person who would have to wake him up. He pushed himself hard, but when you're a kid, you don't understand your parents at all—they just are the way they are. Later in life, you look back and can say, "Ah well, that's what was going on."

My dad never had a relationship with his father, who died when he was five. My dad had a brother, eight years older, who had more of a relationship with their dad and more memories. My dad hated his brother. My dad was sick as a young child, so he was seen as a momma's boy and a pussy, so he came to hate weakness. His uncles picked on him and it left psychological damage. A lot of the traits I saw my dad frown on, he had himself. Overall, my dad was a good person, a strong guy; he had a lot of good values, a lot of intelligence and was capable of so many things, but his main flaw was not having dealt with his childhood.

My dad got sick of his highway job and he and my mom had this idea they thought would transform our lives. My mom loved animals. She was amazingly, and strangely, good with animals—a horse-whisperer kind of strange. She had been helping the vet, caring for horses. So my parents started developing this dream of getting more involved with horses and getting their own acreage.

They bought some horses and boarded them at a racing stable that had this house out back. When I was in grade 3, we moved there and lived in it. It was a two-bedroom house that had originally been for the help. It had a bathroom in it and was a nice house. We were basically "coat-tailing" off some rich guy that owned it all. My mom did chores on the farm and also worked for the veterinarian who ran the neighbour's operation next door. She was wrapping the horses' bandages and learning things. It became a really good situation for her. She was getting a great "horse education" and because she was so good at getting the horses healthy, she was developing a good reputation. As I grew up, I started working for that vet too. I got the chance to learn how to do a lot of things and I got the chance to see a lot of really nice horses.

Then my dad bought ten acres down the road. There was nothing on that land. The idea was that we'd buy the adjoining forty later. My dad wanted to start his own horse business. We'd board racehorses when they got burnt out at the track. Living like athletes is tortuous for horses and they get so they don't want to run anymore. My parents wanted to provide them with what the vet called *the green doctor*. The owners could send the horses to the farm for a couple of weeks and my mom would bandage their legs and get them in shape and ready to run again.

Our lot was in the middle of the mud. We didn't even have a road approach; we had to drive in through the farmer's field. The summer between grades 3 and 4, we packed up literally everything we had in our car and trailer and drove to our property. That first night, my dad gave us a speech about how we were going to be pioneers and then he started building. He put up four poles and made a little lean-to with a roof over it and a bench inside. He built that thing in ten minutes. We had a Coleman stove and we'd eat our dinners on the bench. This was our home. We had no toilet, no running water, and we slept in a tent. That first night, my dad bought a bucket of chicken for dinner and the dog ate half of it. Today, I don't enjoy camping because back then we were camping for survival.

Next, Dad made our first one-room shack. It was small—maybe twenty by fifteen feet. By then, it was the end of summer and getting cold, but all we had up were the outside boards. We could see the stars at night through the spaces between the boards. My dad used a combination of sawdust and newspaper for insulation, then he put up the inside plywood boards. He wrapped the shack round and round with many layers of tar paper, put a screen over that so the tar paper would stick and stapled it all down. It was supposed to be temporary, but we lived in that shack for the next six years while we were building up the farm. We never had an indoor toilet or running water. This was a really hard time for our family.

We had the place set up, but we weren't there very long before my mom and dad had a complete breakdown. My dad was losing it, coming apart. It was the stress of the road (he was still truck driving), the drugs, the long hours, and the pressure of making the transition before winter. He and my mom also had their own problems going on at that time—probably sexual. She just wasn't turned on by him anymore and so was moving away from him in that way. Even though my mom and dad were starting the horse farm together, they were, at the same time, moving apart. My dad didn't react physically; he never hit my mom, but he was verbally abusive. It just wouldn't end. It was terrible.

My dad decided to leave, and he put me in a tough position by telling me to make a choice: stay with my mom and sister, or go

We had no toilet, no running water, and we slept in a tent.

with him. I told him I was staying. It was a game changer for him and me. I took a bit of a beating that day. I saw my dad in a very poor light, really for the first time. I was in grade 4 and I took it hard. I was terrified.

My dad came back home and somehow my parents pulled out of it, but it was emotionally hard on us all. My dad would feel guilty about beating me up and act all nice, but he would still go back on the road driving his truck again. He kept busy working on the farm too, but he didn't know how to manage the money. He wasn't business savvy. But he was living his dream. Meanwhile, my mom was stranded out in the middle of nowhere, with a couple of kids, working so hard but not having much money, because it was all going into the horses—but she was making it work.

When my dad would come off the road, he should have been sleeping, but he'd only sleep an hour or two, take a handful of pills and start swinging the hammer. He was giving it his all, he had to. My dad did show me some good lessons—how hard you have to work if you want something and how you can do anything. My dad went to the guy who sold us the land and bought an old World War II army barracks that was on that land. He cut it in half, figured out how to put dollies underneath and pulled those forty- by thirty-foot buildings all the way to our farm five miles down the road. My dad was very smart, very creative and did everything the hard way. He put the buildings back together and gutted them, then he used the lumber to make the stalls to house the horses.

My parents brought their reputation to that little dug-out of a farm they started. The racehorse owners kept bringing their overflow horses to us and our business was booming. My dad decided we needed to expand. He bought another barn and hauled it next to the first one, built a centre piece joining the two and redid the shingles just nice. Now there were fifty-two box stalls and we filled them all. The stable looked state of the art inside, as good as any other barn in the racehorse business. Top of the line. But my dad wasn't caring about us in the same way—we were still in that same shack with no running water.

Once we had a reputation for fixing horses, my dad decided we were going to breed horses too. We bought a stallion named Jack's Charger, which was a really smart move. It was a well-bred horse, a direct descendent of one of the most famous horses in the world: Bold Ruler. We bought the offspring of his brother, Bold Bidder. The only reason my dad could buy the horse was because it was uncontrollable. My dad found a way to control and train him, and because his bloodlines were so strong, we had a lineup of mares for breeding with him. We bred fifty-two mares with him in one year. Some owners would bring the mares back to foal with us as well. One year, my parents' business was even named Manitoba Breeder of the Year. My dad would sleep with the mares at night or, if he wasn't there, I would. I was probably thirteen and I was handling a lot of responsibility.

By the time I was sixteen, we'd upgraded our house a bit. It was a bigger shack, an older building that my dad hauled onto our land. This one had running water. I think we were all brainwashed on this type of life and into thinking that horses were all there was in the world. My parents were horse nuts. I was a horse nut too. Still am.

At that time, my mom was sleeping with my dad with her jeans on. From what I remember she went a whole year without taking her jeans off—probably without having sex with him too. One day, my sister and I went out to the movies with our uncle. My dad must have lost it because when we came home, there was a bit of a scene. My dad was literally raping my mom in the front yard. We got there right in time to stop it.

That was the final straw. She left him right after that. When she left our family behind, she had someone to go to—my dad's best friend. She got a tiny apartment in the town of Stony Mountain. For the first time in my life, I saw that my mom had freedom and independence. My sister and I stayed with my dad, but then my mom took my sister later. When that first guy didn't treat her very well, she moved on and found a younger guy. He was eleven or twelve years younger than her. He seemed like a nice guy, and they settled down together for several years.

I left home when I was seventeen, in the spring. I had quit high school after grade 10 and had been working on the farm for free. The day I left, I had a fight with my dad. I don't even remember what started it. There was probably something ignorant I said to him that made him mad. I was probably standing up for myself. He literally punched and slapped the piss out of me. He was sitting on top of me slapping me when the phone rang. It was like getting saved by the bell. He went to answer the phone and it was my mom. I remember this as clear as day. I could hear him begging her to come back. I just thought, *What a pathetic piece of crap.* I grabbed a chair and just went to town on him. It was the very first time he was scared of me. My mom could hear my dad getting destroyed and she got scared that I was going to get killed once my dad got up. So she called the RCMP. She probably did the right thing. As I was leaving, the RCMP came in the yard. They held my dad back while I got in my car. (Things with the cops were different back then.)

I went to my aunt's, my mom's sister. She and my uncle were really good people. (They're still my favourite aunt and uncle.) They knew what I was going through. I stayed with them for a good month. They always had a couch for me to lie on and never a question asked. After that month, I found myself a job selling vacuum cleaners door to door for Filter Queen. It was easy. The company had good leads for me. I started making $300 a week. I bought a nice shirt and tie, and a pair of sneakers. I looked ridiculous, but I was trying my hardest to be a salesman and I expected to sell a vacuum on every single call. It was a very competitive business—there was a little prize and a photo on the board in the office for whoever was the seller of the week and everybody wanted that. I won that quite a few months. Eventually, they put me out towards Fisher Branch, calling on farm families. It was out in the middle of nowhere, but I liked the freedom.

What I didn't like was lying to people about them needing a big piece of equipment. I remember this one person calling me and getting mad at me because I sold a little old lady a $600 vacuum cleaner and all she had was one small rug. But I kept on because of the benefits I was getting: I had a car, I had freedom, and I was making money. I was on the road living in a motel. I did that for a year, and during all that time I didn't talk to my dad. I was going to hate him forever at that point, but my dad missed me and missed our relationship, so I ended up going back and living with him for about six months. My dad remarried—the first lady that came along. She was terrible. They blew all the money. (The farm was still making money at that time.)

Next, I moved in with my mom and sister in Stony Mountain. My mom wasn't home much; she was going back and forth to her boyfriend's place. I had to stay with my sister who was going to high school. After selling vacuum cleaners, I ended up getting a job working in a warehouse, unloading box-cars, moving bags of rice and nuts until my fingers were raw. From working at home on the farm, I had a good work ethic. I thought that ware-house job was easy so I got a second job unloading trucks for Purolator. I still had enough energy to do that for three hours a night. The work didn't seem hard.

If I hadn't bought a Harley, I probably never would have ended up being around the gang. Sometimes I think about how different my life would've been if I had just stayed with the Japanese bikes.

THAT'S HOW I HAD THE MONEY to buy a new motorcycle and that's when my life really changed. I bought a Japanese motor-cycle, a Honda. At first, I was happy with it, but by the end of the year, I traded my bike in three times until I bought the bike I really wanted—a Harley Davidson. If I hadn't bought a Harley, I probably never would have ended up being around the gang. Sometimes I think about how different my life would've been if I had just stayed with the Japanese bikes.

There's only a couple of Harley shops in the city. You either go to the expensive shop or you go to the guy who has the garage business where you can get deals. That guy was in the gang. He was initiated because he could service the gang members' bikes. He was the friendliest— wasn't a tough guy or anything like that. He was only in the gang because he could twist wrenches. Having my Harley was how I ended up meeting everybody in the gang, because I had it in there getting fixed and members are always scoping for new recruits.

One day when I was hanging out with the gang, there was this Tough Man Contest where you have to fight one guy after another after another, until you are the last guy stand-ing. I was not really well trained for it, but I went in anyway, against a much older, bigger guy. It was '82 and I was twenty. I had been in good shape from unloading boxcars, but that job had ended and I was on unemploy-ment insurance. I was already partying a bit too much, starting to do a few drugs, staying up all night and not taking care of myself. When I fought this guy, I knocked him out before the bell rang. I should have been disqualified. After he got up off the ground, the fight continued because the guy wanted to. I did really well, but I didn't win the fight because you had to win by knockout. To be honest, I was lucky just to survive that first fight because I wasn't prepared to fight anyone. I didn't understand what it takes to be that kind of athlete: you've got to be in good shape. The gang knew me a bit before, but once they saw me in that competition, I drew some attention, including from the president of the club at the time.

It wasn't the money that motivated me to be interested in the gang. It was riding the motorcycles and the tough-guy image more than anything, because I had such a weak image of myself. I was hooked on having my bike and riding with a biker crowd. It was very family-like in a way, and I wanted to be a part of it. You've got the harmless everyday bikers—the enthusiasts—but then you've got the "one percenters." They're the outlaws, the criminals—that's who I wanted to be with. It was such a powerful, badass image, but I

didn't see myself living long enough to bother caring. Thirty is old. Seeing guys in their thirties and forties, I'd think, *I won't live that long.* I just accepted that.

I spent my first year just hanging around the club. I didn't go to any clubhouse. I was just meeting guys at the motorcycle shop. Then the president invited me to the clubhouse. He was a pretty tough guy, always going to jail, putting the gang at risk, so a lot of guys didn't like him. My first role was as a striker, another word for a prospect, but half the guys didn't like me because the president had brought me in. It was hard work to not let myself get picked on. Some guys would get tough with me, but I had to take care of myself without being disrespectful, so I played it safe. The club had hunting rifles and my job was to sit with other strikers and do shifts on lookout. I did that for maybe another year. I'd go to meetings, but strikers had to leave part way through.

I got my rocker—that's a term used for the label with the gang name on the back of the vest. It's a striker patch. At that time, I had just started to date my first wife. She had no idea I was hanging out with a gang. I just came home with a vest after the meeting.

Next, I tried to do collections for a while—really, that's extorting. I could beat up a guy, but I couldn't do it in front of his wife or kids, so I wasn't very successful. I was supposed to get half of everything I collected, but I never actually collected anything. There were plenty of times I refused to do things the gang wanted me to do. I never once folded. Some of the things I saw were very disgusting, so I steered clear of that kind of stuff.

That was a time when things were going mad and wild with the club. I was caught in a crazy world of lucky to be alive. See, there were a lot of things happening that I didn't know about when I joined. The guy that brought me into the club was making all these deals and getting a bad name. I didn't know about the deals that were going on. Our club and another big motorcycle club had amalgamated. We were small players compared with some of the big, bad clubs out there, but our guys beat up the guys in the other club, shut them down, made them take off their old patches and that was it. The old club was over. Our club took a handful of them and patched them over to our club. We just kept the drug dealers because they could make money.

So we weren't a tight group. No one trusted each other. No one liked each other. There was a lot of animosity and cliques. I was more like an outsider, hanging out with other strikers. I never got close to anybody. I was really scared at that time because you just didn't know who might show up or whether you'd get blown away. Everybody was beating up everybody else, for anything. The punishments were rough.

When we were at our biggest, there were sixty-five guys. You put that number of people in a room and no one's going to agree on anything. There was nothing but problems.

Cocaine was brand new on the scene. It was really pure and there were only a few guys in our club selling it. Three or four were making a lot of money off it, turning all their brothers into addicts and making them peddle their asses on the street to make their money back from their drug debts after getting into it. They were all using each other. There's no "let's do this together and split the money." It's a few guys, parasites, using their friends (gang members). Thank God I didn't like coke, because none of us knew the danger then. I'd do a line here or there sometimes, get high, and then feel so sad afterwards.

Guys were really getting hooked on it. I saw so many people's lives destroyed by cocaine. Hash was more my thing.

I was making my own money separate from the gang, so I didn't need to sell dope for them. I had been working with a friend, stealing money. My friend was a safe-cracker. We were doing sneaky, through-the-wall stuff. This guy didn't believe in hurting people, didn't even want to hold a gun. I liked that; it was smart.

The next thing I know the club had a meeting and I was kicked out. They lined all the guys up and told us *yay or nay*, telling us we were in or out. I was given some bullshit reasons why and I was thrown out. I couldn't figure out what was going on. I was a good little striker and I was very confused— what had I done wrong? There were a lot of false accusations and then the club broke up.

I just slid out of that scene and right into jail. My buddy and I did a robbery and it went bad. I ended up getting a year and a half in Headingley. My buddy got longer. I went to Headingley after Christmas in 1983. I spent New Year's and my February birthday in jail.

Then, I got paroled in May '84. I was only in for a short time because it was my first offence. During that time in prison, I remember wondering if this experience was going to change me. I probably did have good intentions of changing as soon as I got out, but I didn't.

Once I was out, I got a call. "Hey, we're rebuilding the club, a whole new chapter." The club was supposed to have broken up, but a few of the founding members were getting it back together. There were only fourteen or fifteen members, so there'd be less people fighting each other. Seeing that I hadn't been a member when it folded, I was brought back as a striker. I was the only one. Then we had one meeting and I was brought in as a member. There was nothing spectacular about getting my patch.

It was crazy, because after I got out of jail and I was on parole, I was supposed to be staying away from the club. I'd tell my parole officer that I wasn't hanging around with the club, but I was living that life every day. I was going to the clubhouse. I had a

During that time in prison, I remember wondering if this experience was going to change me. I probably did have good intentions of changing as soon as I got out, but I didn't.

common-law girlfriend and a one-year-old son at home. My son was born just after I got out of prison in 1984. I also had a second girlfriend, so I was being nomadic, living from place to place. That's nothing I'm proud of. (It's considered normal in the club to have a wife or a permanent wife-type relationship with family and then have a girlfriend too. Most gang members were polygamous if they had the opportunity. That's accepted in this sub-culture.)

That first year after prison, even though I was hanging out with the gang, I lay low and didn't have any problems. At the time, I had one foot in the gang and one foot out. My son was born and my father-in-law had got me a job doing roofing. Everybody was pulling for me to get out of the gang and start over. I was starting work again, but I was also flirting with the gang.

I was trying to stay out of sight, but I would take a chance and go to the club meetings. The police were watching me. They could see that I was doing this and would mention it to my parole officer, but I would say, "I'm not doing anything. They're saying that because they don't like me." I didn't give a shit. I was laughing about most of it. It

was a game. The cops could have pulled me in for violating my parole, but that would've taken me off the street only for a little while. I would have gone back to jail, got more friends, and more experience. In jail, you get even more connected with gang members and that life, so the police don't want to arrest you for something small.

EVERYTHING CHANGED on the May long weekend in 1985. It was my last weekend of parole. Our gang was going on a bike run to a campground and partying for the weekend. Our gang had four mandatory runs a year. I could have been exempt because I was on parole. The gang had told me not to worry; it wouldn't count against me if I didn't go. But I said F-it. My girlfriend wanted to go and I wanted to go too. I wanted to party.

So I went. Most of it was fun. We were just partying and driving motorcycles around the camp. We had a barbeque and then I napped. When I woke up, I was fresh, not even drunk at that point. It was evening, so I went back to the barbeque. Three different biker gangs were there and the guys were all old fogies: thirties, forties, fifties. I was twenty-three and with a young girlfriend. We wanted to be where the young people were, so we left our campground and went to the main party ground. Our gang had never had a run on Crown property before; we'd always been on private property. It was a big mistake. And because of me, they never did it again.

I remember the scene clearly: Me, my girlfriend, and another friend (a biker with a broken arm) walk up to a bigger crowd and start talking to everybody. We're both wearing our patches, and I feel totally in sync with the crowd. (I hadn't even had one drink.) They are friends and I'm not some intruder. I see a pick-up truck coming very fast with a bunch of guys on the back. They are local guys, all hockey players. They had just finished off the playoffs and two were drafted to the NHL. They're blowing off some steam, but I didn't know any of that then. The truck stops and a guy jumps out. I don't know this guy at all. I find out later that he was a tough guy, an enforcer, a fighter in the hockey league. He's the cocky guy coming through our group and he breaks in between me and my friend and smashes us. My buddy's got the broken arm. And this guy stands in front of us like a stupid jerk, laughing. Both of us are eager to fight. I say, "Hey man, what's your problem?" and smack him in the face to dummy him up. Instead of backing down, he explodes; the fight is on. I grab him in a head-lock and I'm punching him and he's trying to hold me. He grabs for my knife, but I grab it so he can't get at it and now his buddies are there very quickly. I feel them pulling my hair, punching me and pulling me to the ground. I start stabbing as I'm falling backwards. I think I stab three times around his armpit, but I only get him once. It's in the stomach area, under his rib cage, through his heart and into his lung.

What happened after is that I had the guy in my arms and I lay him down. I didn't know the damage. I just thought he was going down from losing blood. I looked at his buddies and said, "You happy? Is that what you wanted? Now, get this guy to a hospital." Then I walked away. I didn't run. We got into the car and we drove out of the campground. As we drove, we passed a continuous flow of police cars and emergency vehicles (ten or twenty) driving in. Later, I found out that they had taken our whole gang and lined them up in the spotlights of the cars. The police had all the witnesses going up and down the line to identify. They picked out the suspect that night.

I was gone. I hid that night with my girl-friend and my buddy. The next day, I went to our gang's clubhouse and I remember one of the vice-presidents saying, "Garry, did you have to kill him?" I didn't even know he was dead. I had no idea. They told me I had better get out of there, so I went into hiding for one more day. I don't think the cops knew it was me yet. I had decided that I would turn myself in the next day. I told my girlfriend that I didn't think things were going to work out for us anymore. And I had to go see my common-law wife and my son to fix things up with them.

The next day, my wife and I went to the clubhouse. We were going to meet my lawyer and then I was going to turn myself in, thinking that maybe I could get bail that way. So I'm sitting in the clubhouse with my wife and my buddy, drinking Caesars. My sister had my son at home with her. My lawyer never showed up, so I suspect that he just called the cops and told them where to pick me up. The police SWAT team came in and took me down. It was pretty scary.

I had some assets tied up in our home in the North End, but it wasn't worth much. The lawyer wanted everything. He told me if I gave him $50,000, he'd for sure get my charge reduced to manslaughter. I didn't have that kind of money, so I went with legal aid.

I waited almost a year for my trial and spent it all in solitary confinement in Headingley. Each of those solitary cells had old gallows, so there were once people who slept in those cells and then died in them. It was really shitty—very hard psychologically. Really, really terrible.

The trial was pretty straightforward. The lawyer made it look like he was defending me, but I wasn't really being defended. The Crown had the guy's bloody clothes and gory pictures of his wounds. They had a knife and said it was mine. This really impacted the jury. But it wasn't my knife because the night of the murder a couple of gang members I was close with had got rid of it. They threw it down a crevice between two giant rocks at the campsite. They told me no one would ever have found it. The knife in court had blood on the handle, but it wasn't my blood type. That knife had been used by the group to butcher a stolen cow for our dinner. Still, they tied me to the knife because it was all the prosecutor had. There was no DNA testing back then like there is today. They had a clump of my hair, but could only say it was "consistent with my hair." Again, no DNA technology. They really had no evidence tying me to the murder. I was the right guy, but they were just a bunch of lying sacks of shit lying to get me in jail. They got the right guy, but the narrative was totally wrong, 100 percent wrong.

They offered me a manslaughter charge if I turned my friend in (the one with the broken arm who was with me that night). He'd already done five or six years. He was a young guy, one of those guys abused in jail. He didn't deserve to go to jail for something that he didn't do. Maybe for some, the easiest thing to do is sell out another human being and save yourself, but I knew I was guilty. I had enough integrity. I didn't rat on him. Everybody wants to be the best person and do the right thing, but I actually told the truth. I was directed by my lawyer to say I was innocent; he insisted my only chance was to go for an acquittal. I was very uncomfortable at the trial. I wanted to take the stand and tell my side of the story, but my lawyer said no. Then I got the life sentence and ten years (meaning that I was eligible for parole in ten years). I never blamed my lawyer for my sentence; I blamed myself. I was fucked.

After the trial, they held me in Remand waiting for the appeal. I had the grounds for an appeal, but the appeal process was a joke. At the appeal court hearing, they laughed at me. They told me right to my face that I was going down because of who I was: a gang member. The club name was just booming at the time, so they were happy to send me to prison. I accepted it because I understood that I was paying for an entire lifestyle. I was paying for every wrong choice I had ever made.

After the appeal, I was to be locked up in a maximum-security facility. Stony Mountain didn't have that. The maximum lock up in Stony is basically the hole (solitary confinement). They don't hold guys there very long unless it's extreme, or they can't go anywhere else for their own safety because everybody wants to kill them. The two automatic places for lifers in Western Canada are Kent and Edmonton. If you don't have family there, they don't give a shit. Then after a couple of years, they phase you back to medium security. In my case, my lawyer fought very hard for me to stay in a high-medium security because that's what Stony is. I was lucky; they let me go to Stony because I had family in Manitoba. (I deserved to go there, but you don't always get what you deserve from this world.)

When I went away for the second prison sentence, it was totally different than the first. I just gave up that I was ever going to get out. I couldn't see the light at the end of the tunnel. When I was sentenced, I cried and cried. When I was first in Stony, they gave me pretty much every chance to make it. The guards were pretty good and the staff wasn't gunning for me. A couple of prisoners had killed a couple of guards there—this was before I arrived. Before that, guards used to look the other way a lot when it came to drugs and alcohol. There was a new tone set in the prison after those killings. But regardless I felt almost free after having been in solitary confinement for eleven months. Solitary was so much worse than the regular prison that I was pretty happy at Stony. I was eating all the crappy food and loving it. Everyone was kinda laughing at me.

First, I was in general population for a few weeks, just for processing. I had just been moved into my new cell and then I must have looked at a guy the wrong way. I found

out later that he was an informant in on a name change, total witness protection. This guy was important in some case and they needed to keep him alive. I didn't know what I had done wrong. The guards questioned me and wanted to know why I had it in for this particular guy and had told him I'd wanted to kill him. I didn't know what they were talking about. I used to tell the other inmates not to look at me or talk to me. You got to be cruel when you first come into the prison because you don't want to start talking to the wrong person.

Often the first people that try to be your friends in prison are the worst people, because they're the outcasts and needy. Friendship in that environment can truly be min-max—the maximum that you can do for me and the least amount I'm going to do for you. (That's how friendships are based anyway, but it's even more so in prison.) Later, I would end up with a crowd of lifers that were pretty nice to me.

So I was thrown into the hole in Stony. Since I'd already done close to a year in the hole, it was tough. The entire three weeks

> Often the first people that try to be your friends in prison are the worst people, because they're the outcasts and needy.

I was in solitary, I was very angry. I would say I became psychologically estranged from myself. I think a weaker person would have gone insane. My input was negative, so it became negative in and negative out. I was totally in harmony with my surroundings, which were terrible. (Although if you're not in harmony with your surroundings you're in a lot of trouble too.) I was aware of the psychological damage being in the hole was doing to me. It broke me in a way. I knew I was becoming institutionalized. Before, I had been living this unstructured life, then prison and solitary. I started to feel comfortable with the cage closing at night. I knew there was a psychological play that was going on that would need fixing or rebuilding down the road. I had to de-program myself later on when I needed the doors to be open. You gotta find your way out. It's a very deep rabbit hole.

Finally, the internal security guards realized that I was just really dumb about what was going on and I really didn't know who this guy was. I think he was skittish. He was transferred to another prison. The prison administration let me out of the hole, but I ended up with this "incident" with this guy on my file until just a few years ago.

So now I'm back out of the hole and I got a second chance, but the administration put me on the Native range. It was a cultural range and I was the only white guy. The other inmates didn't like white guys. They didn't even like half-breeds; they were considered second-class citizens. But I don't think I was put on that range maliciously. The prison was just full and it was probably the only spot.

One thing that helped me fit in right away was my love of hockey and being a good hockey player. Stony had a hockey league. Growing up my best friend was Cree, so I didn't look down on my Native inmates. But I didn't understand their culture, so I was having troubles tolerating it. The inmates were always banging their drums and burning their sweet grass. One of the guys on the range told me, "You have to learn to exist here," and then he showed me how.

At that time in my life, I was spiritually empty because I had given up any idea of God or the dogmatic system I was raised on. My life had been about doing whatever I wanted and having fun. I didn't give a shit. I had a closed mind to all religion, but this guy got me hooked up into something that filled a void in my life.

I saw guys going to sweat lodges and, you know what, I got curious. I wasn't planning any outcome of a spiritual nature; I just thought it looked fun. My second year in the jail, I went to my first sweat lodge. I went respectfully, but not looking for anything. I respected the customs, the people, the process, and the potentiality of what might happen there. I had no idea people could have visions there or what that would feel like. I fasted, I think, for a few days before, so I was tired and weak. I was dehydrated. And then when I got into the sweat lodge, I was hallucinating. I was mentally separated from my physical self.

While I was in there I had a vision. It was not something that I *saw*; it wasn't a picture. Instead the vision that came to me was a *knowing*. It was something that I needed. It was a wake-up moment where I knew I needed more. The vision that came to me was that I was going to play football in the CFL.

After the sweat lodge, I went to the showers and I was trying to make sense of what I was feeling, what I thought. It had all been so weird. I had a good cry in the showers, a bit of a mental breakdown really.

At that time in my life, I never cried. I had just started seeing a psychologist and the very

first thing he said to me was that if I had an opportunity to cry, I shouldn't hold back. He said that holding back was really unhealthy. I had been doing that for so many years. I was running from my pain in such a profound way that it was very damaging to the people around me and to myself. So it hit me that day—*boom*—I had a big cry. I let it happen just like the psychologist had said and it felt good.

So I started crying whenever I felt I needed to. When you're in prison you can't admit you're scared or sad because the guys around you can't allow that weakness in their lives. So guys put up these walls and won't cry. But they do. You hear it when the doors are locked and the lights are out. When it's 3 am. That's when you hear men crying, crying like babies.

Shortly after that sweat lodge, I woke up one night at three or four in the morning, shaking like a leaf. Terrified. Never been scared like that in my life. I'm sitting on the edge of my bed, two years in on a life sentence; the minimum number of years for release was so far ahead of me. And I think to myself, *What the fuck have I done?* I suddenly regretted every single thing that brought me to that moment. It wasn't just a single incident, it was the combination of the way I had lived my life, the bad energy.

What got me out of that moment? I made a commitment to change. I actually made a promise to myself and a deal with my Creator. *You give me football and I will work with kids.* It's something I committed to and did: coaching football, jiu-jitsu, working with youth. Later on, there were a couple of times I stopped working with kids and the football disappeared. But then the phone would ring with another football opportunity and I'd get back to working with kids again. While I was on the Native range, I got to know my Native brothers. You could see the social injustices against them, just by the numbers. I started to understand their situation about three years in and, by the eighth or ninth year, I could really understand my Native brothers around me.

So I had this dream of playing football professionally. I didn't listen to logic. I didn't even have a plan. But I started training like an athlete every day. The food was not good in prison. You can't build a body on Kraft Dinner and wieners and beans. So I was sneaking a dozen to eighteen eggs a day. One of the guards would let another of the inmates steal meat for me every night. Some guys were scamming dope; I was scamming food.

I was fighting against the mentality of some of the guards and guys I sat with to eat, who found this all entertaining. These were guys that never went nowhere in life. My dream was completely outside of their level of understanding. I was being ridiculed by them and so I stopped talking to them. Instead of arguing, I'd just tell them that one day, they'd see me on TV. Really, those guys helped me because they pushed me to work harder.

In the beginning, I did some drugs, but then I quit everything in my last five years in jail. I was never into heavy drugs, so it was easy to quit. I was 100 percent no drugs, no alcohol. I had this good reason to let go of that lifestyle. It was a way of making me feel, while I was locked up, like I was in control, even though I wasn't.

I married my common-law wife in 1988 while I was in jail. I was really trying to rebuild my family. My wife was bringing my

> I actually made a promise to myself and a deal with my Creator. *You give me football and I will work with kids.*

son to visit every week. I started taking university courses inside too. I had only grade 10, so I applied as a mature student. The idea is that life experience can take the place of high school, so for a few of us that was the case. For the majority, no. Most people were working on basic literacy. Your marks have to stay at a certain point, so that takes hard work and commitment. Thirty-five people dropped out and that left six of us. I had a hunger for knowledge and I studied really hard—as long as it was a subject I was interested in: psychology, philosophy, sociology. I never finished; I'm five credits short of a university degree—but I had more courses than my case-management worker in the prison.

In '92, my daughter, Cheyenne, was born. I had conjugal visits with my wife every three months when I was in prison. It was all earned. My behaviour had to be good inside. By then, I was just training and I had the luxury of being left alone. Cheyenne has been special to me since the morning the guard woke me and told me she'd been born. A guard handed me the message on a piece of paper and I put it beside my bed because when I woke up in the morning, I wanted to make sure it wasn't a dream.

While I was in Stony I was president of our Children's Wish Foundation group inside the prison. During the six years I was actively involved, we raised enough money each year ($5,000) to grant a wish to a sick child. Helping those kids was a way for us all to feel good. We raised money a few different ways. We tie-dyed t-shirts and sold them to guys in the prison through the prison's canteen. Then I contacted the Manitoba Boxing Commissioner, who was a really nice man, who allowed the prison to host amateur fights inside (using amateur boxers, not inmates) to raise money.

WHILE I WAS IN STONY, I met Tim Jesse, a runningback from the Winnipeg Blue Bombers Football Club. He volunteered with our lifers group. He was a kind guy and curious about us. He had a full salary from the Bombers, but was getting towards the end of his career and wasn't playing much. They were keeping him on the injury reserve list in case they needed him, so he had lots of spare time and came every week to the prison to hang out with us. Any guests that came into our lifer group were immensely important to me. I couldn't wait to wrap my head around their conversations. (The educational system was the same for me too.)

The first thing Tim said to me when he met me was, "Holy shit, you ever play football?" I was 6'3", 305 pounds. He didn't even know I'd had the dream in the shower. No idea.

I said, "Well, I have a desire to." I had these big plans, but, at that moment, I didn't even put two and two together, that this was a guy who could help me.

In 1994, when I was up for day parole, Tim Jesse introduced me to Urban Bowman the interim head coach at the Bombers. I was given a private evaluation. Coach Urban Bowman wrote a letter of support to the parole board stating I was the most incredible physical specimen he'd ever seen in thirty years of coaching football and that I was officially invited to preseason camp if I got parole. It happened while the head coach, Cal Murphy, had been in the hospital for heart surgery. When he got out and heard about the evaluation and the team's interest, he decided not to sign me.

> Coach Urban Bowman wrote a letter of support to the parole board stating I was the most incredible physical specimen he'd ever seen in thirty years of coaching football and that I was officially invited to preseason camp if I got parole.

I was up for this day parole and the Board had told Coach Murphy that they'd give it to me if the Bombers would give me a job. He didn't like that kind of responsibility. There was too much hype. No one else comes to a team with that kind of stipulation—*we'll give a guy parole for murder if you give him a job.* I never held that decision against Coach Murphy.

When I got day-paroled I went to the penitentiary's Pacific region, which includes BC. It was a progressive liberal region with good case planners. When I reported to them, they told me they could let me go and that they'd heard I was going to play football when I got out. I told them I was thinking of contacting the BC Lions, but I played that down because I didn't want to get my parole turned down like before in Winnipeg. They said, "We wish you luck and we're celebrating." I thought it was a joke, but it was real. I cried. I'd been inside for eight years.

I was trying to start my life over. I was looking over my shoulder, not because I was doing anything wrong, but because I wasn't used to living unprotected. I felt vulnerable and naked. But this time, when I got out of jail, I made a firm decision to leave the gang. I was not going to fuck around.

So I contacted the BC Lions and they put me in their first mini football camp. I tried out for the defensive line. They brought a whole busload of hungry linemen wannabees in from Seattle, Washington. They lined me up against ten guys, no equipment and made me do one-on-one drills. It was brutal: guys ripping off shirts, grabbing lips and skin. These were skilled guys. I got beat up really good. To be honest, I got my ass kicked. The coaches just wanted to see if I was tough enough—and I was.

After the mini-camp I met with Head Coach Dave Ritchie. George Chayka, the director of marketing, got me my first meeting with Coach Ritchie. Coach Ritchie asked me how I'd got there. He knew, but he wanted to hear my story about Urban Bowman and Tim Jesse. He also wanted to know why the Blue Bombers hadn't used me. I told him there'd been a lot of hype in the media (because I'd been in jail for murder) and it didn't work out.

I didn't know it at the time, but the BC Lions' owner liked me and had told the coach to make sure he gave me a shot. Coach Ritchie told me he didn't know what to do with me, but he said, "We have a free agents camp next week and the week after, we have a rookie camp. If there's anything left of you and if you make it and there's room on the roster, we'll add you."

The rookie camp was the hardest. There we were wearing football equipment, something I wasn't used to. It was bulky. I hadn't worn equipment since I played football for two years in high school. (I only played for grades 9 and 10 before I quit school.) The other guys were tough, tough, tough people. I was the only O-lineman at the rookie camp. There were two very good D-linemen. I had to try out with this guy, Doug Peterson, who turned out to be one of the best D-linemen in the league. All the rest of the rookies were receivers or runningbacks. I remember that the first time I lined up on Doug for a drill, I got him really good. I literally ran him over and he landed on his back. My offensive line coach was freaking out he was so happy. The coach built my confidence up. Doug and I ended up playing together and becoming friends.

I did really well at the camps. I showed I could play football and be valuable somewhere. The team could have got an American player better than me in one day, but they had only so many American spots to fill and the rest of the roster had to be Canadians. The teams were paying the American players almost nothing to play in Canada. The Americans wanted to be seen so they could hopefully get back to the NFL. They were using the CFL as a stepping-stone.

It's tricky because there're only so many spots on the roster: thirty-nine for the team and sixteen spots on the reserve and practice roster. Sometimes the teams use all the available spots just to hold good guys, so they don't have to give away players they like. The BC Lions signed me to their practice roster instead of taking a chance on losing me to another team. I got in because I am Canadian and I worked as cheap as the Americans. I was the oldest rookie in the history of the CFL. I was 32.

The management called me in and said, "You're probably not anybody we can use regularly this year, but you know what… we could use you if everyone on the O-line becomes injured." The truth was, I had just got day-paroled and had been out of jail for only a few weeks. I was locking up in a halfway house every night, so I couldn't have travelled with the team. I'd practise with them every day and get locked up every night. I really couldn't have made the team anyways, so there was not the same pressure. The only pressure was if the team did need me to play in an away game, I'd have to get a special pass or be locked up in a halfway house somewhere close to the team's hotel. I was insurance. If someone got injured, the team could pull me up to the active roster as a replacement at any time.

The coaches said I was good for the team. It was an older-than-average-aged team and a lot of the older players liked me. They hung out with me and guided me. They took me through my rookie year, where you have to sing songs and be ridiculous; the kind of fraternity stuff I missed because I never went to college. It was a wonderful group of people. Amazing. I remember sitting in the hot tub after practice and guys wanting to hear stories about jail. I don't know why; there's nothing exciting about jail, trust me.

I was the oldest rookie in the history of the CFL. I was 32.

I was trying to get away from that part of my life, but I was happy that they were interested because at least I had acceptance. Some of the guys would take me out after practice, but I was always afraid. I didn't want to blow my curfew. I had far more fears than the young kids had. They were adults, but in my mind, they were kids compared to me. I'd been through the shit hole already.

A sports team and a gang represent two contrasting worlds. The only thing that was similar was the togetherness. The sense of "family" with the team was very much like with the gang and the celebrations seemed the same, but the activities were far different. The football was honest. The guys were so hard-working; they were physically tough people, that's the difference. I have so much respect for any football player, anybody that can go through the league for two or three years. They are legit. I think football and training prepares you for anything in life.

After putting my body through those camps, I was beat up pretty good. I looked like the whole team had just gone at me: you could actually see the finger marks up and down my arms. I was bruised. I was seriously messed up. One of those days, I was sitting on the couch, my knees in an ice bath, watching the bloody football movie *Any Given Sunday* with my son when he says, "Dad, now you're going to the main camp!" (My son's so proud I made the team.) But I couldn't move. Honestly, I thought at that moment that I wasn't going to be able to do it. I knew I'd be going into camp with all these veterans and they were fresh. They'd been training in the offseason, all their past season's injuries fixed up. I knew that I'd be coming in a way behind everybody in physical training.

The funniest part is that I still, deep down, expected to make that team. I always did. I never look back and I always have blinders on. It was my strength and my weakness— still is. I was lucky: every step of the way it could have been over. I was scared of not making it, but that fear drove me on. My attitude from day one was that I was physically better than the other guy in front of me. (I didn't realize then that there was this mental part of football too.) I felt I was going to out-beast anybody in front of me—if you're fast, I'm going to be faster. If you're strong, I'm going to be stronger. I had some success with that. It got me in the door. It made people curious. I didn't realize how lucky I was to even get the chance to try out. I should have been too old for the CFL. I was never satisfied with anything. I wasn't satisfied with any success; it'd always come with wanting more. I even thought I was going to play in the NFL too. At that time, I didn't have a filter for my dreams. Later on, I would even have a meeting with Joe Gallant, a famous NFL coach. He actually had the courtesy to meet me—in a Starbucks in Vancouver—but he told me "Son, you're just too old."

So I had my blinders on about the football camp. I started using the practice roster time wisely: lifting weights, running, and conditioning. I had to learn how to move and run plays. I had to learn the game and its psychology. I started to learn that I didn't always have to smash the guy into the dirt; all I had to do was make him off balance so we could run the play successfully. Once I understood that, it was easier.

In '94, I played in one preseason game, a local game against the Las Vegas Posse. I played at the end. They put me in for maybe six plays. It was probably less than two minutes. It went by so fast. I felt like I didn't even know what I was doing out there, but when I saw the game film after, I had done

everything right. Sometimes I would feel like I barely got a piece of the guy, but then when I looked at the play, that one piece of the guy made the other player lose a step and that one step made a hole for our runningback to get away. When my name appeared on the practice roster, the media thought the Lions were using me as a stunt—just to get people curious and watching the team. They didn't realize everybody was dead serious.

That year the Lions won the Grey Cup. I saw what a winning attitude was like. The coaches were smart. And they knew what they were doing with me too. I didn't hold anybody back.

During the football offseason, my family and I were living in Vancouver, so Cheyenne and I spent a lot of time together. She was still in diapers. In Vancouver, you don't want to lose your daycare spot. I'd take her there in the morning, go to the corner store, and then come back and say, "I'm taking Cheyenne home for the day." We were officially there on the books, but more times than not, I was busting her out of there. We'd go to Stanley Park and the aquarium just about every day. We'd visit the bottlenose dolphins and the beluga whale. She'd ride on my shoulders.

We'd go to movies or a restaurant. I'd put juice in a wine glass and spoil her. It was incredible. Eventually I would not live in the same city as Cheyenne, but we've always been able to maintain that close relationship.

Then comes 1995. I'm invited back. Now I can actually compete for the job because I'm out of the halfway house. At camp, there were fourteen guys for six spots. All the guys in front of me were CFL veterans and American linemen the team had brought up from US colleges. I had an advantage over the Americans because I was Canadian and I was working cheap so I had some value. Those two things made me lucky, but I had to really compete hard against the other Canadian linemen. I don't break—that was my attitude and I just kept going forward. I had to beat out a lot of good names. I made the active roster as the sixth guy. That meant that if the first guy went down on the O-line, I'd be a replacement. It blew me away. By the end of the season, I was starting and then in '96, they started me for the game opener.

My first practice after the '95 camp, I showed up early at the stadium. All the media were there to do a story about me. I don't know if they got together ahead and planned it or what, but they all lined up and shook my hand. There were eight of them. They apologized. They told me that they truly thought it had been a stunt the year before, until they realized I was a good football player. I was blown away. They did a big article on me in the paper.

In '95, I played a preseason game in Winnipeg against the Blue Bombers. Funny thing was, a number of the guards I'd been ridiculed by in Stony were at that game. The Lions started me that day. I played two quarters and I was even brought out for the coin toss. Wow. In one way, it felt so good—it was a *fuck you* moment. But in the end, I would never get off on those kinds of moments like my original intentions were. When I got to the moment, it just didn't feel right. The thought of revenge felt kinda empty. Instead I felt sorry for those guards, almost pity.

So '94 was a camp year. Then I played for the Lions in '95 and '96. In 1997, I got cut and then picked up by Hamilton and had a camp there. I played a couple of games, but then I got cut, too late to be picked up by another team. I remember when I went to Hamilton, I came in looking for a starting job and there was a guy a year younger than me who was already retiring. He'd already had fifteen years in the league. I was old, but I wasn't giving up.

My personal life was a bust that year too—my marriage fell apart. Things hadn't been good for a while. My wife would say or do anything. And that could be really dangerous for someone doing life, especially when she was calling my parole officers.

In '98, I had a staph infection and was too late to catch a tryout so I didn't play. I lived in a nice apartment in West Van and took the kids off my ex's hands a lot. I also coached the O-line on my son's football team. They ended up winning that year.

The next year while I was still living in Vancouver, I played for Winnipeg. My parole officer knew everything that had gone on between me and my ex, and he suggested I move away from Vancouver. He said if she made many more complaints, I could have some trouble. He suggested that I think of moving back to Manitoba permanently. I suggested this to my mom and my sister and they were thrilled. So we bought a house together.

I played in Winnipeg for a couple of years after that, but I was getting old. I played one last year in Toronto in 2002. I was forty then.

I retired at the end of that season. I don't even think about that time in my life anymore. Sometimes I get called to do alumni work, maybe with kids, and then I go for the day. I'll put my cleats on and hold the blocking bag. People tell me I look like I still know what I'm doing. My body's better than ever from my martial arts. I have agility. I've slimmed down. I'm 220 now. But now I'm accepting old age. Before, I was in denial and that put me at risk of injury. Being realistic now, I am being more careful. I'm fifty-four.

I BEGAN BRAZILIAN JIU-JITSU TRAINING in 2002 after the football season. I got into the training to stay in shape. I also went with the intention of training to become a mixed martial arts fighter. My master is Sylvio Behring. He lives in Brazil. I was under one of his instructors when I first started. I am extremely, extremely lucky to be training with him. There's no reason I should be. I'm a very good black belt, but I don't have the refinement of a Brazilian professor. He's an eighth-degree master. What he likes about me is that I'm always striving for perfection.

I can't go two days in a row without my jiu-jitsu. I need the mat. I need to roll.

Jiu-jitsu is a very different martial art. It's 100 percent fighting. This martial art has the ability to destroy another human being. I could choke the life out of someone in two seconds and so have the choice whether they live or die. In our sport, the tap represents death. No one wants to admit they're caught and tap out, but if I do get caught, I have to face up to it. Either you tap out to be freed or your opponent taps out. Fighting for your life is scary, but the feeling afterwards... wow! That's a weird but empowering feeling.

If you go too hard and try too quickly (like in a street fight), then you're tired in two minutes. That's why it's so easy to fight a non-jiu-jitsu player. Jiu-jitsu is like chess, it's not just about using and stopping aggression. It's about breaking grips and being patient. You have to breathe and have a certain sense of relaxing while trying to choke the life out of somebody. I also have to relax while someone is trying to hurt me and take me down. Fighting for an hour is hard until you've learned the pace. But at the end of a roll, I have to get in my hot tub. I can barely lift my limbs. The feeling is complete muscle depletion, like when I used to play football. It's such a good feeling.

KEITH LEVIT

Today, I am the Manitoba representative for Brazilian jiu-jitsu at my gym, Academy 64. As I age, I want to do what Master Behring is doing now and move to more of a coaching role. I want to have more students winning bigger tournaments. I want to take them to the Worlds.

KEITH LEVIT

jiu-jitsu to their students in their Ojibwa language. Those kids are happy. Their bodies are healthy. We've got kids that used to be fat from drinking Pepsi and eating chips. Now they're training. Jiu-jitsu has a lot of structure and it's good for kids. My goal is to take jiu-jitsu to the reserves in Manitoba where there is a lack of resources, depression, and poor nutrition, and give the kids there something to do so they can feel hope and stop trying to commit suicide. Jiu-jitsu and its training can change lives. Who knows what they're capable of? I want to be the spark of a bigger flame, not the flame. I want everyone to feel excited and happy that I've come there for a seminar.

I'm so lucky because my girl, Christina, and I have been together ten years and we're still planning our future together. Everything changed when I met her. It's a stable relationship and has led me to a more secure place in my life. We met probably fifteen years ago in 2002 when I was forty-one and she was twenty-two. (I had told myself that I needed someone in my life who was younger, not because I'm a dirty old man, but because I needed someone with enough vigour to stay with me. I'd already missed so much of my life.) We were intrigued by each other. It was

Right now, the two Manitoba locations under my direction are doing well and our students are happy and satisfied. One of my former students runs our sister club in Transcona, Tapout Martial Arts, where we are at capacity. Another student of mine was 200 pounds, could barely walk up the stairs, and had Type 1 Diabetes. Now he's an instructor and he's accomplished his dream of becoming a police officer. We are also part of a community jiu-jitsu project in Roseau River First Nation. The two instructors are teaching her short shorts that I looked at, but once we started talking, even though she was young for me, I thought wow, but nothing came of it. We ran into each other maybe three times in four years. We'd stay in touch and talk on the phone—she'd call me when she wanted to talk to somebody. But at that time, for whatever reason, it was not right to date, but we really liked each other as people.

A few years later when I bumped into her again, I invited her to come to the gym sometime, so she came down. She never went home that night; we talked all night long. We never left each other after that. Christina's so bright and so energetic and so goal-oriented. She was already doing Muay Thai, so I suggested jiu-jitsu. She became very skilled at Brazilian jiu-jitsu and got her black belt. She competes and she lays herself out there. She teaches at the academy. She has students that really look up to her. Master Behring invites her on to the mat to spar—that's an honour. And she's a really good mom. We had our son Jett together in 2012.

I'VE DONE A FEW DIFFERENT JOBS since I got out of jail. I drove a tow truck for five years in Vancouver in the football offseason. After I moved to Winnipeg, I opened my first jiu-jitsu gym in 2005 when I retired from football. I had an insurance policy coming in and I had some money saved, but then two years later, I lost the gym. After that, I was a bouncer doing security for a nightclub. But when I met Christina, I wanted to get out of the club life, so I became a caseworker at Stony for a while and I also worked for a few different social enterprise organizations where I was helping gang-affected youth become employable and get work. I was getting burnt out, so, in 2013, I quit that job and I'm at home with our son while Christina works full-time. It was also a good time to leave because I could also take care of my sister, Kathy, and my mom.

My sister was in a car accident in 1990 and has been in a wheelchair since. She's a quadriplegic. (I had been in prison four or five years then, but Stony gave me a compassionate pass so I could see her. She had broken her neck and she was in a halo.) My mom and sister moved in together, they travelled together, they were besties. Eventually we all shared a duplex in the country. My sister and I co-own it. We bought it together a long time ago. Kathy and my mom had the downstairs, seeing that Kathy's in a wheelchair. Christina and our son and I have the upstairs. It's a big house so we each have 1,500 square feet.

My mom did most of the care for Kathy, but then Mom was diagnosed with COPD (a lung disease that slowly progresses over the years) and, after that, cancer, so she couldn't take care of Kathy anymore. And, of course, she needed help too, so I took care of Mom and cooked for her. My mom died in February of 2016. We're adjusting. There was lots of good, but the worst memories are of her deteriorating state. She died at home.

I am still my sister's caregiver. She's very independent. She can cook and do lots of things herself. She's okay on her own for a few hours, but I help her with all the hard stuff, getting in and out of bed and driving. I want to do this. It really works for us. Our relationship will only be over when her life ends. My sister and I have a good situation.

My dad died from lung cancer in 1998. The last time I saw him was '96. My sister and I went out to the farm and had dinner with him and his wife, Karen. They lived in a small house trailer I had bought him when his life wasn't going so good. I felt like I had a family responsibility to my dad. (If he wasn't doing good, I felt like I had to help him. But it's funny because I never thought that he should feel the same about me. He never took care of me. I always took care of myself. Always.) The place was terribly filthy. He was talking down to Karen, just like he had to my mom in our childhood. Nothing had changed. Whatever child was locked inside him was damaged and had never had a chance to break free and heal itself. He had an alcohol problem at that point too.

I gave him a game tape of me playing football and I invited him to a game in Winnipeg. But he told me he couldn't come because he didn't want to leave the farm—he never wanted to leave the place. He was very selfish that way. He had grown up without a dad and he didn't understand what his own role was in my life. I left him the tickets, but he never came.

It was a good visit though—friendly. But I felt more pity for him than anything else. I was happy about where my life was at. Our lives were a contrast. I stayed in touch after that. We talked on the phone. When he died I couldn't find the tears to cry. I thought I might later, but I never found those feelings of loss like I did when my mom died.

I'VE BEEN OUT OF JAIL TWENTY-ONE YEARS. But I have this sentence of *life*, so I am on parole for the rest of my life. It makes me feel vulnerable. What if there was a policy change, like maybe we should just lock up all the lifers for example? Overnight my life would change. I'm not saying I don't deserve everything that happened— I did my time. Life is life and I still can't get a pardon, but I can apply for a suspension. I'm working on that right now. One good thing has already happened: my file in Ottawa was changed a year ago. The police still had on my file that I was an active gang member, even though my club had been non-existent for so many years. (It had been absorbed into another gang.) It took everybody's signature (mine, my parole officer's) to get it off my file in Ottawa, but we accomplished that.

When I look back on my younger self, it's like I'm looking at part of me and I own it, but that person is also detached from who I am today. I've had a lot of gradual change and growth. The guy I am today would take that younger guy I was and throw him off a cliff—first chance he coulda got. That's how I feel about that guy today.

I've always been a work in progress. My goal is to be a new, better version of myself. Making that kind of change is not easy, but I'm working to let go of all the things that hold me back (insecurity, ego, and pride, for example). Today, I am very comfortable because I have a balance of give and take. I'm taking good stuff, but I'm giving it back. I want people to be happy. I want to make this world a better place. I keep taking little steps forward. Sometimes, I don't even know I'm doing it because it's just the mode I'm in. Now, I get off on benefitting society. It gives me unlimited purpose and makes me happy. I'm paying my way forward. There's no other way.

In 2015, this guy messaged me on Facebook. He seemed to know a lot about the murder. He told me he forgave me. I messaged him back and said, "What do you forgive me for? Did I hurt you? Did I do something to you?" I told him that the thing he was talking about, I did to someone else. I gave him my number and told him to phone me. He called and explained everything. He was the victim's best friend. He explained himself very clearly. He wanted me to know that he thought I was doing good from what he could see on my

Facebook profile: working with kids, with First Nations, and all that.

He said, "I believe that people can change. I've put it away."

This guy wasn't at the party when I stabbed his friend. He showed up right after. He had regrets thinking about that night and if he'd been there on time, he might have been able to prevent it all because his friend was a hothead and he was always getting him out of fights. I'm not saying the guy deserved to die, but it explained a lot why he was so aggressive and ready to fight me. He was causing trouble for sure.

I asked this guy what happened to everybody. I wanted to know how they were all affected. In my mind, I had ruined this guy's life and this guy's whole family. I knew the victim's girlfriend was pregnant at the time. There was this burden. He said that the girlfriend hooked up right away with this new guy. They're still together and they raised the kid as his own. He said, "Everybody's moved on with their lives." I felt so emotional because I knew they were all okay. I just cried and cried.

IT DOESN'T EVEN MAKE SENSE that I'm here today in a situation where I have so many good things in my life. But even with everything I have—all the happiness—I can't look back and say that I have no regrets. My biggest regret is that I took any of this gang shit seriously. I could have avoided the whole life and become an athlete right from the beginning. I regret that part of my life big time. I regret quitting school, it was a bad decision, and I regret allowing my dad to push me into it. I wanted to stay in school. But I was supposed to be part of the farm and then it never happened. My dad lied to me. I regret cheating on my first wife and all the things I did to her. I regret being absent to my older son, Clinton, even though we worked everything out. I'm cool with him today and it's a beautiful relationship. I don't deserve that, but I got it. I got daily regrets every time I look at my younger son and think of the things I do with him that I didn't do with my older son. Also, I am vegan today, so I even regret eating animals. But meanwhile, if you look at the whole, I got everything. I got more than I deserve.

Yes, I got more than I deserve, but at the same time, it could disintegrate in one moment. That already happened to me once, in the campground, that night years ago. You have to be always looking forward, always being better. Am I perfect? Hell no. I've got all kinds of flaws, but I don't let anything get away from me. I have had issues with anger my whole life, but I can control it. You betcha, 100 percent. If I'm disrespectful and rude, that means I have to come back to that point and either make amends or find out why I acted that way.

I wouldn't recommend prison to anybody to work out their problems and to get their career straight, but it worked for me. There's a lot of change that can happen in jail. Probably most of my growing up was inside, because really, you don't need perfect conditions to grow, you just need to be willing.

I live in the moment and only in the moment. The present has a solid connection to the future, but the past is a re-creation of memory. It's an interpretation and it's flawed. The present moment is much more critical and much more alive than the past. It's precious right now. I'm happy today. Right now, life is wonderful. It's not perfect, but it's wonderful.

Garry is a person of contradictions. His demeanour is serious and intense, yet he laughs easily, especially at himself. Besides being a dad to his daughter, he is a father to both a thirty-five-year-old and a five-year-old. In his pinnacle of football training, he could press 1,000 pounds (with his toddler son sitting on the weights), but later he cared so tenderly and compassionately for his mother in her last days. He's been both a bouncer and a stay-at-home dad. He is physically strong and has a dominating presence, but his favourite jiu-jitsu class to teach is the one with children. I saw an unbelievable video of Garry sparring with a four-year-old girl. There's this giant man taking down, rolling with, and later being pinned by a four-year-old. Garry was so gentle.

Other Side of the 49th is an excellent documentary about Garry's life that was released in 2015. It was directed by Ervin Chartrand, a filmmaker and participant in this book.

ERVIN

My first memories of childhood are of being lost. Very lost and alone, even though I had my mom and my brothers. It was almost a fend-for-yourself type of environment. When my mom got her welfare cheque and went shopping, the cupboards and fridge would be full and I'd get a few bucks for allowance. We'd all be eating and drinking as much as we could because we knew it wouldn't be around for long. Then, *boom*... all the milk was gone, all the food was gone. By the second week, there'd not be much left and really we'd be fending for ourselves. We'd go to 7-Eleven and shoplift for food. And in the summertime, we'd raid gardens. The big thing was rhubarb dipped in sugar.

My dad was from Camperville, Manitoba, a Metis community about four, four-and-a-half hours north of Winnipeg, past Dauphin. But I never knew him because he died of stomach cancer when I was about six months old. My mom is from Pine Creek First Nation, just outside Camperville. I am the youngest of six kids. I had four brothers—Paul, Sid, Ernest, and Pat—and one sister, Loretta. After my dad died, my mom decided to move into Winnipeg to be with her sisters. That's where things took a turn, I guess you could say. My mom thought that support would be there for her, but her family was going through some hard times because of alcoholism and their experiences in residential schools. Her sisters were drinking a lot, so she started partying with them. I used to watch my mom go out and at times, I would wonder if she was ever coming back. In the morning, she'd be all bruised up from getting into fights or falling while being so intoxicated. She worked, but it was not consistent—she would do sewing and cooking for people to make extra money. Welfare wasn't much.

When I was a kid growing up in the '70s, it was easier to see poverty. Back then, there weren't the resources and different community outlets there are today. Nowadays, I see kids, poor kids, but they are all dressed properly. I grew up with torn jeans, no socks and no shoes, almost like a hobo. The clothes I had were sewn and patched hand-me-downs from my brothers. My mother had to stitch a length of fabric around the hem of my jeans just to make them a bit longer. So there'd be all different coloured pieces sewn onto the ends of my jeans. She sewed up everything. Even though the patched clothes looked poor to us back then, I realize now that, for some reason, my mom had a sense of style. That's not something you just pick up.

Today, I see my mom as a little old lady who's a firecracker. She's a strong woman, kind and resilient. But she's been through a lot. My mom is a survivor of residential schools. I wish she would speak to me more about what she went through so I could understand where she came from, but she never has. I really don't know her story. The alcoholism and all that abuse she did to herself, obviously now when I think back, I know it was because of the experiences at the residential schools and I see she suppressed them through alcohol. Later on in her life, she was part of the information gathering from residential school survivors for the Truth and Reconciliation Commission. I remember one day, she was getting ready to go to speak to her lawyer and did not want to go. My brothers convinced her to, but when she got back home, she went straight to her room, closed the door and shut down. She

> I grew up with torn jeans, no socks and no shoes, almost like a hobo. The clothes I had were sewn and patched hand-me-downs from my brothers.

didn't want to talk about it. She was almost like a child again. She asked us why she had to go through this. She didn't want to share. I know through my brothers that there was abuse, but she didn't open up to me and say what happened. Anything I know is through other people's stories.

I saw violence early. My brothers were fighting and I was getting into fights too. And then, I saw my brother Sid get stabbed right through the front door of our house. That was pretty traumatizing. We lived at Victor and Ellice, near where the University of Winnipeg is today. Sid was sixteen or seventeen and I was about eight. Sid got into a fight with a guy because the guy used to date the mother of Sid's child. The other guy got jealous that she was back with Sid, found out where he lived, and came over to our house. I was upstairs and heard them, so I came down and watched on the stairs. Sid was inside arguing through the screen door, and this guy was standing on the steps outside. He pulled a knife out of his jacket and stabbed my brother right through the screen. My brother slammed the inside wooden door and we locked all the doors and turned out the lights. I remember running to my room and

hiding under the covers. I was pretty scared. I don't know how we phoned the cops because we didn't have a phone at the time. I guess one of us went next door to use our friend's phone because the cops came and questioned my brother. They found the other guy hiding under our patio deck in the back.

My brothers didn't hang out with me much, but I saw them go through a lot of pain. I did hang out a bit with my brother Ernest who is four years older than me. Over time, he became the father figure in the house. By the time we were living on Young Street, around 1980, my brothers were in street gangs. I would have been about ten then. That's when I was introduced to gangs. Patrick joined a gang of maybe six to eight guys. They used to take off their shoes, tie them to their belt loops, and roller skate all over Winnipeg all night. My brothers were into building roller skates with parts they bought: trucks, boots, wheels. I don't know what they did on those roller skates, but it probably wasn't good. And my brother Ernest was part of another gang. There was this place called the Hamburger House where the gang hung out and they used to sell drugs out of there.

One summer, back in the early '80s when I was fourteen, I was just hanging out with a group of friends and we decided to form a street gang. It was partly boredom. We were a group of friends who really didn't think anything of promoting violence and drugs. We wanted to cause some trouble. I looked up to that kind of life because it was around me all the time. There weren't really a lot of solid role models, but belonging to a gang was one thing I wanted to achieve. It's just the way we thought our lives were going to go. It was good to be part of a group and hang out with my friends. It gave me some pride that people looked up to us, even if it was for the wrong reasons. We saw the action our older brothers were getting in their gang and we wanted a piece of that action too. We picked a name similar to that of my brother Pat's gang because we were all younger brothers of those guys. We wanted to hang out with them, but we ended up causing them more trouble than anything else and so they told us to find a different name because we were causing heat on their gang. We'd go to other turfs and get into fights with other street gangs. It wasn't like we were trying to take over a turf or sell drugs there; we were just fighting and

hanging out, smoking weed and getting high. I think we were only together that one summer because our older brothers took a few of us aside and said we had to break it up. So we each went our own way after that, although I still hung out a bit with the guys.

At that time, I was trying to go to school. I was fourteen and I went to RB Russell for a while. I even enrolled in drama class. I remember my first day, I walked in the class and they were doing a play. All these kids were on top of desks with chairs acting like it was a ship. They even had swords. I got overwhelmed and never went back. It was just too crazy for me. I was a very shy kid so it was out of my comfort zone.

I watched my older brothers in their gangs. Pat was interested in his gang to hang out with friends and party, while my other brother Ernest got into the business side of his gang, selling drugs and making money. My interest in being in that first gang was basically about selling weed and making money to get by. After we broke up I started selling drugs independently at school and downtown. A gram of weed cost me ten dollars from the dealer. I'd sell it for fifteen and keep the extra five. Someone told me that I should get an ounce and start making my own money. Back then, you had to get certain drugs off certain people. At the time, one of my brothers was an enforcer for a motorcycle gang. Eventually, I found that I could use his name to keep people from bothering me. So I picked up an ounce from a friend whose father was a big time weed dealer. He fronted me and I sold it, paid him off, and bought another ounce, and soon I started selling my own stuff. My business took off quickly. By the end of the summer, I had guys running for me.

I spent lots of time partying with other street kids. Some nights, we didn't go home, we would stay out, put our money together, buy some booze and rent a hotel room. The hotel we usually partied in was the Super 8 Hotel at Stafford and Pembina, but it's gone now. The owner would let us stay even though we were a bunch of kids. When I started making my own money, I began to separate myself from those street kids. I started working my way up the ladder, hanging around with more independent drug dealers, guys in biker gangs, and other organizations.

I started working my way up the ladder, hanging around with more independent drug dealers, guys in biker gangs, and other organizations.

One night, I went to a party and hung around with my old RB Russell friends. By then I was seventeen and I had dropped out of school. We were standing out back smoking weed and drinking beer. I had this one friend, Howard, who came out of the house drunk and he staggered past us and walked across the alley to this derelict garage that was leaning sideways and looked as though it was about to fall over. He stood beside it to take a leak and we heard a smashing noise. I guess he'd put his hand through one of the windows and smashed it. Then we heard dogs barking and lights came on. As he walked by us into the house I could see he had cut his hand and blood was trickling down it. We didn't think anything of it. Then lights shone at us out of nowhere. I guess the cops had been slowly creeping down the alley. Everybody scattered.

I just stood there. I thought, *I didn't do anything, why should I run?* I didn't have any drugs on me, I was just drinking. The cops came up and grabbed me right away. They threw me on top of the hood of their car and started rifling through my pockets. They yelled at me, "Did you smash that window?"

I said, "No, I didn't smash any window."

Another cop said, "You fit the description: long hair, Indian, wearing a leather vest, black shirt, and jeans." I was standing around with five other guys who looked like that. (Back then, leather vests were in and people wore them whether they were Indian or not.)

So they grabbed me and I said, "You can even check my hands, they aren't bleeding."

One of the cops grabbed my hand and actually hit it with his billy club and said, "Well, your hand is bleeding now." So they handcuffed me, threw me in the back of their police car, and arrested me for mischief.

I'd been charged with mischief before as a kid, and those charges always got thrown out of court. This was different. It was the first time I ever got charged, so I went through the court and justice system. I didn't have a clue about any of that or the Youth Detention Centre. No one was supporting me or making me go to court. I was very naïve and thought this legal hassle would go away, so I skipped my court date six times. It got breached

I was very naïve and thought this legal hassle would go away, so I skipped my court date six times.

every time and then there'd be a warrant for my arrest. The mischief charge lasted until I turned eighteen and was an adult. I tried to get mediation through my lawyer so I could meet the people who owned the garage, have them see me, and say that I wasn't the guy who smashed their window. But before I could do that, the courts finally caught up with me and gave me a fine option. Back then, there was this option and if you didn't pay your fine—I think it was $300—you had to go to prison to work it off. When I didn't show up for my fine option, I was sentenced to sixty days in jail. Of those sixty, I actually did only twenty days, which I served in the Annex in Headingley.

THE ANNEX IN THOSE DAYS was in the town of Headingley, just outside the fenced-in part of the prison. It was made up of these big orange buildings almost like boxcars. There were two wings of dorms with a kitchen and cafeteria in the middle. I'd say there were sixty guys in those four units. This is the place where you can meet bigger drug dealers and make more connections. I was terrified because it was my first time in prison and I didn't know anyone. That fear was the same kind I'd have when going to a new school for the first time. When I was a kid, I switched schools sixteen times and every time I'd be afraid of how I was going to fit in and who I was going to know. Being in prison for the first time was basically like that.

The first few days I was in a place they call the fish tank. Everybody goes there when they first arrive. They ask you questions, do a blood test, get to know you, figure out what level of security you are, and where you want to work. The fish tank is near the front of the prison and at the back of it, there's a door with steel bars so you can see the outside stairs that the guys from the general population take to the gymnasium. So everybody floods that area to look in the door and see who's coming into the fish tank. You feel on display. That first night I was scared, but I was also intrigued. I thought to myself, *Wow, I'm actually lying in prison and when I get out people will recognize me!* That was kind of exciting. But then the next day started and the fear returned. In jail, there are always people fighting, getting assaulted, being intimidated, and giving up what they have.

You gotta protect your back. When I got there these two guys threatened me and robbed me—that's called getting muscled. They took my lighter and my baseball cap. That may sound small, but it felt like a big thing to me.

I tried to stand my ground and act tough. You have to look angry, frown, be tough and intimidating, like no one's going to mess with you. That was the whole prison environment: anger and rage. I did carry some anger within me from all my trauma and it did come out when it needed to, but I wasn't walking around with a chip on my shoulder. Some people, they just cannot be happy, they are constantly full of rage; I wasn't like that. I had to wear that mask of constant anger in order to fit in and to survive. There is a lot of anxiety that comes from carrying all that anger and that kind of energy.

I got out in twenty days, but it felt like a lifetime. My God, my first few days in there felt like a year. After the fish tank, when I got out to the Annex, I sat on my bunk—it was the lower one—and I didn't know what to do. But then I had these two big guys full of tattoos sit down on either side of me. I thought *Here we go again...* But they gave me a kind of kitty with some smokes and food.

I thought I knew what that meant for a new person going into prison—they were going to own me. But it turned out they gave it to me out of respect for my brother, Ernest. He was pretty well-known and had all this cred from the streets. They told me to let them know if anyone messed with me and they'd take care of them. As soon as I heard that, I felt a relief, like acceptance. Back in 1988, the gangs weren't controlling the prison system like they are today. There were just a lot of independent drug dealers, car thieves, and break-and-enter artists.

When I came out of prison, I felt more in charge of my life. I had done my first prison bit and had been accepted. Once you're out of prison, especially when you hang out with a younger crowd, your status goes up right away. And then you have this ego that goes right along with it. It's almost like going to university and graduating with a BA. It puts you on a different level and gives you cred. It shows people on the streets that you aren't a rat, that you're reliable and can do your time. You can show your "employer" what you've got.

I had just turned eighteen when I was released. I went to live in a halfway house, but went right back to selling drugs again. Only this time, I started selling cocaine. My mom was living in Dauphin, so when I left the halfway house, I was just sleeping on friends' couches. Eventually, I was making really good money and I stayed with my brother Sid, giving him money for rent.

Then my reserve bought the old Flamingo Hotel at the corner of Notre Dame and McPhillips and made this bar called the Pine Creek Inn. They hired my two oldest brothers, Paul and Sid, to do security and they also hired me, my brothers Pat and Ernest, our cousin and some other guys. There were thirteen of us bouncers. Once I started working there, I brought my business there too. It was okay for us to sell out of the Pine Creek Inn because we were the bouncers. My two older brothers eventually quit, but my cousin's friend, who was a big-time drug dealer, came on as the head bouncer and so we started selling drugs for him. He told us that we had to start buying from him, but that was okay because he gave us really good prices.

Some of us were getting muscled and robbed by other gangs because we were independent. Other people started trying to move in and sell drugs there too. We had to have some sort of protection, so one night we got together and formed a gang. That's how our gang started, in the Pine Creek Inn. We were wearing these jackets that had patches on them that said "Bouncer" and had the four traditional colours: black, white, yellow and red. My brother was the first to cut out this patch and sew it on the back of his vest. Everyone else followed suit. We decided to call our gang after our reserve's hockey team. My life changed after that; I became part of organized crime.

We had to move big. We branched out to other territories and gangs. The first two years were pretty violent. Warfare went on with other people who didn't want to give up their territories. We moved into a lot of bars, chasing out drug dealers and other gangs. And there was one set of crew that didn't want to move out of the Merchants Hotel bar and that led to violence. There was a point when I didn't know what the hell I had gotten myself into, but the status was great. We had automatic status wherever we went because we were wearing our colours. You walk in with six or eight guys and no one is going to mess with you. Sometimes, we'd go into a bar out of our territory and all the bikers would show up. People would wonder why they came, but it was just to drink together with us. We never went to war with the bikers; we only went to war with the other street gangs. Of course, that did mean longer times in prison. I did some provincial time, mostly for cocaine and lots of weapons charges.

BY THE SUMMER OF 1998, I was starting to think about leaving the gang and wondering what I could do to get out. That's a common thing most guys think about. But getting out is hard. Most of the time, the answer is just *No, you're not leaving.* And if you really are going to leave, you have to pay for it. It's about respect. Leaving is a sign of disrespect to your brothers and the club. You can get beaten out, stabbed out (if you are in prison), or take a shot in a drive by. And you have to get rid of your gang tattoos—either burn them off or cut them out. But for me it

> Leaving is a sign of disrespect to your brothers and the club. You can get beaten out, stabbed out (if you are in prison), or take a shot in a drive by. And you have to get rid of your gang tattoos—either burn them off or cut them out.

was a little different. I helped create the gang. I was the last original member of the thirteen, so who should tell *me* what to do. For me, the gang had been all business and retaliation; I didn't go out of my way to hurt guys. But if I left, it would be an opportunity for the guys who didn't like me and were jealous of me to cause me harm.

So I had one foot in and one foot out. I was still a member and none of the guys knew what I was thinking about. I had a reputation on the streets and all my friends were still involved in the gang. But I also didn't really trust anybody at the time because word on the street was that someone in the club was trying to set me up to get me done in. I wasn't selling drugs, but I was still using. I had an actual job doing foundation work and I was trying to straighten out, but I also didn't have enough money. I was trying to distance myself, but it was a hard thing to do.

And then there was the sweep: Operation Northern Snow, November 4, 1998. It was run by the gang unit of the Winnipeg Police Department. One day, I was supposed to go to work and the cops kicked down the door of the place where I was living. I was staying with friends and their mom, Val. We were all brought to the living room and our hands were zip-tied, even Val's. I thought the cops were coming for my friend—they came for him a lot—but they arrested me. They read me my rights and all my charges. I was totally shocked. The police told me there had been a two-year investigation. I told them that my lawyer would get me out tomorrow. They said, "Not this time." I was one of the first people they put in a cell. Then they put another guy in next to me, side by side. Slowly everybody started coming in. In total, there were fifty-two people arrested. But they housed all of us from my gang in those two cells. It was just jam-packed.

I was terrified because, as I already said, I had been trying to distance myself from the gang and had not seen those guys in a while. But seeing them again, I had pretty much no choice—it was like, *Okay, I'm back in it.* I hadn't ever said I'd quit the gang, but when they asked me where I'd been, I said I wasn't selling anything, I was just working. That pretty much got passed over because everybody was more concerned with what charges they'd have and with getting out. We all made a pact to stick together and not rat each other out.

They built this big multi-million-dollar courthouse in an industrial park in Fort Garry. It was a warehouse they converted into a friggin' courthouse. It was so annoying because it took hours just to get us there from the Remand Centre downtown. They transported us like cattle first thing every morning. We'd go downstairs one individual at a time, our hands and feet were shackled to our waists, and when we were sitting or riding in the vans, we were also shackled to the floor. There were maybe six to eight guys in a hot, cramped van and there were thirty-six of us, so we were in a convoy of vans. Then we'd be stuck in the holding cells. Every day was like that. I think they were trying to break us, to see who would crack and roll over and rat each other out to take a plea bargain. There were one hundred and twenty informants giving info to the police. That's a lot. We found out that two full-patch members were informants and that two other club members had also rolled over.

I had seen my lawyer and was looking at only two-and-a-half years. I was vice-president (second in command) of the gang at the time, so I wanted to jump all over this and take the deal. But I went to talk to the other guys in the gang: the president, the sergeant-of-arms, and the treasurer. They said I couldn't take the deal and if I took it, I'd set a precedent and everyone else would be charged. These senior members were all looking at a significant number of years and they wanted less time than that. But even though I was vice-president, the police didn't have much information on me. When I was selling drugs, I was really low key; I wasn't a heat-bag showing my money everywhere. So I didn't have many people informing on me, but the other senior gang members said I couldn't take a lesser deal than them. They said, "We gotta stick together."

But then this guy who was one of our enforcers and a full patch member rolled over and took a deal. He had a lot of information on me because he'd done a lot of business for me. He knew every single person I had dealt with: business contacts, assaults, collections, and drug transactions. He made a sixty-page statement against me. Then my lawyer came to see me and said the Crown lawyers had changed their minds. They were now asking for fourteen years, instead of two-and-a half. *What the fuck?!* I went straight to talk to the other senior gang members. I could have taken a two-and-a-half-year deal, but they had told me no. Now I was basically looking at the same jail time as they were. I was pissed off. People were stabbing each other in the back and talking. It was a very unhealthy environment to be in. I was charged with living off the avails of prostitution, conspiring to transport cocaine, possession of firearms, fraud, and assault. But looking back, I guess this was a good thing because it gave me the motivation to get the fuck out of the gang.

I took a nine-year deal without the gang's knowledge and really distanced myself from the gang members after that. I spent fourteen months in Remand, which got counted as double time, so that was two-and-a-half years off, leaving six-and-a-half years in Stony Mountain Institution. When I got there, I was in the fish tank for the first three months, which is standard for a federal prison. Even though Stony is federal, their fish tank is similar to the provincial one at Headingley. They were doing assessments and stuff, and I was in there with another guy, named Spider, from my gang. He also took a deal because he wanted out too. We

> I took a nine-year deal without the gang's knowledge and really distanced myself from the gang members after that.

were trying to get a transfer out to a place called The Farm (Rockwood Institution, a minimum-security facility adjacent to Stony Mountain) because there was no one from our gang out there. The prison staff eventually decided our security levels and sent us there. Then six months into my sentence, they called me into the office, put cuffs on me, and took me back to Stony. Another inmate from Rockwood had escaped and when he got picked up, he wrote a statement saying I had muscled and intimidated him. He said that was the reason he took off, but I knew that was a lie. The gang wanted me back in Stony. There is a zero-tolerance policy so the administration acted on his allegations without any discussion.

Once I was back in Stony, I was pretty scared. While I was in Rockwood, a television crew from CBC was filming a documentary about gang violence in Winnipeg and talked to a few of us guys. While I was being interviewed, I denounced my gang status. Everyone saw it. My anxiety kicked in, especially because of this one guy from my gang—he was an instigator and knew how to manipulate people. He had threatened me the whole time we were both in Stony. He worked the library cart so he had access to my unit. He'd say, "This is your day," every fucking day. He wanted me stabbed up and done in. I'd be walking on the breezeway or wandering to the gym and would wonder, *Is this the day?*

This guy told me to remove my gang tattoo, but it was a big tattoo and hard to remove. He said he was relaying messages, but I knew it was just his idea. I thought, *Seeing I was one of the original members that started the club, why should I cover up my tattoo?* I didn't care what they said. I felt that I'd given up a lot already and the tattoo was something I wanted to keep. It was a pride thing.

I tried to get transferred back to Rockwood, but they said I would have to rat someone out and give them a name. If I had done that, it would have put me in an even worse situation. I felt like I was going insane from the mind games the gang was playing on me. There was a lot of pressure. I feared for my life every day. Sometimes I used to think, *Either die by the sword, or die by my own sword.*

So I started working out and doing a lot of Aboriginal ceremonies. I connected to the Lodge (sweat lodge) and that's what kept me sane. Without that, I think I probably would have killed myself.

I attended my first sweat lodge while I was in the fish tank at Stony. I'd heard of sweat lodges, but I didn't really know anything about them. I didn't grow up with that kind of background, so it was all new to me. When I went to my very first one, it was the most powerful feeling I had ever had in my life. At first, I was anxious because the doorway was closed off and it was totally dark in the little hut. The rocks were glowing and hot. The elders started singing and it was almost as though I could feel things dancing around me. Then I sweat so much, it was like having a big bucket of water poured over top of me. My body felt heavy and weak, like everything from my head to my feet had just drained out of me. And I cried and cried and cried. I couldn't stop. I cried through the whole thing—three-and-a-half hours. I felt like burdens were

> The sweat lodge felt like such a safe place to be. It awakened my spirit and I felt connected to myself.

lifted up, things that were troubling me. The sweat lodge felt like such a safe place to be. It awakened my spirit and I felt connected to myself. It was an amazing feeling.

After my first sweat, I participated in all the ceremonies. I went every time. There were sweat lodges every week, so I went to at least a hundred, maybe more during those two-and-a-half years at Stony before my parole. I connected with the elders and the spiritual advisors. It was a place where I could feel safe for at least a few hours and be among others who wanted to be connected with their Aboriginal spirituality.

It made going back to the pit (the prison) easier. I knew there were a lot of things that could happen to me and I still had anxiety, but I was learning to leave everything at the sweat lodge. I felt protected for some reason. I prayed to the Creator and I also felt someone watching over me spiritually. I think it was my father.

But then something happened that was almost like a godsend. I felt like it was spiritually given to me, but I don't know why. There was a feud in Stony at that time between my gang and another Aboriginal street gang. A bunch of pool balls went missing and the guards said that they had to be coughed up or everyone was going to be locked down. Nobody coughed up the pool balls and there was a big fight. The guards fired a warning shot and people got arrested. I was in my cell, but I heard about it. They shut the whole prison down and took out four instigators from each gang. That guy who was giving me such a hard time was one of them. These guys were sent to Edmonton Max (maximum security prison). It was just a big weight that got lifted off my shoulders when he left. I was so thankful. Some of the guys from my gang apologized for the pressure. They would catch me in the breezeway and talk to me when no one was around. They were sincere about it.

I got transferred out of Stony to Pê Sâkâstêw Centre, a healing lodge in Hobbema, Alberta. It is a federally run, minimum-security centre based on Aboriginal culture that's for healing and reintegration of Aboriginal offenders. I did seven months there. From Pê Sâkâstêw, I returned to Winnipeg to begin my parole and lived in a halfway house for a while. I was still drinking and came home drunk a couple of times. One of the stipulations of my parole was not being under the influence of any kind of stimulants, so I went back to Stony three times, for three weeks each time. That was horrible. Before, I had had my own cell made into a little house with a TV. When I went back, the cell I was put in was bare. I had nothing. The last time I got out of prison was April 2003.

I hung out with my brothers, Pat and Paul, when I got out. I had stayed with Paul on weekends when I had passes from Stony. My brothers were out of the gangs way before I was. I kept that kind of stuff away from my family. I didn't want them to get into trouble or to be worrying about me. If I was going down, I wanted to go down by myself. I also went to visit my mom a lot at that time, but didn't see much of my sister. She has lived a transient lifestyle and has stayed in Camperville mostly. She is my blood and I care about her, but we are not that close and I barely ever see her.

Once I was back in Winnipeg, access to the same Aboriginal teachings and elders and that whole environment I had in prison was hard to find. Back then, that was a common problem for guys coming out of prison. I went to Thunderbird House in Winnipeg a few times. My cousin was an elder there. But then I started connecting with sweats at Birds Hill Park and Peguis. And I went on about four different vision quests. These quests provide a kind of cleansing based on Aboriginal teachings and the basic idea of them is to find meaning and purpose for your life. I went on my first quest while I was in Hobbema. You go out and live alone in nature for four days and nights, setting up a makeshift hut and fasting without food or water. You only take what you can carry. Some teachings allow for a hatchet. And you must keep your fire going the entire time. You have to cut down trees for firewood, so imagine doing that on the third or fourth day when you have no energy.

On one vision quest in Peguis, I fell asleep in my hut on the third day and when I woke there was this silhouette of a man on the other side of my fire. He looked identical to my father and seemed to be coming over the fire at me. I got scared, jumped up, and put my hands and a foot out because he was coming towards me. And then he was gone. When

Once I was back in Winnipeg, access to the same Aboriginal teachings and elders and that whole environment I had in prison was hard to find.

I first saw this, it looked like a real person, but then it became a vision. I can't explain it.

Connecting to my Aboriginal spirituality gave me identity and purpose in my life. It protected me. I was searching, wondering, *Who am I?* First Nations, Aboriginal, Metis? I am an Aboriginal man, but what does that mean? Connecting to that spirituality and, I guess I would say, to my ancestors and my mom's family helped me to stay positive.

THAT FIRST YEAR after prison, I met this Aboriginal RCMP cop named Dean Fontaine. He asked me to do these gang-awareness talks in schools with him and his partner. Their mandate was intervention and prevention. I didn't distrust Dean, but I couldn't believe I was actually doing these talks with a police officer when I was fresh out of prison. At first when I was with him, I was so friggin' scared. I was trying to quit the gang and get out, but I wasn't far enough away. So when I was with Dean, I felt like I was doing something wrong, like I was ratting someone out. But I told myself, *I have to do this...I want to do this.* Later, that experience opened up a lot of doors for me. It was one of those things that came into my life at the right time and was an important piece of the puzzle and added to all the tools I needed to progress forward.

Throughout my parole, I saw a psychologist named Dan Beaudette every two weeks for the first three years I was out. That was helpful. I saw my parole officer too. He was also a positive influence. They reassured me. But I still had one foot in the door of the gang and I could have easily gone back to the gang lifestyle.

Then, about one year after I got out of Stony, I had a turning point. I was still in the halfway house, working at a dead-end job that I wasn't that interested in, and so I was thinking about whether I should sell drugs again. I went to this house party with guys from my gang. I got into a bit of an argument and a fight. I got a beer bottle smashed over my head and I went into the bathroom and two or three guys came after

> I was searching, wondering, *Who am I?* First Nations, Aboriginal, Metis? I am an Aboriginal man, but what does that mean? Connecting to that spirituality and, I guess I would say, to my ancestors and my mom's family helped me to stay positive.

me. My shirt was ripped and I was bloody. They left and I started washing up, but then they came back at me again. The next time I woke up, I was in the bathtub and there was a lot more blood. I didn't know how long I had been out. It must have been a while. The music was loud and you could hear lots of people in the house. I decided to make a run for it. So I opened the bathroom door and ran through all the people and out of the house. I heard someone shout, "There he is, he's getting away." As I ran down the sidewalk, there was a cab coming down the street, so I flagged him down and got into the back seat. When I looked back, a bunch of guys had come running out of the house, but I was already gone.

I took the cab to my close friend at the time, Shelly's, house, and from there, she drove me to the hospital. I was already doing those gang talks with Dean, so I had called him to come to the hospital and talk to me. He wanted to know what happened. Sure, I was doing the talks with him, but I wasn't going to give him any kind of information. So I said I was in the wrong place at the wrong time and got jumped. But he was a good friend to me. We had this heart-to-heart talk about where my life was going—I had gotten my grade 12 at Stony in 2000 and I was now doing the talks with him and also going to broadcasting school. Our talk made me think about a lot of things in my life.

On the way home from the hospital, I broke down in Shelly's car. I was at a cross-roads in my life, with one foot in the gang and one foot out. It was a tug-of-war. I was so confused. Good things were happening, but it was also hard to walk away from the gang, to be called a bitch and a pussy. Somehow, that would make me feel less of a man. Today, I think differently, but then I felt really vulnerable to everything, like I would be opening myself up. And that was a scary thing. To feel those emotions and breakdown like that, I thought, *What am I becoming*?

When we got back to Shelly's, a bunch of guys came over to the house: ex-gang members, friends, and family. They were rough-looking and from the streets too. They wanted to go back to the party and take care of what happened. I was thinking about that and they were ready, but then I told them to go home. I just knew the way it would be. It would be a vicious cycle. I'd go retaliate and the guys would come with me and then the other guys would retaliate against me. In that way, I'd create more enemies. And if I really did want to get out, then these enemies would come after me. Guys in gangs carry grudges a long time—pretty much forever.

WHEN PEOPLE ARE IN PRISON, they may want to quit the gangs and start new lives, but once they hit the streets, they end up back in. The gang lifestyle is always there, but I was wanting out for real. I was going to school and looking into the future and actually seeing where I could go. I had a taste of what life could be like. Lots of positive things were coming my way. I saw an alternative. So I think this was a big turning point for me, because it was a chance to say, *Okay, I'm walking away from everything.* And I did.

Shelly's mom, Val, had been looking out for jobs for me. She had given me a pamphlet about an Aboriginal broadcast training initiative. The pamphlet indicated that the training involved doing stories and I thought, *Why not?* It had appealed to me because I liked doing the gang talks. So that's how I came to enroll in and finish broadcast school. I had a student loan and Manitoba Metis Federation paid the other part. First, I did an internship with a production company on Marion Street and then one at CBC. But I was naïve, I thought broadcasting would be like filmmaking, but it wasn't. The formats are totally different and broadcasting is not creative.

So in 2004, I applied to the Faculty of Social Work at the University of Manitoba. But I also had a friend in Calgary who said he could get me a job on the oil rigs, which meant I had options. My parole officer, Mike Schroeder, had also set up an interview for another internship with Lisa Meeches and The Sharing Circle, an Aboriginal television documentary series. He told me I could make up my mind after the interview. A whole crew of people came with me: Mike; Dean Fontaine; my psychologist, Dan; my councilor from MMF; and Belinda Marintette, who worked for Bear Clan National Patrol. It felt odd to go in with all the support, but it felt great too. At the end of the interview, Lisa offered me a paid, one-year term. MMF would pay fifty percent of my wages. My parole officer said it was a once-in-a-lifetime opportunity. It felt amazing to have all these

> The gang lifestyle is always there, but I was wanting out for real.

people come and support me, pushing for me and believing in me. I had never had anything like that. I did all kinds of things there: camera assisting, transcribing, shot listing. I made my first two films while I was there. My first one was about a guy coming out of prison and making choices—a fictional story based loosely on my life. I left it open ended. The second was nonfiction about a guy named Patrick Ross explaining prison and the choices he made.

My filmmaking is something I'm really proud of. I am finally sticking to something. I've always been self-sabotaging and have not stuck to things that I thought I was good at. Filmmaking gives me a voice and helps me express the things I'm going through, bringing my awareness to my life at the moment. I was excited to have a medium to show a greater audience and reach as many youth as possible. I would like to inspire youth to change their ways and their lives; to not do drugs and alcohol; not join gangs or go to prison. To do the right thing instead. That's important. In the beginning, I was a self-taught filmmaker. I have made seventeen films in the years since (as of 2016). Now, I am proud to be known as an artist. I

KEITH LEWT

graduated from Film Studies at the University of Winnipeg in June 2017.

When I was first picked up during Operation Northern Snow, I met a woman named Kathleen at the Remand Centre. She taught me literacy and I thought she was a very good teacher: patient, kind, and understanding. I thought she was beautiful too, and it's easy at that age to have a little crush or become infatuated with someone. But then I'd shake my head and think, *Nah—I could never be with a person like this because of where I am.* But back then, Kathleen planted a seed in me that I guess you could say blossomed. She told me to explore literacy through poetry. It's not like every single guy at prison is writing poetry! But I did and it opened up a lot for me. Poetry gave me a purpose other than what I had from gang life and it led me to education.

When I was sentenced to Stony, Kathleen ended up there too. She had left the John Howard Society and got a job as a program facilitator in Stony. We'd see each other in passing, but I didn't take her programs because she said it would probably be a conflict, seeing she had been my teacher at Remand. Sometimes she'd invite me to her office and we'd talk. She wanted to know how I was doing because she'd heard word through the prison about what was going on and was concerned about me. She understood my situation, which was kind of nice. When I got out of prison, I tried to stay in touch with Kathleen through email. But it wasn't as regular as I would have wanted it to be.

Kathleen was interested in hosting a meditation retreat for inmates at Stony and she contacted me about maybe documenting it.

She introduced me to a guy named Michael Pancoe who was running Vipassana meditation retreats out of Beausejour. I was totally interested, but there was a lot of red tape at Stony and it didn't work out for me.

But in 2007, I decided to take this ten-day Vipassana introductory retreat to get the feel of this kind of meditation and see what these guys were going through. This practice teaches you how to meditate through disciplined attention to body sensations and how to recognize those sensations and feelings. That course felt similar to a vision quest, but I also got an internal understanding of spirituality that I had not had before.

In 2011, I decided I wanted to do a cross-Canada walk to raise awareness and money for Aboriginal concerns. I had met this guy, Kevin Abraham, at Stony and had done a documentary with him. He had done another walk and he had the vision of walking across Canada with his grandfather drum. I had a vision of walking across Canada too, so we talked about it but it didn't come together. Eventually, someone introduced me to a guy named Michael Gladue and we decided to collaborate on a cross-Canada walk. Michael organized the whole thing. He got an RV donated from a school in Toronto that he knew about. He called the walk, Walk For Nations. I had a whole lot of things coming up in the film world that I just left to do this walk. I wanted to go on a cross-country pilgrimage and visit many of the Aboriginal communities. It was something I needed to do spiritually.

We started in St. John's, Newfoundland in the spring of 2011. There was a small group of us, maybe ten. It took seven months to get to Hobbema, Alberta. We passed through there because one of the guys on the walk was from there. We stayed with his uncle. While I was there I spoke at Pê Sâkâstêw about my journey since leaving there in 2002. Then someone set us up with a vision quest. On the vision quest, I had a feeling of having come full circle and that the walk was over for me. So I did not complete it. I felt it was the perfect place to end. The walk had been tiring, but also inspiring, motivating, and full of learning from the sharing we did with all the people we met.

When I got back to Winnipeg, someone from CBC radio contacted me to come on the morning show and talk about Bill C-10. Kathleen says she doesn't listen to the radio often, but that day, for some reason, it was on and she heard my voice. I know it wasn't a coincidence. I don't believe in coincidences. It was fate—our paths in life were already chosen. So she emailed me and asked how I was doing. She had emailed me before the walk saying she had a crush on me, but when I emailed back asking for more, she never responded. So it was nice to see an email from her. We set up a time to meet up. We met at Cinematheque because they were showing a documentary about gangs in Chicago slums and I had been asked to give a talk about gang life after the film.

Shortly afterwards, we saw each other again and she invited me to her place. She had just ended a relationship and had bought a house. It was November 2011. We each knew how we felt about the other, but had not shared these feelings. Dating had been far from my mind. It was a long time coming, but once it happened, everything moved forward quickly and there was no looking back. It was serendipitous. We didn't make this happen, it happened because life made it happen. I would never have met up with Kathleen like that if I had finished the walk and not come back to Winnipeg when I did.

The summer of 2014, we went to our first ten-day Vipasanna retreat together. We meditated for ten hours a day. She was always very interested in it, but had never actually gone on a retreat. It was amazing to experience that together. We'd already been meditating and doing yoga together each morning for three years. (I have not forgotten the Aboriginal teachings. I still carry those teachings with me, but my meditation has moved me into a new practice now.)

Sometimes, I still have dark forces like anger, resentment, and bitterness creep in because of the person I was before. That can pull at me and interrupt my positive feelings. But now it's easy to recognize that. Before, I wouldn't even understand why I was acting the way I was and I couldn't acknowledge what was happening. But now, I recognize the dark feelings even before they surface and I know how to control them. It's all because of meditation and understanding body sensations. You learn to feel the sensation of something that's coming: a trigger, an emotion, anything that builds up. Back then, I used to carry the feelings around, like carrying a grudge. But I don't let them build up any more. Now, they only last for a few seconds. I let them go by, acknowledging the fact that those sensations and emotions are there and understanding them. Acknowledging them quickly dissolves them. Meditation brings me back to the present moment and helps me feel calm and rational about what I am thinking. Meditation keeps me focused on my life and my goals. My mind is no longer chaotic. It's calmer and clearer. I'm not 100 percent at peace, but I am at a place I could not have imagined.

Kathleen and I have a love relationship and a friendship. She is someone who can understand me because she has been there pretty much from the beginning, so she knows everything about me. I don't have to explain anything to her. She told me she had been watching the difference in me over the years and she saw a big change.

I just never thought there could be someone out there who could be so together and have such a loving family. And she shares that with me. Everything. I never knew I would be able to have a healthy relationship. It is just amazing. It was a struggle at times, not fitting in because of my background and

Meditation keeps me focused on my life and my goals. My mind is no longer chaotic.

the way I grew up. Then again, our relationship was such perfect timing because I started studying film at the U of W right around then as well. It was good to be with people who were intellectually stimulating. I pick up a lot from being in the environment of Kathleen and her family. The way she lives her life is very healthy.

Often, I see the signs that Kathleen and I were meant to be together, that we have a special connection that is hard to explain. Not long ago, Kathleen cut her finger really badly when she was cooking. Right after that, I jumped into the shower and there was some caulking that was hard and loose, so I tried to pull it off. When I grabbed it, the caulking went far up under my fingernail and it was very painful. It was the same finger and at the same small spot that Kathy had cut. It's hard to believe two people can be connected this way. I feel happy being in sync with Kathleen.

I have a daughter who is twenty and living out west. She is doing really well. She was born in 1997, eighteen months before I was arrested with Operation Northern Snow. Our relationship has been off and on. Our last visit at Christmas 2014 was really good, different from all the other visits because the other times my mind had been distracted. Now, I have a more stable environment. I am thankful for our relationship and I hope we can continue to reconcile and develop a bond as mature adults. I love her so much.

I hope to one day go away and do my Master's degree in Film Studies. Kathleen plans to come with me. I want a different experience, different teachings, and a new culture. I have so many ideas. They are always evolving. I want to tell inspiring stories and now I have the confidence to tell the stories properly. When I look at things through the camera lens, I think they look different and I take the photo or the view differently.

Once I'm more settled down, I'm really interested in working on bikes as a hobby or opening my own business. There is a two-week, bike-building program in the Okanagan Valley that I would like to take. I've always been interested in building bikes. As kids, me and my brothers used to have this bike workshop in our garage, but our bikes were stolen ones. We built a lot of bikes and I was passionate about that. I'd really like to work with inner-city youth and have a bike shop. I know it's not really "up there" like being a doctor or anything, but I have that in my mind. For me, as long as I have my health, a roof over my head, and food in my fridge, I'm pretty happy.

My brother Pat passed away of stomach cancer in 2013. Watching him struggle tore our family up. There is a void in my family now. It feels like Pat's death changed everything. It used to be that we were hanging on to the past and being more of a family. His death made things clearer—we are all going in different directions now. Then shortly after Pat's death, my brother Sid had a severe stroke. My mom was devastated. He and my mom have lived together as far back as I can remember. My mom is doing better now. My brother Sid is in a nursing home, stable and getting good care.

Before the gang life, I didn't know who I was. I was a person looking for an identity, a purpose, and trying to find a place to be happy because, back then, happiness didn't really exist for me; it was hard to come by. Today, I am very optimistic about the future and I can't even imagine doing the things that I did back then. If I was my younger self listening to my older self saying not to get involved in the gang lifestyle, I'd probably tell my older self, *You are fucking crazy, coming to me and telling me that I need to straighten out.* Then I'd say to my older self, *How'd you get where you are in the first place?* So I don't spend time wishing I could change the wrong choices I made when I was younger because my younger self could then say, *So why are you telling me to change my life when you are sitting where you are now because of the life you led?* If I were to have changed at seventeen, I'd probably be somewhere totally different today. Instead, I lived in the struggle and now, I can say that everything I went through back then is the reason that I am where I am today.

Before the gang life, I didn't know who I was. I was a person looking for an identity, a purpose, and trying to find a place to be happy because, back then, happiness didn't really exist for me; it was hard to come by.

I first met Ervin a few years ago when he came as a guest to a board meeting for a charity I am a part of. He was introduced as a filmmaker who might consider doing a short piece on the school that is associated with our charity. He brought along a representative from the National Film Board. He came across as personable and engaging. I remember liking his sweater and thinking he had a good sense of style. I did not know or have any inkling of his past, nor did it matter. I have seen most of his short films and read some of his poetry. His eloquent work serves as a bridge to higher understanding and opens our eyes to the life of struggle he passionately wants to share.

Ervin kindly invited me over to the house he and Kathleen share. While there, they proudly showed me their expansive backyard that they have lovingly transformed from a now invisible weed patch. It was beautiful, carefully landscaped with reclaimed rock, water space, and multiple gardens in flower. I could not help but feel these peaceful and blooming gardens were a metaphor for their relationship.

IAN

It happened on December 23, 2013. I only remember bits and pieces. I was driving down McPhillips; I think I was going to my mom's. Just after I turned the car down a back lane behind a Mac's convenience store, suddenly everything went black. When I snapped out of it, I realized that the car had crashed—and then I saw my arm flopping and moving. I couldn't control it. I thought, *What the fuck?* I was so confused. And I started yelling. Two old ladies came up and asked me if I was okay. I remember yelling to them to call an ambulance. Just thinking about that time bothers me still, but it needs to come out.

Later, I heard on the streets that there had been four guys standing right there as I turned the corner. I didn't know who they were. I think they were standing on the road, but I didn't see them. Apparently, one of them pulled a gun real quick and shot at me while I was driving. I didn't even hear the bullets. They must've thought I was somebody else.

The bullet went through the metal of the car, but somehow it turned. It entered my left side and went in sideways behind the back of my heart, travelled up and got stuck in my right trap (trapezius muscle) and made me paralyzed. The injury is called a C6 ASIA A. At the time of the accident, I was paralyzed from the neck down. Today, I'm in a wheel-chair and I can use parts of my arms—my biceps and a little bit of my triceps. I have no movements in my hands, but I do have some wrist movement. I can feel my organs and a little bit when someone touches my legs. That bullet should have killed me. It was a big one. That day, there was an angel or something watching over me because that bullet could have hit me right in the heart. I'm lucky.

> That bullet should have killed me. It was a big one.

WHEN I WAS A KID, I was always outside, never inside. I used to play and go exploring. Sometimes I'd go hunting with my brothers. I loved that. I am the youngest of five brothers. We'd hunt gophers and rabbits. Sometimes, we'd see a deer, but I never shot one. We had guns, rifles and 22s, but they were always locked away. I also went snaring with my brother, Matthew. We caught a few rabbits in our day. My dad came with us a few times, but he was gone a lot. My dad was married before and had two older kids, Brent and Tyler. They never lived with us, but I consider them my full brothers. My dad met my mom and he got divorced from his first wife and then he and my mom had my brothers, Dwight and Matthew, and then me.

I also loved horses back then. I still do. When I was about eleven or twelve, Matthew and I trained and broke them ourselves. We didn't know nothing about training horses, but we had cousins that had them, so one cousin came and showed us what to do. We took the horses into deep snow so they couldn't buck so much and then we just got on and let 'er go. Me and my brother Matthew were really close. He's one year and eleven months older than me.

I was born in Winnipeg at the St. Boniface Hospital. As a kid, I lived back and forth between Winnipeg and Swan Lake First Nation, two hours southeast of Winnipeg. We'd go wherever my dad could get work. He was a truck driver. Sometimes during the winter, there were no jobs and he'd get laid off. He couldn't sit around. He's the type of guy that needs to work, so he'd be driving a school bus or a water truck for a while. But we'd always spend our summers in Swan Lake. My dad didn't want us getting into trouble in the city; it wasn't a good place to be in the summertime, when he was working long-haul truck driving. We had lots of aunties and uncles in Swan Lake. And my grandma and grandpa were there too. I spent a lot of time with them. I was happy.

There were no gangs on the reserve, not that I knew of anyways. My dad clicked up with a biker gang, but just for partying and hanging out, drinking and fighting. He had stopped hanging around with them before any of us were born. So I never saw much violence growing up, just a few kids fighting and getting beat up or an older guy beating up on a younger kid. That probably scared me the most. I used to tell the older guys to leave the younger ones alone. Fuck, they were just kids. I didn't like violence. I still don't. I wouldn't wish it on nobody.

We took the school bus from Swan Lake Reserve to the town of Swan Lake to go to a school there with mostly white kids. They would tease me about my parents because I had a Native dad. They were bullies. I fought in school and swore at the teachers, so I'd get kicked out sometimes. That started at about age eight or nine. I wouldn't take shit from nobody; I didn't care who they were. I didn't

like getting picked on so I just stuck up for myself. I'd only fight others when I had to, if they threw the first punch. I wouldn't go out of my way to hurt anybody. I won some of those fights and lost some. I wasn't the biggest kid, but I wasn't the smallest. I'd get in trouble for fighting, though; when I got home from a fight, I'd get a licking for doing that.

Around the same age, I smoked a bit of weed with my friends from the neighbourhood. Their parents sold it, so my friends stole some and brought it for us. They were trying to be cool. My parents were against that stuff; they didn't touch that shit. One day, I smoked it on this thing called a lung, which makes the high more intense. There was a whole gram in there and, when I smoked it, I got really high and the world started spinning on me. That made me really scared. Afterwards, I was never the same. Before, I could concentrate on things and be good, but after that I couldn't pay attention in the same way.

So I was getting into trouble because I didn't pay attention in school. I also liked to joke a lot and have fun. I guess you could say I was more into fucking around. The teachers wanted us to be serious. But as a kid growing up, who wants to be serious all the time? My dad was working driving trucks so he was gone weeks at a time. But when he was home, we'd get it for fighting with each other or for getting in trouble at school. He'd hit us on our butts or legs with the leather part of his belt. No kid should be hit, but that's how my dad grew up—when he was a kid, if he did something wrong, he got a licking with a belt or a spanking with a broom, at least that's my understanding. His mom, my grandma, went through the residential schools. I don't know if my dad did; we've never talked about that.

As I got older and my dad was still away a lot, I started to get mad at him for being gone. He was always working and I missed him, for sure. I felt distant from him and neglected. I would see all these other kids with their fathers doing things together and then there's my dad—gone. I knew he needed to support us, but then I thought maybe he could have done more with us. I didn't blame him, but I hated him. When he was around home, he liked his bingo and a bit of drinking. He was a happy drunk. I actually preferred him when he was drunk. My dad has never hit my mom, never. Now, he has diabetes and he doesn't drink at all. My mom has never drunk. As I got older, I felt so distant from my dad and I felt neglected.

My mom was always around. She didn't like what was happening and she argued with my dad about the lickings he gave us sometimes. She'd say, "You got to stop doing this to the kids." One day when I was twelve and Matthew was fourteen, my dad threw a shovel at us. I don't remember the argument, but my dad was mad at Matthew so he threw it. Didn't hit us, but it scared us. Matthew was protective of me, his little brother, so he told the Child and Family Services office. It was across the road, close by our place. They moved us out of the house. I thought that was a good choice. I wanted to teach my dad a lesson that he couldn't do that again. We moved in with my cousins for a couple of weeks. Then my older brother, Tyler, said he'd take us. So me and Matthew moved to Morden, Manitoba, a small town close by the reserve. After my dad threw the shovel and we got taken from our home, he never laid a hand on us again.

I REMEMBER THAT WE MOVED TO MORDEN around my thirteenth birthday. I stayed until I was fifteen. Matthew and I joined the cadets and I started playing hockey right away. I had skated before, but never played hockey. I really got into it. I played left wing and was good at that. Back then, my favourite NHL team was Pittsburg and I'm still a Pittsburg fan. Hockey took my mind off everything and that's what I focused on mostly: hockey and school. Tyler was fantastic and his wife, Toni, was a nice woman. He got so emotionally attached to us. But there were still a few problems. Once, I got into a fight with Toni about eating junk food before dinner. I headbutted her and was sent to a foster home in Brandon for a while, maybe a month. That was one time when I didn't have Matthew with me. I felt uncomfortable living with people I didn't know and so I ran away and started to walk back to Morden. The RCMP picked me up and I ended up going back to Tyler's. It was nothing serious.

Morden was a white town. I got bullied there. I went to the junior high that was connected to Morden Collegiate. Matthew was protective of me, very protective. We always had each other. He's still like that today.

When I'd get bullied, Matthew would step in and ask what was going on. He'd always throw the first punch and I'd go in after. We'd take people on together. We didn't have a choice; we had to do that, going to a white school. There were only three of us Native kids and most of the others were racist. I developed an anger-management problem. I didn't know how to handle it back then. Now, I've had courses and know the symptoms and what to do when I get agitated. I've realized the triggers and how to avoid or control them. Some of the triggers are people talking shit about my parents or my brothers or people being racist. I hate those things.

There were only three of us Native kids and most of the others were racist. I developed an anger-management problem. I didn't know how to handle it back then.

When I lived in Morden, I smoked cigarettes. I only drank once in a while and usually only a glass of wine, just with family. I was not allowed to drink to get drunk.

Morden was good until 2004. I was fourteen when my brother Matthew moved back to Winnipeg. He returned to live with our parents and Dwight because he didn't like the rules at Tyler's house. I stayed in Morden because I wanted to keep playing hockey, but

I missed Matthew. That really got to me, so I stole a car and ran away to the city. Some of my Winnipeg friends were car thieves and I had listened carefully when they talked about it, so I just did what they did. Matthew hid me in our parents' house. If someone was coming, I'd hide under the bed or behind the curtains in Matt's bedroom. My dad was out working all day and so we'd come and go while he was gone. We stole cars and got money for food.

My parents and my family were worried. I could hear everything they were saying since I was hiding there, but no one knew where I was except for Matthew. After two weeks, Matthew sent me back to Morden because the cops were looking for me. Everyone had been worried sick wondering if I was okay. I was arrested for stealing the car and spent one night in the Manitoba Youth Centre in Winnipeg. My brother, Matthew, was already in there. He'd got picked up right after I left. When he saw me that night, he cried. He told me that later. He said that he had never wanted to see me in there, so he was hurting a lot that night.

After I got out, I went back to Tyler's place. Tyler wasn't mad at me for running away. They knew I missed my family, missed my brother. They understood. Tyler and Toni sat down and had a serious talk with me. They told me they'd take me to visit Matthew, all I had to do was ask. They were like that. They wanted to make me happy. They loved me. I knew they did and I felt bad I had done that to them. I apologized and they asked me to please never run away again.

While living in Morden, Tyler would take me back to visit with my mom in Winnipeg. I missed her, but not my dad. He had never come to watch me play hockey, but I didn't really want to see him either. I stayed in Morden a little bit longer and then I moved back to Winnipeg to live with my parents and with Dwight and Matthew. I was still mad at my dad, so we weren't really talking. My dad was gone a lot and Dwight came and went as he pleased between friends' houses and home, so mostly it was just my mom, Matthew and me.

IN WINNIPEG, I went to Elmwood High School. I had lots of friends there from growing up and going back and forth. At fifteen, I started to get into real trouble. First, I started stealing cars. I did that because of boredom and because that's what the kids I hung around with were doing. I wanted to fit in. Seeing my friends stealing cars and getting money from doing it—that got my attention. It was negative, but at the time I thought it was good. When I stole my first car, I was nervous, very nervous. But then, once I got the hang of it, it was *bang-bang-bang* and I just kept on doing it. I don't know how many I stole. I don't know if I should even say, I don't want to get myself into trouble. I'll just say that I stole a fair number of cars in my day.

I was hustling too. My brother, Dwight, sold drugs, but he didn't get me into that. I just did it myself because I had seen it done. I stole some crack cocaine from him and I went to the North End neighbourhood and hustled it off. I stole five pieces, flipped it, then bought an eight-ball, and then flipped that into two. Then I flipped the two eight-balls into half an ounce, to an ounce and to five ounces, and then away I went. I made lots of money selling drugs. I bought my first car. I had fat gold chains, gold bracelets, and diamond earrings. I had ten rings, one for every finger, but I only wore six at a time, three on each hand. Yeah,

> When I stole my first car, I was nervous, very nervous. But then, once I got the hang of it, it was *bang-bang-bang* and I just kept on doing it.

I even had a gold grill for my teeth. I was a heat bag—going to school with all that would bring a lot of attention on me and I know that people wondered where I was getting my money. It felt good to have all that money at the time. But I think now—all those people I hurt when I started that shit...

At that time, I was partying and drinking, but I didn't do any drugs. I sold them, but I didn't take them. Later on, I'd do drugs though: coke and some pills. I wasn't into it too bad though, just partying. But I never touched crack.

That same year, a group of us formed a gang. At first, it was just a couple of guys and then it got really big. We did it because there was this other gang and they were always trying to pick on us. We had rankings: president, vice-president, and then there were council members, patches and strikers. Another guy was president before me, but then he got locked up. He was older and went to the Remand Centre, so his position got passed down to me and I became president. I loved the power because guys respected me. They looked up to me. I was the leader, so I knew I had to show them how to be smart, organized, and respected. In gangs, it's all about competition and being better than other gangs. It's about the best cars, the most money, more jewelry, and better women. Being in charge felt good.

Our gang was affiliated with a bigger organized street gang. We were a younger crew that worked for those guys. You could say we were their flunkies or their bitches. They never got into trouble for things that we did for them. The younger ones do all the dirt. That's the way it works to this day. They'd give us the drugs and we'd sell them, give a certain amount of money back to them, and we'd keep our profits. You had to be eighteen to join the bigger gang.

I got arrested at fifteen for stealing cars. I went to the Youth Detention Centre. It was scary at first because I didn't have my mom or Matthew there. But I knew a few guys. While I was inside, I found out who my real friends were on the outside. Some guys didn't care, didn't help me out. School was mandatory. It's held inside the Youth Centre because we weren't allowed to leave. I was remanded—that's what they call it when you're waiting for your court date. So I had to stay in.

My lawyer told me they had me on the charge of stealing cars, so I pled out and got bail. In court the following month, I got eighteen months of probation. The courts put me on curfew, so I was allowed out of my house from 7 am to 9 pm. But then the cops raided our house for drugs and Dwight got caught. He went to Stony and did his time. The night of the raid, I wasn't home, but I had seen that the cops were at my house so I ran. I shafted them. But then a couple of weeks later, me and a friend were driving and got pulled over. There were three pieces of crack in the van and we had 1,500 bucks on us, so they charged us with trafficking. That was the first time I got charged for drugs. I got locked up at the Youth Centre again, pled out, and went to Agassiz Youth Centre in Portage La Prairie. They have a program there called Positive Peer Culture (PPC). Guys check each other, meaning they call each other out on their actions. So, if a guy doesn't like the way

> In gangs, it's all about competition and being better than other gangs. It's about the best cars, the most money, more jewelry, and better women. Being in charge felt good.

you look at him, he can say, "I don't like the way you're looking at me, so you're checked." You gotta march to the beat in there. That place was messed up. After that, I went back to my thing—stealing cars, bagging hoochies, and selling drugs.

When I was still seventeen, almost eighteen, I got into a high-speed chase. I was driving a stolen SUV—a Tahoe or a Yukon—and I had my friend with me. These cops spotted us and chased us all the way up McPhillips Street. I hit black ice and almost lost control. But I got from the north end of McPhillips all the way around to Chief Peguis Trail, then down Henderson Highway to Elmwood. I thought we shafted the cops, so I parked the SUV and we started wiping it down and taking everything out. Then their white police truck with the dogs showed up. I yelled, "What the fuck" and we started running. We were running through yards and hopping fences. The truck was flying up and down back lanes trying to find us. I ran to this automobile shop and my friend ran the opposite way. He got caught. Then the canines started sniffing me out. I hid for a bit, but all of a sudden, I heard the sound of a panting dog. The dog found me and took a chunk out of my leg. I stabbed the dog in the head, but the cops caught me and apprehended me right away. They knew my name; my friend had ratted me out. I got charged with dangerous driving and stealing an automobile. The high-speed chase was fun when I thought I was getting away, but when I was running from the dogs I was scared. I got locked up in the Youth Centre again and I did my time: nine months.

RIGHT AROUND THEN, my son, Isaiah, was born on January 7, 2008—one month before I turned eighteen. I had been out of the Youth Centre for three months. His mother didn't know who the dad was; there were two of us, me and this other guy, David. The other guy was there at the birth and got to cut my kid's umbilical cord. I got to go to the hospital later on that night Isaiah was born. When I got to see him and hold him, I was happy and joyful because I just knew he was mine…I just knew it. I had brought my baby picture to the hospital and when I held it up to his head, we looked identical. I cried staring into his eyes. A couple of weeks later, I took a paternity test and found out he was 99.9999 percent mine! David was pretty upset about that at the time, but eventually we became friends; we're actually really close now—that's weird, I know.

I was excited about Isaiah and wanted to spend time with him, but I was still young then. I had to learn about how to be a father. Back then, my gang was my family too. I felt that leaving the gang for my son would be like picking between family. It was hard to pick one over the other at that time. Today, my boy comes first for everything.

When I turned eighteen, I joined that older street gang. My president ranking in the younger gang got passed down to another guy. Everyone in my crew knew that when you turned eighteen, you moved up to the other gang because we were clicked up with them. When I moved to that gang, I had no initiation because I had done lots of things for them—sold drugs, made them money—so I got a patch right away. I was happy. I felt like I had more power because the younger guys respected me even more.

From 2007 to 2013, I was in and out of jail. I was in the Youth Centre, Agassiz, Brandon, Headingley, Remand. There were a bunch of different charges: stolen cars, theft, assault (just one), drugs, that high-speed chase, and breaches. Lots of breaches. I'd skip court or not show up. Then the cops would have to come and get me. The cops are so frickin' greasy. They would come and knock on my door, but I wouldn't hear them because I was sleeping, so they'd leave and fucking breach me. Such bullshit they did to me, those cops. I enjoyed the rush and the thrill of stealing cars, driving fast and getting away with it. It was fun. I was happy, but at the same time, I knew it was wrong so I did have mixed emotions during those years.

And then there was my kid's first birthday; I'll never fucking forget that. I was out of jail and we were having his birthday party. Isaiah's mom called the cops and accused me of domestic (abuse), but it never happened like that. She was trying to rip my gold chain off my neck because she was jealous of other girls. We were dating on and off again around then. I grabbed her hand and told her to let go of my chain. But she called the cops anyway. They came right over because there is a zero tolerance on domestic abuse. Four cops dragged me out of the house in the middle of my kid's party and beat me up in front of him. Four on one. They sucker shot me when I wasn't looking, in front of my kid. That was uncalled for. They were hitting me in the face, kicking me and shit. My brother came outside to try and stop the cops. He was holding Isaiah. I told him to take the baby inside. The charges were dropped three or four months later in court.

I got out of jail for the last time in October 2013. My gang did nothing for me when I got out. When you get out of jail, you're supposed to have friends be there for you, doing things like getting you new shoes, giving you a little money, helping you get back on your feet. Nobody did nothing like that for me. I'd seen so much greasy shit— guys mistreating and manipulating other gang members. And after all the dirt I'd done for them, I thought, *Fuck that, I'll just do my own thing*. It was a reality check. So I told myself I was done with the gang, but I didn't tell the gang. I just did my own thing and didn't hang out with them anymore.

I called my other friends who weren't gang members. I bounced around from house to house. I didn't think leaving the gang was hard. I didn't *have* to go and nobody gave me a hard time for leaving. If anybody had tried to fuck with me, I would've just knocked them out because I was a fighter back then. I had been into mixed martial arts and I knew how to fight. I was good at it and I was fast.

I was trying to get my life back on track. I had my boy. He's the biggest reason I wanted to change. I didn't want my son going through what I went through: growing up and not having a father around, because sooner or later I probably would've ended up dead. I've lost seven or eight really good friends. Like my good friend who got shot in the back of the head—executed—while he was at a restaurant. That was fucked up. He told me he knew he would be dead at the end of that day. He told his other friends, *I'll take this one, you just run*. He stood there and took the heat. Every day, I think about the friends I've lost. It's a touchy subject. They have kids. What if that had happened to me? And I knew it could've been me, even I had lots of enemies.

And then, just a few months later, I got shot.

The guy that shot me got caught. He got charged and he's locked up for eleven years. He was in a gang that is bitches for a big motorcycle gang. But the thing is, I never had a beef with him. Apparently, there were four guys there. And apparently, there are three different guys that say they shot me. That's what I'm hearing from the streets.

Some people think it's blood in-blood out for gangs and a drive-by shooting could be what a gang would do if you want to leave. That wasn't what happened with me. I was not shot by a guy from any of my old gangs. Maybe for some other gangs that type of thing would be the case, but it wasn't like that for the crew that I was with. In my gang, if you want to leave, you tell them you're leaving. That's it. You're done. No hassle. Now, if you owe money and you're trying to leave, then you're going to get a beating. But if you're leaving clean cut and you're good with all the guys—maybe you want to leave and just be a family man—guys respect that.

Of course, I'm upset and hurt and sad about the shooting. I still have dreams about it. Sometimes I feel like screaming or crying. But I'm trying to be a more spiritual man. I'm getting into my culture, smudging, trying to practise my traditions. I think now that the right way would be to let it go, pray for the best for the shooter. If I was the old me, I'd want revenge and I'd want them to take a bullet, all three of them. But if I saw them today, I'd say to them, "Karma's a bitch and you'll get what's coming to you." I can forgive them, but I'll never forget.

Life is too short to dwell on the past. You need to live life and just move forward. Helping people—that's what I want to do. If I could help make a change for three or four people in the world, I'd know I did my job. That's why I like telling my story and speaking at workshops. I really like doing that. To young strikers and bitches hanging with gangs, I'd say, "Just think man, it's not the right way. Hurting other people, victimizing, or even being the victim is not a good feeling. Right now, you might be thinking you're going to hurt this person because of a beef or because you're getting paid to do it. But later in life, you're going to regret it." Some kids don't think about that; hanging with gangs is just normal to them. If I could see the people I've hurt, sold drugs to, victimized, I would apologize. I wish I could take all that back. I'd offer to help them later, if they needed an extra hand. I'm trying to live a better life, not just for me, but also for my son.

DOES BEING PARALYZED affect my abilities to be a good father? No, not at all. Never. I'm not a quitter. I never was and I never will be.

I'm trying to teach Isaiah and to show him the right way. Isaiah lives with his mom, but every weekend he comes to be with me. His mom and I are civil; we're good. His mom is a great mother. She knows how to raise a boy; she has two others. Everyone gets along. I don't want him growing up the way I did. I will never hit my kid the way I got hit.

Isaiah's a good kid. He's nine years old now and so supportive and loving and mannered. It really hurts him when I go to the hospital. He's always calling me and coming to visit. He wants me to be okay. My son says he wants to be a doctor someday so he can fix me. Isaiah doesn't even know I got shot. He thinks it was a car accident. I don't tell him about my gang stuff. I'm not going to lie to my kid though. When he asks more or reads this story, I'll tell him the truth. But if he ever wants to join a gang, I won't let him. There's no way.

My life can be unpredictable. I have to go to the hospital a lot, sometimes every second day. I get a lot of urinary tract infections and I have to be dis-impacted (stool removal). I usually have to visit the hospital to get it done. The nurses won't come out to the house. The WRHA nursing manager says it's unsafe due to the gang-related nature of my injury. That's ridiculous. The aides that wash and care for me come to my house regularly. My mom is my main caregiver; she does it pretty easily.

IN THE SUMMER OF 2014, we had a fundraising social for me. I was hoping it would turn out good and we'd raise money, but it didn't. The social basically just paid for itself. I thought lots of my old crew would've come, but only a few did. There were maybe fifty or sixty people there. We were hoping for 250 to 500. The social was on Aboriginal Day, so other things were going on in the city. Also, people were talking shit about the social, saying it was going to get shot up. And the cops were there. They sat outside the whole fucking time. That just killed it for me. I would like to have another one, but I need help setting it up and I don't really have that right now. A few guys came to see me after the accident. The guy that showed me the ropes in my old gang, he still comes. He's a real friend.

I did have some tough times after the accident; I felt really low and in a dark place. There was a time where I just wanted to be gone from the world. After the accident, while I was still in the hospital, I smoked some weed and did some coke. My friends and family helped me with that. I had been depressed and bored. It was a spur of the moment thing to have some fun and pass the time. It only lasted for a week or two, but then I just stopped. The drugs were affecting me and I decided I didn't like that. I didn't need rehab or anything. The support and the help I had from my friends and family, that made me realize life's too short to feel down all the time. I tried to stay positive, to be creative, and be joyful. I told myself, *Don't let go.*

I tried to stay positive, to be creative, and be joyful. I told myself, *Don't let go.*

But being positive and happy usually comes naturally for me. When I wake up, I just feel good, especially when my boy calls me. It gives me joy, that good feeling. And when I see my mom and my family happy, their positive feelings help me to be positive too. If I'm feeling down, I always try to joke and make them laugh and find something to do that's positive and makes me feel good.

Today, my relationship with my dad is fantastic. I love my father to death. He has changed. He's such a good guy. It started when his first grandchild was born. He did a one-eighty and he wants to be around the grandkids all the time. Then when Isaiah was born, my dad started taking him places and doing things with him. I could see my dad was trying to make up for what he hadn't done for us; he could do it with his grandkids. That's when I started to forgive my dad. Just seeing him with his grandkids—he's great with them. He spends so much time with them, doing things and playing with them. He's loving and caring. I don't even care about what he did to us when we were kids because what he does now makes up for that. I guess it's just the grandpa thing.

I don't talk to my other brothers much. One is out in BC. But I'm still close with Matthew. He lives in Winnipeg and calls and texts me throughout the day. He's my best friend.

WHEN I DREAM FOR ISAIAH AND ME, it's to live in a big house and be happy, stay positive, to do new things, and to look forward to facing challenges in life. I never graduated from high school; I only made it to grade 11. I'm going to graduate. I can't just sit here and tell

Isaiah he has to graduate, with me not having graduated too. The thing I am most proud of is having my boy. I'm so proud of Isaiah, of what he's accomplished and what I've accomplished. Love is a good feeling. It makes us who we are. Without love, you're lost. You have to love; if you don't, what's the point of living?

A mutual friend introduced me to Ian after I heard him speak at a gang-awareness workshop. Ian had been shot just five months earlier, but was already eager to tell his story, especially if it could help others. When I eventually interviewed Ian, it was in his bedroom at Ian's parents' home where he lives. Ian lay on his hospital bed while we talked. The bedroom is filled with medical equipment and personal items. There is a beautiful photo collage of Ian and Isaiah laughing as they goof around in a variety of poses.

Ian is funny and charming. He had a girlfriend who he started dating shortly after his accident while he was in the hospital recovering. She lived with Ian and his family for almost three years. They recently split up and he says he has moved on.

ANONYMOUS

I am sharing my experience of being part of a street gang in Winnipeg. I want to honour my story and to be honest about the realities and the sacrifices. I want to take ownership and speak from my experience, but I don't want to speak for or about other gang members. I am speaking specifically about my experience with other people—my shared experience. A valuable lesson I have learned is to never talk about other people. So, this story needs to be 100 percent me. Otherwise, it is open to interpretation... and people's reactions can be unpredictable.

I was born in a small city in southern Sudan in 1984. The civil war between the north and south of Sudan had just broken out in 1983. South Sudan later got its independence in a referendum in 2011, but back in the '80s, people were getting killed and it was really a dangerous time. Many south Sudanese joined or supported the liberation movement. Some of my extended family members on both sides supported the movement and its causes of independence and self-governance. My grandfather, my mother's father, had been a police chief in our city. He said he did his part to make sure the rule of law was in effect, to keep the streets safe and the people treated fairly.

Because it was not stable where I lived, we moved north to the capital city of Khartoum with my mother's family when I was four months old. My dad's family stayed behind. My parents hoped we would have a better life in Khartoum. They were recent graduates with professional backgrounds and had just started their careers. My father lived with us in Khartoum but was working three jobs, so he was gone a lot.

We stayed in Khartoum until I was about eight. I went to kindergarten and primary school there. During that time, I spent a lot of time with my grandma, my mom's mom. She is from a local South Sudanese tribe and her culture and heritage are important to her. She used to say, "Your culture and your language are part of you, never forget it." We would garden together. She taught me how to cultivate the land and to watch for the vegetables to grow out of the soil. That took time. At first, I didn't have the patience for that, but that's what she taught me—patience. We grew corn, tomatoes, and different kinds of fruit including watermelon. She taught me what types of plants to grow, how to space them, what to do about bugs and weeding, how often to water, and how to recognize when the fruits and vegetables were ripe. That was an awesome time. My grandma is an assertive, self-sufficient, task-oriented person. She knew how to control things, but she wasn't a control freak. She'd just say, "This is what needs to happen. This is the reason."

WE'D SEE VIOLENCE IN KHARTOUM: soldiers dressed in green, riding around in their army trucks. They came to our neighborhood pretty much every week, harassing us, tearing our houses apart looking for papers or weapons. My first specific memory of violence was at age six or seven. I remember seeing people dead in the street—shot, cut with bottles or stabbed. At night, we could hear the gunshots. But our Arab (northern Sudanese) neighbours were never bothered; the soldiers came only to the homes of the south Sudanese. Sometimes they took people out of their homes, beat them up,

> My first specific memory of violence was at age six or seven. I remember seeing people dead in the street— shot, cut with bottles or stabbed. At night, we could hear the gunshots.

or took them away and then we'd never see them again.

Adults lived in fear of being targeted all the time. I had one uncle who did as the northern Sudanese government requested and converted to Islam, but he went missing anyway. I didn't understand all of this at the time. I was just a little kid with my own little world. I'd just play and go to school. My family tried to shelter us from the war. Some days our lives felt very normal, but other days I was not even allowed out of the house because it was so dangerous outside. In hindsight, that time was the peak of the war. I remember cleaning this one uncle's weapons—taking his gun apart and putting it back together. And I knew about RPGs before I knew what the letters stood for (rocket-propelled grenades). They were one of my favourite things—I just thought about how cool it was to watch them fly. But I never knew the huge damage they could do until I was an adult.

There were other hardships for us kids. The city was divided in two. On one side, there was fighting and complete rubble with no running water—a crazy ghetto area. The other side was beautiful, with schools and kids playing. It was two completely different spaces. We lived in the poorer side and would cross over to go to school on the nicer side. We were Christians, but we went to a Muslim school where we had to learn the Koran. Southern Sudanese are very dark skinned and there was racism there, something I understood from a really early age. I'd get into fights because our family was discriminated against. Our neighbours used to throw garbage at our house and they'd speak poorly to us kids, saying things like: "You're not supposed to be here." And their kids used to say, "We're going to wipe you out."

I'd get into trouble at home too. If I did something wrong, I'd get a whupping, usually from my teenage uncles. They babysat me a lot. My mom says I was a very active kid, getting into fights, hurting other kids, jumping off things. For punishment, my uncles would make me hold bricks up in my hands and as soon as I let my arms down they'd whup me. I have a few uncles I actually hated. I'd think, *You know what, wait until I grow up, I'm going to kick your ass.* My dad wasn't around much, but he would occasionally give me a whupping, but not a bad one. Same with my mom.

My grandma also gave me a lot of whuppings. She was strict and structured. I loved her for that. My grandpa was so chill. He taught me to read and I spent a lot of time with him during the day while my mom was out. My grandfather sold groceries out of a little shop. He never, ever hit me. He never put my grandmother down, but he'd say, "I'm going to teach you a different way." He'd want to talk. He'd ask me why I did something, ask me lots of questions. Then he'd let me explain and figure out why. It would sound like I was having a conversation with myself. I'd go on…and on…and on, and eventually figure out what the problem was.

THE LAST TIME I saw my grandfather and grandmother was in 1992 when I was eight years old. That year my mom, my siblings, and I moved to Cairo, Egypt. We needed to get out of the capital because it wasn't safe. There was a genocide happening in Sudan. Looking back, 1992 was the most violent year of the war. My grandparents were patriotic. They said they'd survived other wars and didn't want to leave their country. My dad stayed back in Khartoum too, but I don't know why. (I didn't see him again until maybe 1995 when he visited us in Cairo.)

I'd describe our time in Cairo as crazy. First, we stayed at my uncle's house for maybe a year, with him, my aunt, and my cousins. There was something wrong with my aunt. She was a nice lady but I think she had mental health problems. She couldn't afford to get medical help. It was sad. There was also a lot of domestic violence in that home. I never understood why that was going on. I'd try to just avoid it—to be outside the house, either at school or off playing soccer. It was a small space and things were intense there. As kids, we had no control over anything and that affected us all. I was restless and always worried about what would happen next. I was afraid to let my guard down.

After that year, my mom and us kids moved around a lot, staying with different uncles and other relatives. More family members, uncles, and aunties were coming from Sudan, fleeing for safety. It was a hard time. Our house was always full of people and we didn't have enough resources, so we had to share everything. It was just my mom by herself with us trying to cope with helping these family members. She was working two jobs and absent from home a lot.

At that time, I never understood what was happening—things were so emotionally unstable—but I was very responsible. I had to help out watching my younger siblings and do a lot of shopping. I remember being nine or ten and having to walk across town to get bread for my family. That was dangerous because it was a two-hour round trip and I could get jumped and robbed or beaten up. I was always afraid, but I couldn't say no to my family. I had to go. I'd had that thinking instilled in me by my grandmother. Back in Khartoum, she used to say, "You have to be a task-oriented person. Sometimes you do things because you need to, not because you want to, but because you've been chosen for the job." I had to figure out how to be smart and resourceful.

I went to Catholic school in Cairo. Actually, I did really well in school. My mom used to say, "School is what's going to save you." But I got into a lot of fights. I had no choice—I had to either learn how to fight or get my ass whipped. People were always wanting to beat us up, hurt us. I remember being angry a lot. The thing is, Egyptians don't think of themselves as African. They're Muslim. We weren't Muslim and we were in their country. That created a lot of tension. Having to face that situation changed me; before that, I didn't even like fighting but I had to find a way to be tough.

In June of 1998, we left for Canada. By then, I was fourteen and I didn't want to leave. The last day I was crying. My mom and dad told me, "We need to go. It's good. Canada is good." Just before we left, my good friend killed herself. She was Sudanese too, the same age as I was and a nice person. Her parents were planning to marry her off and she didn't want that. She talked about drinking poison. I was the only one listening, but I couldn't really grasp the concept of having to get married. I asked her why she couldn't just tell her parents *no*. Then a couple of days later, I heard that she was dead. Looking back, I realize that her death had a powerful effect on me. At first, I couldn't process her death. A lot of other things were happening so quickly and I didn't have the chance to deal with any of it: the move, my friend's death, everything else. But those

> In June of 1998, we left for Canada. By then, I was fourteen and I didn't want to leave. The last day I was crying.

events shaped me. I went through it all but, you know, I was in survival mode.

WHEN WE FIRST CAME TO WINNIPEG, we stayed downtown. We frequently played at Central Park. It was hot and sunny and I saw a lot of kids and people playing. My siblings started going outside and playing in that park too, but I'm kind of a reserved person so I didn't go out for the first few days. I was just observing my surroundings. (I've always been like that. I like to take my time and figure things out.) Later, I spent a lot of time hanging out and playing soccer in the park. Even though I was fourteen then, I didn't see the other things that were happening around there. I guess my parents knew about the gang activity—they were probably told about safety measures at orientation—and they made us come inside at certain times.

The friends I made around Central Park went to a few local junior high schools, but I didn't end up going to school with them for long. My family moved to the North End of Winnipeg in October and I was put in grade 9 at a school close by. I went to the English Second Language (ESL) class there. That class was really good because I had a great teacher who had an impact on me. She was really nice. There were other kids from different countries in that class and I felt at home there.

I had learned some English in Egypt but I hadn't practised because we didn't speak it at home. In class, I didn't find English hard to learn. Within a year, I was pretty fluent. Reading and writing were easier than speaking. My teacher helped me and I also learned English from my friends.

In the fall of grade 10, my teacher told me I needed to get more involved in the school, so I took a dance class—hip hop and break-dancing—and other fun classes like shops and electronics, besides taking math, English, and science. My phys-ed teacher told me I should try out for the soccer team. I remember that a teacher I liked took me to Walmart and bought me some shin guards and soccer cleats. So I played on the school soccer team and we won the championship that year.

But by the spring of grade 10, things started changing and getting crazy at home. My parents were going through stuff they didn't want to share with us kids. All of a sudden, a lot of Sudanese community elders and uncles were coming to our house. I'd hear them talking for hours. Everyone was getting into shouting matches—my parents and also the community elders. Things were intense. Looking back now, I think there were both transitional and financial issues. People were getting laid off. My dad was driving a taxi and working at a furniture manufacturer. My mom was working there too, as well as doing cleaning and translating. They were sending money back to Sudan. During that time, my uncle from Kenya came with his family and they were living with us. My mom had sponsored them so they didn't qualify for social assistance.

My dad started drinking. His dad had died in '99 of an illness and I don't think he'd processed that. My father has suffered, has lost a lot of people and seen a lot of tragedy, but he doesn't talk about that. And then, he was a professional in Sudan and wanted the same career in Canada, but he ended up driving a cab here. I never saw my dad drink back home, but again, he wasn't around me much when I was a kid. I go by what I saw, so I think he started drinking when he came to Canada and then it developed pretty fast. He became an alcoholic. His drinking caused fighting between him and my mom. It was an unhappy place for everyone. I didn't want to be there.

That summer, I was really upset because I didn't know how to process what was going on. Whenever I spoke up about my parents' fighting or tried to calm my dad down, it would get worse, so I was angry a lot. That summer I started hanging out with older guys who were drinking. I would drink a little with them. I couldn't wait to get back to school in September and start grade 11. But when I went back to class, my mind would wander because I was thinking about all my problems, so I began skipping. My teacher kept trying to encourage me to go to class, and the school would call my house and my parents would be upset and tell me I had to go to school. I tried to stay in school, but I was angry and confused about all my problems. I was a good basketball player, competing in pickup games against university players that I knew. I tried to play for the high school basketball team, but I couldn't be coached because of my attitude so I was kicked off the team. Then I started getting high. My friends had told me that weed wasn't addictive.

That winter, I made some friends who were in a local gang. I wasn't in it, but I would hang around with them a bit. One of the leaders—he was African—would come by where we were shooting hoops and he'd watch me. I remember he was one of the few people I knew who was going to jail. I was shocked and couldn't wrap my head around someone I knew actually going to jail. He told me I was a good basketball player and not to be seen in the same place as him. He told me not to do the things he was doing and that I had an opportunity to make it. He even paid for my community club basketball registration because I couldn't. That was a chance for me to do something positive.

But then, in the spring of grade 11, things started to get even more intense at home. My family was in crisis, but my parents wouldn't admit it. They would say they were trying to deal with things, but it wasn't working out. One night, I came home and found my mom crying and bruised. My dad had hit her while I was out. Then I got into a fight with my dad and punched him. My mom said I couldn't do that to my father and told me that I had to leave. My mom's response made me even angrier. One of my uncles came and picked me up and I had him drop me off at Central Park, at the convenience store close by. I stayed there all night. I started couch surfing at my friends' places. I also started getting high more often.

It was 2004 and I was twenty years old and trying to find a way out, so I just took off. I left Winnipeg for Western Canada. I had cousins there and I went to spend the summer with them. I worked there for a while in a factory that made packaged food—lasagna and macaroni. I also worked a bit for the travelling fair when it came to the city. I played a lot of basketball and smoked a lot of weed. Before I left Winnipeg, I was smoking joints (weed rolled in papers like a cigarette) but my cousins were smoking blunts (a cigar that's been hollowed out and filled with weed). It's the strongest way to smoke it. I went from semi-smoking weed to smoking blunts every day. I wasn't getting into trouble; I just wanted to get away from things. But in early August, my mom told me I had to come back to Winnipeg and go to school. When I moved back, my uncle said I could stay with him. I got a job working at the same furniture manufacturer as my parents and uncles. I planned to go back to school, but then something happened that changed everything and I quit school before grade 12 started.

I've had twelve close friends in Canada die in ten years. All murdered. The first one to get killed was my very good friend, N. I came back in mid-summer and N got killed shortly after. By the time I returned, N was a member of a gang made up mostly of African youth and he was dealing drugs. His death was a direct result of gang rivalry. The thing was, he was hanging around people who had problems and he was getting into trouble: engaging in criminal activity, promoting gang values, not listening to anyone, and living in the moment. People were using him. They would have him in charge, stationed at a crack house— that's a house belonging to someone who is an addict and, as long as they get drugs, they open their house for others to deal crack or cocaine. N was selling drugs there all night. I think he just made a choice. He chose to be someplace where the opposing gang knew that his gang members hung out. He got shot and died instantly. The people who were with him, their lives were changed. So was mine.

N was just a young teenager and he had been my little homie. He looked up to me and always wanted to play basketball with me. He was very funny—and so naïve. When I first came to Canada, I believed that my life was being rewritten—as a peaceful and good one. And, at first, my life in Canada reinforced that, but when N was killed I was so shocked; I never thought that people could die in a violent way in this country. His death was the first time I understood the gravity of violence in Canada.

After N's death, I went to adults in my community to try and discuss his death, but they didn't want to talk about it. They just told me to be careful or I'd turn out the same way. The day N was killed, he'd been in contact with the police but they didn't hold him or ensure that he got home safely, so he went back to the crack house. My friends and I started thinking that people, police and other adults, didn't want to protect us, and if they weren't going to do it, we were going to do that for ourselves. I thought, *What the hell!* I wasn't part of a gang, but some of my friends were. This set of conditions is what brought people together to form a separate gang. None of us wanted to be alone; it was about sticking together. From the beginning, it was a different formation, not a formal one. It took us a while to

…when N was killed I was so shocked; I never thought that people could die in a violent way in this country.

settle on a name. There were no initiations or rankings. A few guys were older, twenty-two or twenty-three, and they had connections for dope and weapons. Everyone else was younger, sixteen or seventeen, and some were as young as twelve.

Guys had different reasons for joining. Some came from other gangs and some, like me, were new. For me, I joined because I wanted to protect my neighbourhood and my people. I had moved out of my uncle's place and he had helped me move into a one bedroom downtown. I couldn't see a purpose in my life at that time and I felt this was a calling. That was my frame of mind. Some of the members of our new gang had weapons, but in the beginning, I didn't carry. Later on, I did use violence when I needed to. That's part of the cycle. If another gang did something to us, we had to do something back. If you don't enforce things, no one's going to respect you, you know.

The gang I joined wasn't like other gangs in Winnipeg. It ended up operating on one city block because most members grew up in that area and lived in the apartment buildings there. It started with a small group of guys, but grew quickly and, in two to three months, there were close to a hundred members from many different African backgrounds. Most of us were living day to day, just trying to survive, but we were all taking care of each other too. Like I'd be selling dope on this same block that others were working and we didn't interfere with each other; we were all making money. Of course, there were other spots—crack shacks—that I could go to stash drugs and weapons and maybe go to when I was getting paid. (There are a lot of crack houses in the West End of Winnipeg.) Once you're in the gang and know these things, it's hard to back out and just go back to living with your mom and dad. I don't think I understood what was happening, what I was getting into. It all grew so fast. By then, it was too late.

I don't think I understood what was happening, what I was getting into. It all grew so fast. By then, it was too late.

I was constantly around people who were dealing drugs, but at first, I didn't deal. I was still working at the furniture manufacturer. I was making $500 every two weeks at that job and I was trying to save. But after a while, I ended up dealing—the money was so much better. I had a driver's licence and a car. After work, I could make $500 in one call (drug sale). It just didn't make sense to me, to be spending hours at work when I could be dealing and making more money.

IN LATE 2005, about a year after I started selling drugs, I was charged with trafficking and I went to the Remand Centre. The gang I was in started to have internal disputes. I wasn't in the centre of the conflict leading to these disagreements because I was in custody. Some people wanted structure and initiations, some thought new members should pay their dues to the OGs (gang members who were there from the beginning), and some people wanted to get into prostitution and selling guns. And then there were some who wanted just to be together. That's what I wanted. But there was no real leadership then. Things were unpredictable and that's the biggest thing about being in a gang—it's unpredictability. That's why people die. I don't think anyone asks for that. It's always about choice. You make some kind of choice that puts you in a dangerous position. Some of the gang members would carry weapons to places when that didn't make sense. Then again, I chose to be part of that.

Lots of our members were getting targeted by police, getting arrested, and going to jail. When I was inside the Remand, I tried to keep the peace. There was lots of tension in the gang, but when we were on the inside, I wanted our gang members to be organized and not to fight so we could have respect from other gangs on the inside. I was a person who didn't cross others, so some of the influential guys on the outside gave me a message that I had to take the lead on the inside, getting guys organized. It was for their best interest. I had to get our gang a table in the eating area, organize seating for meals, take control over a phone in the jail so our guys could make calls, prevent other people stealing from our members, make sure members were not taken advantage of at the canteen, and be responsible for managing banned substances and communication entering the prison.

Sometimes people in a gang can rise in rank through intimidation, but that doesn't last long because someone else might be

It's always about choice. You make some kind of choice that puts you in a dangerous position.

much more violent. And with intimidation, you create a lot of enemies. I don't like to fight or yell, that only creates more anger. I am not a violent person, I like to negotiate and use common sense. But I recognize violence does play a role in the gang lifestyle. Violence creates a cycle. People who become valued leaders are the ones who are charismatic, who know how to deal with people and can hold a group together—and who have a strong reason, a motive to hold them together. But mostly leadership is about the ability to connect with people. I think that's the reasons I was able to become a leader. I didn't seek it—that's the thing. I'm not a violent person. I don't like violence; I'd rather solve things with critical thinking. There were other people around me who were violent, but I didn't need to do that. I never craved power; it was about respect and mutual understanding. Sure, sometimes you have to be authoritative, but if you abuse power, it will come back and literally bury you. The whole reason I joined the gang in the first place was to try and keep people together because I didn't want what happened to N to happen to anyone else. My purpose was to help out, be there, and protect my people.

Correctional officers in the prison saw how the gang leadership was working. They wanted to separate the high-ranking members, so they broke up our gang in jail and sent some of us to different places and also to isolation. I was one of those people. I was sent to another Manitoba prison and was put in isolation for the whole eight or nine months I was there. It was pretty long. They put me in lockdown twenty-three-and-a-half hours a day. I got only half an hour during the day to shower and call someone.

The first few months in isolation were pretty hard, but after a while, I got used to it. I read a lot, wrote, worked out, drew. Isolation also helped me by giving me time to think about my life, process things that had happened to me, and prepare myself for what was ahead. Everything in a gang is always in a heightened mode, so there's no time for processing. My mindset was changing. I was beginning to reform myself. Isolation helped me process. I could

> There were other people around me who were violent, but I didn't need to do that. I never craved power; it was about respect and mutual understanding.

see changes in our gang too. Most members didn't care about each other, and some even wanted to kill each other. The reasons I first joined the gang—wanting to protect and to have relationships—were gone. I kept thinking *I want to leave the gang. I can do this.* Realizing all this at an early stage was a turning point for me and really helped me later when I was trying to stay out of the gang. I had always been a decision-maker and I returned to wanting to take control of my life. I was feeling trapped in the gang, but I also knew I could get out of it.

I was moved back to Headingley and put in isolation for my first two months. All the time I was in prison, I wanted out of there. I knew I had messed up and I was down on myself because I was in such a restricted state. I was diminishing my potential. I wanted more for myself and I knew I was capable.

My dad sent me some money and visited a couple of times while I was locked up. He told me, "You've put yourself in this situation and I can't help you. You broke the law and now you have to deal with the consequences." He also picked me up the day I got out of prison in the fall of 2007 and drove me home. He doesn't talk a lot, but during the drive my dad told me, "anybody can be reformed." That was the first time I'd ever heard the word reformed and I didn't know what it meant, so I asked him to explain it. He said, "Anybody has the ability to change if they want to. If you really want it and you believe it's possible, there's a chance. You just have to demonstrate that you can do it." (I would add, it is only possible if you like yourself.) He was saying that if I really wanted to change, I could do it. At that time, I couldn't grasp the truth of that. I was trying to understand if it was possible for me to change after everything that had already happened.

IN MID-2006, while I was incarcerated, I got a letter from Immigration Canada telling me I was eligible for deportation because of my conviction. After I got out of jail, I had a deportation hearing in court in early 2008. My lawyer argued that I had been in jail most of the time since I got the letter and had not yet had a chance to demonstrate my actions. (I got my lawyer through legal aid, since I never had any money to pay for one.) I remember thinking, *I'm twenty-two years old, where would the government send me, back to Sudan? I wouldn't know where to go.*

The judge asked me what I wanted to do if I was given a chance to stay in Canada. I said I would redirect my life and I'd go back to school. She decided to stay the deportation for five years and give me a chance to demonstrate that I could change my life. She had a set of conditions: I had to stay away from gangs, go back to school and get some training, get treatment for my addictions, and not catch any new charges. I also had to visit the immigration offices every three months for review.

I didn't realize that staying away from my old gang friends would be so hard. They lived in my neighbourhood and they followed me around a lot, like to school. Shortly after I got out of prison, when I was at an Immigration meeting, I was charged with assault because someone said I had hit them. The charge was considered a breach and I had to go back to Remand for a few weeks. Later, the charge was stayed, but it was that charge that cemented my decision to stay out of jail and away from my gang friends. There was tension—I had told them I was staying out, but I was afraid of being shot or assaulted. I had no protection. I felt naked. Sometimes, I prayed. I thought, *I can't be afraid of my decision. Now is the time. I'm walking straight.*

Getting rid of my addictions was even harder. I didn't realize I had a serious substance abuse problem until I started to try to sober up. Primarily, I had used marijuana and alcohol. Sometimes, I did other recreational drugs, like ecstasy, but I didn't touch the hard drugs because I knew what cocaine and crack do to people. I started trying to quit in 2008 after going to my deportation hearing. First, I got off marijuana. It was hard. I started cutting down. I'd try to stop completely for a while, but end up going back. Then someone I knew was killed due to a drug-related dispute that led to me firmly decide: *I'm not smoking again.* That was 2010 and I was finally able to quit for good. I went to AA (Alcoholics Anonymous) for my alcohol addiction. When I first went there, I thought, *This is not for me, I'm not staying here.* I left and it took me a while, but I returned. I came back a few times, just a couple of months here and there—I did whatever requirements were

> I didn't realize that staying away from my old gang friends would be so hard. They lived in my neighbourhood and they followed me around a lot, like to school.

needed to meet my deportation request—but I didn't actually sober up until 2012.

Alcohol addiction goes way back in my family. There are my dad's struggles with alcohol—and that created an unhappy home for all of us. And when I was six years old and living in Sudan, my uncle died of alcohol poisoning. He was generally a nice guy, intelligent and very quiet. At the time, I didn't understand why he would become a different person under the influence of alcohol, but I can relate now. I remember the night he died. I hadn't realized that alcohol had that much impact on my life. Eventually, once I started attending AA regularly, that realization is what helped me sober up. I had a really good counsellor there. She was a nice lady.

During all this, I had a girlfriend and we had two children together. Today, I am a single dad. Child and Family Services had tried to apprehend our kids from their mom. I was already on the road to addiction recovery and in a position to be able to take full custody of them. Their mom is going through her own personal challenges and her own journey of recovery. I understand why she is the way she is. She grew up in a refugee camp most of her life and has had a lot of traumatic experiences. Shortly after coming to Canada, she was taken into CFS care herself. She's not healthy, but she's there for the kids when she can be. She has to go through her own healing process. I try not to blame her and I tell her that in person when I can. I say, "You have to keep trying." She can see them any time. If I can change, hopefully she can change too. She's still very young—in her early twenties. I'd like her to be around the kids. I'm just worried that she's not okay.

My parents split while I was still in prison. Culturally, they are not allowed to divorce, so they are still husband and wife. Their families see marriage as a bond my mom and dad can't break. But they are separated. My dad moved back to South Sudan. Now that I have kids, my mom supports me sometimes by looking after them.

It took me four years to finish my grade 12 and get my high school diploma (GED) from Adult Ed. I took a credit here and there because I was dealing with my addictions and working full time at two restaurant jobs. (I could have done it all in one year if I'd been in a healthy place.) In 2013, I earned my GED and also got my diploma in an Addiction and Community Service Worker course. I was attending those college classes in the evening while I was in my last year of Adult Ed. I loved going to that college. It was full of opportunity. That program opened my eyes. In my first class there, the teacher asked us why we wanted to be counsellors. I told him that I wanted to help people. What he said has always stood out for me. He told us that if people are coming to us for support, they're opening up and vulnerable and we need to remember that. We had to be careful not to let our own unresolved issues get in the way of helping others; we needed to put their needs first. He said that sometimes we'd be asked to work with someone who hurt others or with people whose choices we disagree with. He asked us to think about whether we could help people like that. I was like, *Man, this whole thing is different than I thought, but I want to stay here.* I still wanted to help people and I understood what the teacher was saying—if a person is looking to help others, all his work should be around what they want. Willingness to serve people is the main thing. It's all about service first. Everything else will come after.

My teacher's comments also made me realize you need to look at yourself, and help yourself first. If you're counselling, you should always have someone to see, a counsellor of your own. I've been to therapy. I'm really happy I did that. I think it helps to have a professional to talk to in life. In this field, you can really get burnt out. My counsellors help me work through a lot of things. They're still helping me.

While I was attending classes, I did my practicum placement at an immigration resettlement service provider in Winnipeg. It offers a variety of supports and services to newcomer families. It was a full-circle moment. I wanted to give back to newcomers and make sure that I helped prevent some people from getting addicted to drugs or going to jail. I understand what those things mean both personally and professionally. I wanted to create awareness and support them through their transition to Canada. When I got out of jail, I also had a lot of guilt and I needed to heal. I felt lucky that I could get out of the gang and sober up, although I did work hard for that. I just wanted to give back. I wanted to give back because I had done things that were not nice. That's why I sometimes felt guilt; it was related to unresolved issues.

The executive director at the time hired me as a youth worker after my placement. He gave me a chance. I had a criminal record, but he said, "What you are doing is making a difference." He actually looked at both sides. He looked at the value of what I could bring in terms of my former gang lifestyle and he also looked at my academics and how I was demonstrating that I had changed. He recognized that I could add value. He believed I was redirecting my life and he believed in the work I was doing, so he provided me with an opportunity to start my career and take care of my family. I did not expect someone to hand me a job. My lived experience gave me a different perspective and added value. Being hired by that executive director changed everything for me. I don't know who else would have done that. He helped me gain the confidence that I needed to know I could make a difference

When I started at the workplace, I worked directly for the manager who was in charge of youth programming. He also helped me a lot and provided me with leadership. He understood why it's important to have a role model and how to give feedback. But he also let me figure out what I wanted and how I would fit in. He mentored me and introduced me to a lot of people. He looked at me and my former lifestyle professionally, in terms of what I could bring to the table. It was like I had credentials.

I think it is important to share my story; it's a part of my life, always. I can use it as proof to show those from a similar background that if they really want to change, it is possible. I recently received a promotion from my employer. The timing of these two mentors entering my life was awesome. I think they were really meant to be there.

At our service provider, we have so many programs for newcomers, youth, and their families. The kids have people who support them and they have options. They are in a better position to make it than I was. Looking back, I wish I had those kinds of supports when I was younger. I remember all we had around Central Park was an arcade where we would drop in, play video games, hang out, and have snacks, but it was a good

> I think it is important to share my story; it's a part of my life, always. I can use it as proof to show those from a similar background that if they really want to change, it is possible.

thing. We used to go after school and all day in the summertime. We almost lived there! There were dangers around Central Park, but I didn't know that. Kids now have protection from dangers around them. I would say eighty percent of newcomer kids have a really good chance of striving and moving on. A small percentage has factors like family dynamics or trauma that make them especially vulnerable. The most important thing I learned is that you've got to just be there for them in relationships. Building that relationship is the most important thing because then when they need to talk to someone, they will come to you.

IN 2013, I GOT ANOTHER LETTER saying that I was eligible for deportation again and I had to submit all my documentation and proof of what I had done over the last five years. The courts set my deportation hearing up for early one morning in 2015. I went in front of the federal Department of Justice lawyer and the judge. Supporting me, there were four managers from my work. Also supporting me were two people from an organization I volunteered with that supports youth at risk and people who want to leave gangs. My executive director had written a letter of support and the judge asked him what he would like to say about me. He said that he had hired me and I had done a lot of good work and turned my life around. And I had—I had graduated from high school and college, had done my practicum, been hired, and was on my journey of sobriety and I was a single dad to my two kids.

The only question the judge asked was if I would ever go back to the gang lifestyle. I told her no. I said, "I think I have accomplished a lot more now." In the beginning, I was doing what the courts asked because, straight up, Immigration wanted to deport me. But after a while, I decided I was having more peace not living the gang lifestyle and not worrying about everything that goes with it. I couldn't comprehend going back to the gang life. I told the judge it was the first time in my life that I was in control. All my life, I had been under someone else's control—first, in my parents' house and then as part of a gang. But now, I had created stability for myself. I had found something in all the rehabilitation that helped me in my life—it was a starting point to change.

The judge told me she could see I had people supporting me, that I'd turned my life around and had demonstrated successful rehabilitation. She also told me that my two kids were one of the biggest factors in allowing me to stay in Canada, since I am the main caregiver. She said, "I don't see a reason that we should stay your deportation two more years. This is the type of outcome that we hope for when we impose these types of conditions. I can see you've given back already with the work that you are doing. I hope that you continue your education. The deportation is no longer valid. Keep the good work up." The whole thing didn't actually take that long. Going into the hearing, I was confident and calm. I have always believed that if you do your part, someone will meet you halfway. I knew I'd done my best and I was hopeful that they'd make the right decision. I didn't want my past to own me.

My lawyer and I hugged. He's a really good guy; he cares about me. He encouraged me from the beginning and he understood me. He's also my family lawyer, so he had helped me get custody of my kids. He's a really cool guy and he's another person who has made a huge difference in my life.

I HAVE PEACE RIGHT NOW and I am continuing to heal. I'm making that choice. Sometime in 2014, I started thinking it was about time to let go of some of my baggage from my friends' deaths, especially N's. What happened to those people was painful for me. I have my scars, both physical and mental. The cycle of violence continues and I am reminded of the reality of that violence often. Now I choose to remember those friends by thinking of their last words of hope and optimism to me. I was angry for a long time, but I decided I have to let this go if I want to have peace and move on. Now, on the anniversary of N's death, I'm trying to respect and celebrate his life. I will never forget him, but I hold his death differently now. It was heavy and I still have feelings of grief, guilt, and anger, but I want N's death to transform me, in hope of it being for the positive.

The other important thing that helps me heal is just acknowledging that there are still people in that same struggle. I've changed my reality, but it's difficult knowing that some of my former friends are still involved in gang life. In the beginning, when I started to change and left the gang, my former gang members were suspicious, but now they leave me alone. They know how I am. I see them, I ask them how they are doing, but I don't really talk to them. Sometimes, they tell me that what I'm doing is good. They say they wish they could do it too. They even tell me I'm a role model and that they can see that I've changed. I don't seek that attention. That was never my intention at all. But their comments have an impact on me. I feel blessed because I am developing as a person, transforming and demonstrating that to myself. The healing process is also about allowing myself to do good. If my former gang friends seek my help, I will tell them that I can do something for them, as long as they are willing to invest. They have to be willing. I can only help in certain ways. I know it will take time to redirect their lives.

Another positive step for me happened in 2013. Through my work, I was asked to join a writing group created by a Winnipeg woman, which helps you heal and understand things that have happened to you. I was still new at work then, but it was evident to me that the people who had already taken the course were not the same afterwards. I wasn't initially comfortable with opening up and talking about myself—I'm more task-oriented—but I like change and transformation, so I was open to seeing what the writing group was about.

The first session was together with my co-workers and I felt immediately that I was meant to be there. We talked about writing our own stories. Storytelling is a big thing in my culture. I grew up with my grandparents sharing stories about life, so I was attracted to the storytelling and to listening to others. We even shared about deep and private things and many of the others' stories resonated with me.

After that, I took a course to become a facilitator in the program, along with co-workers and some staff at a local drop-in centre and safe place for inner-city youth. I graduated in 2015. I am more confident now and I've gained skills from sharing stories with people. It is one of the only places where I have time to focus on myself. There, writing together with others, I am in the moment, present and grounded. I've never had that before. This writing program reminds me that everything starts with me. You've got to love yourself and be okay with yourself. It's important to hear that message. Everything else—raising my kids, working, volunteering in the community—is for others, and there's nothing wrong with that, but it's important to have time for myself. I find strength and hope from my writing.

For the last six years, I have many positive things going on in my life: community, work, friends, soccer, basketball. But I also have to take care of myself. Sometimes, I can't do it alone and even though I am a person who has kept my feelings closed, I know now that I need to tell my story to others and work through them. That gives me peace. I'm still struggling, but it's a good struggle, it's not like before. I know I am here for a reason.

AT THIS POINT IN MY LIFE, I am most proud of my children and the way I am there for them. I remember something my AA counselor told me after my son was born. She said, "Your kid is being a kid. He's doing what he's supposed to be doing and you as an adult are *not* doing what you're supposed to be doing and that is being responsible." Now I understand that being present as a father is important. My dad wasn't around much, but I remember the times he was there. I am trying my best to help my children to be good people. I really respect autonomy, so I want my kids to be their own people and responsible for themselves. I'm trying to guide them, but to also give them that freedom too. They are the best.

My goal is for my kids to have every opportunity possible, just like any other Canadian kid. I am super busy, but I sacrifice a lot for them. When they go to bed at night, I'm there for them and when they wake up in the morning, I'm there too. Being a single dad is the hardest thing, but the one thing I am most proud of. I would also say I'm proud of growing from my life experiences. I'm totally different than I was before and I'm optimistic about my future.

I like to visualize where I am going to go. At seventeen, I said I would start my career at twenty-seven and I did start my immigrant services job at twenty-seven. I used to walk down Portage Avenue and see the University of Winnipeg. I'd tell myself, *That's where I'm going to be.* People would say I couldn't do that because I'm from the 'hood, but I did not put those limitations on myself. I wanted to be there. At the time, I didn't know how I'd do it. But now I am there. Today, I am going to the University of Winnipeg. I am

> I know now that I need to tell my story to others and work through them. That gives me peace. I'm still struggling, but it's a good struggle, it's not like before. I know I am here for a reason.

interested in studying policy-making, environmental law, and land rights. The South Sudanese have underdeveloped land and have been taken advantage of by the North. There is so much potential there. I want to have an understanding of policy knowledge so that I can advocate for the environment and for the people of South Sudan. I love the land. This interest comes from my time in the garden with my grandma.

I want to be a leader in South Sudan. Everything that's happened to me and all the places I've lived have been there for a reason. I'm privileged because I have an ability to help. I have leadership skills, I listen, I can see what it takes. There is still much to learn, but the community needs a new generation. Growing up, my parents would remind us of the Sudanese who sacrificed their lives in order to help our generation have the freedoms and privileges we have today. My generation has to honour that. The people of South Sudan first need to live peaceful and stable lives. I understand that. I've been given things and I must give back. I could even be president someday. It is a possibility. If you put your mind to it, anything is possible…

This participant is a highly intelligent person, detail-oriented, and he values being in control. He considered the wording of this story very carefully. He chose to be anonymous because, as he says, "I am working hard but not everyone will see it that way. I don't want things to be misconstrued." He feels it is safer for him not to have his name attached. He is concerned about how this story could affect his family, his career, and his future. He acknowledges he may be judged and that's not in his control. This participant has made a brave choice to share his story here. His decision to be anonymous underscores the fact that there can be risks involved in speaking out and, at the same time, highlights the courage of the other participants who chose to attach their names to their stories.

This participant was particularly mindful when speaking about the death of his friend N. N's death is central to this story and has greatly affected many of his former friends from the gang. Anonymous selected a pseudonym for his friend. He chose the initial N to symbolically stand for the Arabic word Ya Nas, *which means* The People. *He selected this word as a reminder that what happened to his friend changed everyone's lives forever*

—no matter where they were or which of the rival gangs they were part of. He says N's death continues to affect many today and there is still a lot of hurt.

Anonymous's leadership strengths remind me of something someone told me early on in researching this book: that a leader is a leader. Gang leaders often become leaders in their civilian lives too. The skills used are highly transferable.

In the early days of doing research for this book, before I began writing, I met Anonymous and we spoke about this project. Shortly afterwards, he sent me an email of encouragement. It meant a great deal to me. I wrote most of it on a post-it and attached it to my computer where I could see it every day and read it often. His message was: "Keep up the passion and hard work you are doing to help give voice to a lot of people who at times cannot do it for themselves. Thank you, Anne."

JAMIE

Even though I'm not involved in motorcycle clubs anymore, it still irks me that the cops call them gangs. In a sense, I guess they can be, but for me it was not a gang. Gangs are low peons fighting for a street corner; they're not on the same level as the international motorcycle clubs I was part of. We were moving a tonnage of cocaine.

I had a straight connection down in Peru that was transporting up to BC and right to my doorstep in Manitoba. We were dealing with four other provinces distributing the stuff. The type of money that was coming in was a far cry from anything a street gang made. If you want to look at it from a civilian point of view, I was sort of like a CEO running a business. You can't call that a *gang*. For twenty-five years, I was entrenched in this life.

I was born in Winnipeg and raised in The Maples. My early memories are of playing drums, doing concerts, and going to all the sports I was involved in. I played hockey and football. I started playing hockey when I was three. My dad coached my teams and my mom was always in the stands. When my dad coached me, he picked on me more than anyone else. That'd be anyone's dad, wanting their kid to shine, right? Our hockey team stuck together from age four or five all the way to juniors at eighteen. My dad coached me all the way through too.

In The Maples back then, if you weren't in sports, you were a nobody, so I got attention by playing sports. I was a big kid, 200 pounds in grade 9. I didn't have speed like my dad did, but I excelled, especially in football. I played the whole game: offence, defence, kick-off, and receiving. I played high school and junior football. Sports to me meant accomplishment and they gave me backbone and made me the person I am today.

But my relationship with my dad was more of a friendship; there wasn't really any love involved. There was a disconnect there. I guess it stemmed from his relationship with his dad who was an alcoholic, so my dad didn't get along with him. There was no bond between them. Then there was this special bond between my uncle (my dad's brother) and my grandfather because they drank together. But my dad stayed involved in sports growing up, so that was our connection and how we spent the majority of our time together. But I always got the affection I needed from my grandfather, my mom's dad.

I spent almost every weekend from as long as I can remember until I was a teenager, with my grandparents, Meme and Grandpee. They lived in the North End at Aberdeen and McGregor. Being male and the oldest grandchild in the German culture on my mom's side, I got a bit more attention. My grandfather took me to the jobsite with him while he was doing sewer and water construction.

I had a mini bike in grade 4 and my grandpa used to take me out to the Perimeter Highway to ride it. I got the love from him that I didn't get at home. Plus, school was rough. So I was always looking forward to the weekends, everything was put on pause and it was a happy time in my life.

I didn't really like school. I was an ADD kid. I wasn't diagnosed back then because not much was known about it. (I was finally diagnosed when I was thirty years old.) In those days, you were either smart or you were put in the "rubber class" and that's where a lot of us kids ended up, including me. I wasn't attentive to my schoolwork; my mind would drift off. I have a sister who's one year younger than me and she's really book smart

I didn't really like school. I was an ADD kid. I wasn't diagnosed back then because not much was known about it.

like my dad. She graduated from high school half a year early. Eventually my problems at school would cause a lot of stress at home and a rift between me and my parents.

I had a bad temper as a kid and I got into lots of fights in elementary school. I was a chunkier, shorter kid and other kids taunted me. They'd start it and I'd finish it. I was fighting pretty much every day. But I only fought once in junior high because the principal had a son my age and we played all our sports together, so the principal and my dad were talking on a nightly basis. I couldn't step sideways without my dad finding out what was going on. He would get pissed off only because he didn't want me to get caught. He didn't care what happened, if I wasn't on school property.

When I was in grade 8, my dad got me into taekwondo because of my temper and all the fighting I'd been doing. He thought it would be another avenue to get my aggression out. It helped for a while. I was training six days a week. Today, I have a black belt in taekwondo, Muay Thai, kickboxing and Bissett jiu-jitsu.

I had a pretty good childhood until I was about thirteen. That's when stuff first started going sideways. There was a sort of split in my family. First, my mom turned to my sister and pushed me away. I never really knew the reason for that, but maybe it was because I was a little harder to handle than my sister. Then there was all this turmoil between my mom and dad. My mom was angry a lot, sort of like I was. She'd been like that since she was a kid. (My grandmother talked to me about it.) I remember my mom hitting my dad a couple of times. One time, I dragged her downstairs, threw her in a chair, and said, *Enough.* (When I saw my dad's face all bleeding, I sort of went ballistic.) He would never hit my mom; he just stood there and took it. So I was the one pulling her off. Even though my dad was derogatory towards me, he was still my dad and we had at least that bond over sports, so I became closer to my dad at that time. I saw numerous fights between my parents. Afterwards, my dad would leave the house for a while, but then he'd come back.

My own temper was starting to escalate. I felt resentful that all this stuff was going on. I was in the middle of all that nasty shit. It's not something a kid should have to go through. And I felt pushed to the side. My dad didn't leave until I was eighteen, but the writing was on the wall back then.

My mom and dad never drank, never smoked, but my mom had some depression, which wasn't really talked about back then. She also had a total hysterectomy, but that didn't solve anything. Her mental health issues weren't addressed until later. In hindsight now, I think she had a chemical imbalance that wasn't right, but it wasn't her fault.

Then when I was fourteen, my grandfather died. I became really pissed off at the world because I didn't have him to turn to while all this stuff was happening with my parents. My grandfather had been staying at Seven Oaks Hospital. One evening, I spent the night with him and walked home in the morning. I lived right across the field, off Pipeline Road, close to the hospital, so it was about a twenty-minute walk home. I had just got in the door and the phone started ringing. It was the hospital telling me to come back because my grandfather had just died. Before I left him that morning, my Grandpee had said, "Make me a promise that you'll look after your grandmother if something happens to me." So that was his last wish for me.

At his funeral, I was a pallbearer. Sitting in the church, I said, *Fuck you God*. That was it. I shut my feelings off and went cold after that. All of my emotions were packed on top of each other. It was a really tough time. I could have turned my feelings back to a certain degree, but I wouldn't. That decision sort of pushed me towards the path I decided to take later on in life.

A year later, when I was fifteen, I moved out and lived at my grandma's. It was good for both of us. I'd take her to get her hair done or get her blood work done. I also took her grocery shopping. I did my best to keep my promise to my grandfather, especially while I was young.

There was an episode a week after I moved into my grandmother's. My mom came over and started mouthing off at me. I stood up and said, "Listen, I moved out to get away from you, so I want you to get out of this fucking house." She slapped me and my grandmother stepped in between us. My mom tried to come at me again, so I reached over and hit her. My mom hit the floor. She left,

> Sitting in the church, I said, *Fuck you God.* That was it. I shut my feelings off and went cold after that. All of my emotions were packed on top of each other. It was a really tough time.

but later I got a phone call from my dad. He was swearing at me and wanted to know why I'd hit my mom.

I said, "Why don't you talk to Meme?" So then my grandma got on the phone and started yelling at my dad saying no, my mom had started it. My dad always sided with my mom no matter what she did to me. Right or wrong, he always backed her, so it was a losing situation for me.

I lived with my grandmother until I was eighteen. Then I moved back home. I was bouncing at a club and it was closer to my parents'. I quit school in grade 12, six months before graduation. I'd had enough of school and bouncing felt a lot more exciting. My dad stayed for a little while after I moved home and then my parents split. I lived with my mom until she started dating other guys and bringing them home. One day, I wound up punching out a guy that she brought back because I felt disrespected and also, I felt a bond with my dad. (At that point, I was connecting more with my dad and appreciating the time he'd spent with me coaching my sports.) Then I started working lots so that I wouldn't be home much to see the drama and my mom's boyfriends.

IN MY TEENS, my friends were the guys I played sports with. We were a tight group because our fathers also played senior hockey together. It was like a family type of thing. We stayed together until we were juniors, basically at the end of high school. Then I quit school and went my own way.

I didn't do much underage drinking. I did get caught a couple of times in junior high. Once, we had a flat of beer behind an IGA grocery store before a dance. But somebody driving by recognized me and my dad got a call. I didn't get my ass beat, but I got a good talking to from my dad. I always looked older, so later on in high school, I was getting into bars early. I started working at the doors while I was still underage—seventeen. I was a bouncer. Then I started drinking lots, every night that I was working.

I worked at a strip club, Teasers, on Archibald. A lot of bikers were hanging out there. That's how I met the president of the first club I eventually got involved with. One night, I threw a kid out and his dad came back the next night to try and even the beef out. I was the only male working. The bar upstairs had shut down and I had no back up. All of a sudden, there's a gun on the back of my head and this guy says, "I'm going to do you."

I said, "Well, do what you gotta do." And then this president at the time put a gun to the guy's head and said, "If you do that to him, I'm going to do the same thing to you." When the guy dropped his gun, we beat the shit out of him and left him outside.

This president was friends with the owner of Teasers. He had a booze-can (an after-hours place in a house where people could go to drink) that I used to pop into for some drinks after work once in a while. I had talked to him before. He helped me that night out of respect for the owner because they knew each other. A lot of those guys had known each other for years, even before I was born.

Eventually that motorcycle club drifted apart and moved from Winnipeg to Brandon. I was dating this girl whose family lived in Brandon, so one night I went to a bar out there and, lo and behold, they all piled in. One person recognized me and we got to talking. Within a year, when that same club re-established itself in Winnipeg, I ran into one of the guys again. By then, I had stopped drinking, had toned it down, and was staying away from the drugs. (Coke was something that everybody was doing to stay awake because we were all burning the candle at both ends. I didn't consider using it an addiction.) I had gone back to the gym hard and had put a lot of size on.

So, one day I was at a booze-can on Selkirk where I was overseeing and selling drugs. I had started dabbling in selling cocaine. One of the club members came in and then there was about fourteen of them. I got a call that one had a gun, so I went downstairs myself and said, "Who's got the gun?" I didn't give a shit about who they were or the patches they were wearing. I punched out a couple of them. I wasn't afraid. If you had a beef with me, I was going to deal with it. By then, I was working out a lot and all jacked up on steroids. I was crazy. On steroids, you feel invincible because you don't feel nothing. I was six feet tall, 230 pounds, with twenty-inch arms. I had all my martial arts training and I wasn't worried about too many people. I had been lifting a lot of weight too. Nobody could do nothing to me. People didn't want to mess with me because they knew when it came down to it, if they didn't kill me, I would come back at them and I'd do twice as bad as what they did to me.

That's how my criminal life started. The club wanted me to become a member, but they wanted to see what type of brass I had, how I could enhance their club. So I started working collections and I became a striker. That lasted about a year, but I never made full patch because everything in the club went sideways. The president got killed and the club started bringing junkies in, so it went downhill.

I got my first bike shortly after I got involved in the club. I was twenty-four or -five then. My uncle had gotten into Harleys. He had one he'd built from the frame up. I spent every weekend helping him. He hung out with the Winnipeg Harley Riders Association and that group hung out with some outlaw bikers, so that's how the lifestyle sort of got engrained in me. I thought, *Yeah, I want to be a part of this.* The other appeal of the club was the sense of belonging, like being in a brotherhood. The guys would go out to the bar or do things as a group. I was looking for somewhere to hang my hat and belong. It felt like the same kind of belonging that I'd had when I played on my hockey and football teams.

It felt like the same kind of belonging that I'd had when I played on my hockey and football teams.

I was also working a day job. For all the twenty-five years I was dealing, I always worked a legit job too. I worked at a box manufacturing plant from '92 to '97. My dad was head of human resources there, so when I finally settled down a bit around twenty-two, I worked there. But then I blew a rotator cuff at work and buggered up my shoulder.

I had ten dislocations and three operations. After my last surgery, the company was trying to get guys with re-occurring injuries out the door. My dad was still in human resources and management was putting pressure on my dad to get rid of me, so after working there for six years, I quit.

There was a time after the gang went to shit that I went solo—about '96 to 2003. I was dealing with drugs and collections for different groups around town. I wasn't so much dealing drugs as putting deals together. I knew where to get the stuff and if a guy was looking, I'd take a cut between him and the supplier and let those guys settle a deal together. I was like a middleman.

THE NEXT PHASE OF MY CRIMINAL LIFE would've started around 2003. I heard this biker club was coming to Manitoba and I knew they were a big establishment. They had been in Montreal and then spread down to Toronto. I'd heard they were looking to come out west too. The Internet had started to be a big thing, so I jumped on their website and sent off an email to the club, saying I was interested in helping them in Manitoba. They got back to me and said they had somebody in Winnipeg I should talk to. They must've checked into my credibility and knew that I had a good name on the street. I had that meeting with their guy and was offered the vice-president job. I took it. So he, another guy, and I went out to Toronto, got our patches, and that's what elevated me to the next level of organized crime. I helped expand that club in Manitoba.

It was good at the beginning and then greed took over. The guy who wound up becoming the president in Manitoba was an ex-police officer from East St. Paul (just outside Winnipeg). He had ulterior motives. He would later say in court that the only reason he joined the club was so he could sign a paid-agent form with the RCMP, set everybody up,

have guys arrested, and then walk away with a payday. A paid agent is somebody who signs a contract with the RCMP to deliver guys. The agent gives the RCMP a list of the names of guys who he can put into a position to frame and probably get arrested. The agent is paid a quarter or half of the total money biweekly until there is an arrest and the case goes to trial. The money is big, from $500,000 to $700,000 (plus relocation and witness protection). Then, once the court case is done and everybody's convicted, he gets paid the rest. That's how the RCMP do it now. Let's face it—the cops need help from the crime inner circle. The RCMP can't infiltrate a club. Very rarely do you see that. This ex-cop president was greedy and he had plans. But it didn't work out the way he had hoped. Instead, he and our club ended up in the middle of what became known as The Shedden Massacre in April 2006. There have been two books written about it.

A few months before, around Christmas of 2005, I had quit the club. There was a big rift between our club in Manitoba and the officers of the Toronto chapter. Our president was greasy and he wasn't communicating with our mother chapter out east in Toronto, but I was. I had developed a close bond with the Toronto guys because when they came to town, they stayed at my place. I got to know them really well.

This Manitoba president was weak, a weasel. There was so much shit going down. He was pissing me off. This one time, we sat down with a big North American bike club to barter a truce. There had been a huge club war in Montreal in the '80s that was bad for business on both sides and had created a lot of hatred. We didn't want another one of those here in Manitoba. During the bartering, a guy from the other club started walking all over my Manitoba president, so I took over the conversation. I said, "Hey, listen, you guys are on one side of the street and we're on the other. We're not trading our colours in for yours and getting our club absorbed by your club. If I had wanted to become a member of your club, I would've approached you guys years ago. I didn't. I don't like what your guys are about."

The other guy looked at me and says, "So that's the way it's going to be?"

I said, "Yeah. At the end of the day, I take my vest off, you take your vest off, and we both bleed the same colour. What do you want?" That's when they got up and left. But the truce had already been agreed to by the mother chapters of both clubs, so it went through. I pissed off the local president a bit, but nothing happened between us.

So when I finally told this president in 2005 that I was done, he told me he was going to take my bike. I said, "Good luck. Come get it." He wouldn't have come for it because he knew he would've wound up in a grave out in the country somewhere. He didn't have the balls to stand up to me. I ended up giving my patch to a buddy who burned it for me and then he buried any small pieces that were left.

One day in early April, I woke up and just happened to flip on the TV. I see on the news that eight guys in my old club had been murdered in Shedden, Ontario. *Boom*, there it was, I recognized one of the cars and when I saw a picture of a body in the back of the car, I knew who that was.

The day I saw that news, I went and locked myself in my bedroom and didn't come out for three days. The faces of the dead guys came up in my dreams and I'd wake up in a cold sweat. I'd need to have alcohol and a couple of lines just to mellow out and get through a night. Later, I came to understand that those days were the beginning of my PTSD (Post-Traumatic Stress Disorder). I was self-medicating just to keep myself at level. Since I've been on my healing path, it's easier for me to talk about those days. Time has helped me heal.

Eight of the senior guys in my old motorcycle club were murdered. Six Manitoba guys were sentenced with six to eight counts of first-degree murder at the trial in 2009. All of them were from my old Manitoba chapter, including that ex-cop who was the president. My name was all over the papers while the trial was on because I had a connection to both the Toronto and Manitoba guys.

> I was self-medicating just to keep myself at level. Since I've been on my healing path, it's easier for me to talk about those days. Time has helped me heal.

At the same time, the Manitoba guys had gone out to Shedden to kill the Ontario members, two guys from Toronto had come to Winnipeg to see the guys here. While they were here, I drove them around. One guy was carrying a backpack. I played stupid but knew that there were handguns in it. Later, I realized the Toronto members were planning to kill those Winnipeg guys.

During the investigation, the OPP and Winnipeg's Organized Crime Unit came to visit me three times. I had moved from one small town outside Winnipeg to another, to lay low until I figured out what was going on. In the first visit, the cops wanted to know what I was doing. I told them I had quit the club the December before. I said, "You guys know that because it was all over the computer and you read the emails and I discussed it over phone lines that were tapped." So everybody knew what was going on.

The cops came back three months later and told me they'd found a cigarette butt out at the farm (the crime scene) and they wanted to do a blood sample on me for DNA. I said, "Okay, but you have to put the request on your letterhead and once my DNA's been tested and it's not attached to the cigarette butt, the DNA has to be thrown away and it cannot be used in any other cases."

They said, "You're kidding us!"

I said, "That's the only way you're going to get it." So they did as I asked and they didn't find any of my DNA on the butt.

The third visit was the doozy. This time the RCMP came as well. They said, "One, you weren't stupid enough to go with the club to Ontario. Two, you're lucky that the Manitoba guys had left for Ontario before the guys from Toronto came here to kill them because you would have been an accessory to the fact. Three, you were under investigation for eight counts of attempted murder, but you've been cleared." When I was with those two guys from Toronto, we had happened to go to one of the houses of a Manitoba guy they were looking for. His wife phoned him in Ontario and that call was heard by the police, so the cops knew I wasn't at the murder. My heart was in my throat the rest of the day after the cops left. I needed to null myself out for a while, so I went and snorted an eight ball of coke and drank some beer after their visit.

Shedden was a waste of life. It didn't have to go down that way. It was caused by the greed of people in that lifestyle. Look at what end those guys went to, to get where they wanted to be. Think of how little another life meant to them. Shedden happened because one greedy guy wanted to set everybody up so he could get a payday. Then he wanted to take over everything and have all the power

too. But it turned on him and now he's in jail. Karma's a bitch sometimes.

Then there was the involvement of the mother chapter in Texas. That's where the international president is. The club started there in the '60s. Supposedly they were having difficulties with Ontario—lack of communication or something like that. Texas saw the greed of the Winnipeg president and (I think) saw a golden opportunity to wash their hands of everything and get this Winnipeg idiot to take care of their problems in Canada. Texas left him and his guys holding the bag. That was a bullshit thing. They could've just taken everybody's patches instead. That's all I want to say.

That whole Shedden thing was a touch of reality for me, but you know what? It didn't stop me. As stupid as it sounds, it made me want to build another motorcycle club that would honour those eight guys and be in their memory. I wanted to pass on to other guys what they had taught me. After the murders, I did do some self-reflection and I tried to straighten myself out for a couple of years. I went to work at my day job and buried my feelings. I was trying to hang out with normal people, but I didn't fit in and I quickly became sick of the average Joe Blow citizen. Two or three times a week I'd hear someone talking stupid shit about Shedden that they didn't know nothing about. I had to bite my tongue. That started pissing me off more and more. It was bringing me back into the memories and emotions I wanted to forget and, although I didn't recognize it at the time, it was affecting my PTSD. I was miserable and angry. I couldn't blend into society; I didn't have the tools at that time. Eventually, I thought, *Fuck, I've had enough.* So I went back to what I knew best—the lifestyle of outlaw motorcycle clubs and drugs. That's how I got involved with the next club and started moving up the ladder even further.

A guy I knew well from my last club was organizing something and knew I'd be an asset. I had legit street cred. So in late 2008, we re-formed one of the motorcycle clubs that had been disbanded. At first, my position was VP across Canada, but when things started getting disorganized, I began enforcing my will onto the running of the club and slowly I took on more responsibility. I wound up being international vice-president. I was in charge of expansion and security. I was running western Canada, plus helping the head person down south expand the US operations. I really took a jump up. I still worked a day job too. I was doing road maintenance for a rural municipality. I never relied on my drug money. The money I made on the side, I mostly spent frivolously, although I saved a bit too. I was back living my life the way I wanted to live it.

I really got the right connections and everything fell together so I could sell more coke. It all went good until, like with everything else, greed got involved. I could've moved more coke, but I kept it to a minimum with certain guys and my club didn't like that. I still moved quite a bit—I don't want to say how much, but it was enough that I could have got double-digits in prison. The guys in the club wanted my drug connections to the supplier but wanted to have private meetings on the side. My drug connections didn't want that, didn't want to talk with them. So because I wouldn't make the introduction, I got greased out of the club (pushed out without the proper way of getting voted out by the club) in 2010.

I phoned the president who was running the US and let him know what had happened. We were close and he supported me. The US operation was just getting started and it was smaller than the Canadian one. He hadn't known anything about my being voted out. When he found this out, he collected all the patches and vests from the guys down there and sent it up to the guys in Canada and told them to shove it up their asses—he and his guys were done too.

Then two or three months later, in late 2010, I got a call from this same guy down south about another club that wanted to approach me. They wanted to move up into Canada. I took my time and talked to them on the phone on and off for a few months. At first, they told me what I wanted to hear. I was still pissed off at my last club, so maybe I had blinders on a bit more than I should have. I shouldn't have joined, but I wanted to get back at my last club. So I joined and I ratified over the phone. I got my colours (my patches) sent to me. I already had a custom vest. I became the Canadian national president and a nomad patch holder.

Nomad patch holder means that I was free to travel anywhere without having to report in to different chapters of the club in other areas. In the motorcycle club lifestyle, that means you are the elite of the elite. I could show up anywhere and say, "I'm here, deal with it." There aren't many clubs that don't have a nomad chapter. When they see the nomad patch on a vest, most guys are going to take a second thought before they try something.

But I was under a lot of stress trying to set up another new club. It takes a lot when you're trying to get a club off the ground, and trying to find the right people for the right spots. You've got to deal with the politics of the other clubs too. I was getting burnt out. The fun factor and excitement were long gone. After I got things established in Alberta, I passed on the president position to a guy in Calgary. I made it public through an open phone line (so the cops tapping the phone would know).

In 2012, a guy I knew called me looking for some coke. The amount wasn't out of the ordinary and his call didn't set off any alarms for me. At that time, I was not selling drugs anymore. I had no solid contacts because my business partner had gone to prison. While I'd been running the last club and moving large amounts of coke, my partner got arrested in a drug project. His driver became a paid agent in that case and my partner got double digits (twelve years) in jail. So I set up the deal through my cousin. We did the deal in the guy's car, but I didn't know his vehicle was wired with audio and video. The guy was a paid agent. I got arrested. The cops got my cousin and me: conspiracy to traffic, trafficking cocaine, and proceeds of crime (because I took the money out of the deal).

I had no previous record except for an impaired driving charge. In court, everything got reduced down to one count of trafficking conspiracy and I got sentenced to three-and-a-half years. I was in Milner Correctional pretrial custody for a year, but that didn't count for nothing. So I went to Stony in November 2012 for six months and then I was transferred to the minimum-security Rockwood because I had never been in prison before. I was low risk on everything.

At that time, I became de-rated. That means I had proven to police that I'd had no contact with ex-associates or members of the clubs I'd once been in. I was made inactive on the gang list, but I would still have a gang or club name attached to me for a very long time. I got out of Rockwood on March 13, 2015.

SOMETIMES, I SAY THAT MY TIME IN JAIL was just time, but really, it wasn't. I got my high school GED in prison and I learned about my Aboriginal background and culture. I knew I had Aboriginal blood in me, but I felt no connection to Aboriginal traditions and spirituality. I didn't tell too many people about my background and I didn't really want to dig into it. I was embarrassed. I had looked at Aboriginals like a bunch of drunks. I was responding to what I saw. I was naïve like a lot of other people are who have opinions, but don't try to educate themselves. I didn't know anything about residential schools or the '60s Scoop.

The first sweat lodge I went to was at Rockwood. My old martial arts instructor, Kirt Prince, who had passed away in November 2011, came to me in a vision during the sweat. (Around the time of his death, I knew the cops were looking for me, so I couldn't go to his funeral. Missing his funeral really damaged me. It made me angry too.) I remember that vision vividly. Kirt and I were in a field and he walked across it to me. He put his hand on my shoulder and all this black stuff came pouring out of my mouth. It was all the crap and anger inside of me.

In the vision, Kirt said to me, "Everything will be okay. It's going to take a while, but everything will get better." He had told me that in real life too, years before, but I didn't listen then.

During that vision is when my emotions finally came back to the surface. I cried in the sweat lodge in the dark, with my face in my towel. I had not cried in ten years since my grandmother passed away in 2003. It felt good to cry, to have the release, to let all that anger and bitterness and hatred out—everything that had built up inside. I let go. I cried later that night too, when I went to bed, because I just kept picturing my vision.

I thanked Kirt for coming to me, but I didn't want to face my vision. I was still pissed off that I was in prison. Plus, the elders that were at Rockwood at that time were just there for the payday and weren't investing their time or caring. I tried to get a few things going. I was head of the Aboriginal Welfare Committee at Rockwood and I got the drum group initiated again, but I couldn't light a fire under the elders' asses at that time.

It took me going to prison to finally have somebody who didn't judge me, someone who opened up the doors to teach me about my traditions and ceremonies and help me learn about myself.

Then a couple of good elders came to work at Rockwood: Brian McLeod and Joe Big George. They had a big influence on my life, especially Brian. Nothing seemed to faze him and that intrigued me. The first time we met, there was a connection between us right off the hop. We felt like we'd known each other for a long time. He is such a loving and caring guy. I started spending a lot of time with Brian. Right up to this day, I call him my brother. We try to talk two or three times a week on the phone or we'll meet for coffee. He is a very special person to me.

It took me going to prison to finally have somebody who didn't judge me, someone who opened up the doors to teach me about my traditions and ceremonies and help me learn about myself. It's a sad state of affairs that there aren't more people like Brian and Joe around who open their hearts and their minds and are willing to pass on to others the teachings that have been passed on to them.

When Brian came over to Rockwood, that's when everything started to change for me. Brian would throw questions at me about cleaning up my heart, dealing with my emotions and starting to love myself. Brian told me that if I couldn't love myself, I was not going to be able to love somebody else. He encouraged me to trust in Creator, Grandmother and Grandfather. Brian told me I'd get what I needed when I needed it. It took me a while to let go and start trusting.

I met another great guy who has inspired me while I was at Rockwood: Mitch Bourbonniere. His nephew was there too and he had told me about Mitch and the work he was doing with youth at risk. I was intrigued. So one day when Mitch came for a gathering, I introduced myself. I saw him a few times. He gave me his card and told me to give him a call when I got out. So I called him the day after I got out. It was a Saturday. He was out with a group of kids he helps, delivering mattresses to needy single parents. I told him that I was having major anxiety and needed to get out of my house. He stopped what he was doing, came to pick me up, bringing the kids. I went out delivering mattresses with them that day and our friendship bloomed from there. Me and Mitch have got a beautiful relationship too. He is another person that really cares about me and I care about him.

I volunteer time with Mitch when I can, at sweat lodges or events, or if his staff is having troubles reaching some of his kids, then I talk to them. One day, soon after I got out of prison, I went with Mitch to a sweat lodge. There were quite a few young guys there. I was tending the sacred fire, but on the third round of the sweat (the healing round) Billy Dubery, who was running things, invited me to come in. I prayed about what I was going to say and then I said a little speech. I said that if I could ask for help and support and move on with my life, then these young guys could too. I told them I felt like I had wasted the last twenty-five years of my life. I announced to the spirit world that day that I was done with club stuff. When I made my statement, I put my nomad patch and international club patches from my last club into the fire. The burning of my patches was more significant than my words. The fire had been starting to die out— it was only eight or nine inches high. But when I put those patches in, the fire flared up to almost six feet and it kept burning until I was done speaking. I didn't speak for those kids; I spoke for myself. I didn't know it until the next day, but there were three or four guys present that Mitch was having troubles getting through to.

I had a curfew and had to be home by 10 pm, so I left. But Mitch and those kids stayed around the fire until almost 1 am. They started opening up and crying. Mitch called me the next day and he was so excited. He said, "You have no idea what you did last night, do you?" I told him not really. Mitch had been trying for a year to get those kids to talk and I was able to do it in one night.

Some of those kids needed to hear my story and where I'd come from to show them that change is possible. It's a lot of work, but it is possible. That night they were awestruck. Most of those kids will never see the level of organized crime that I've seen. It is what it is. I've got to use the tools that I've got. But I don't put the emphasis on my past as much as I do on where I am today. Yes, I'm struggling every day, but I still wake up and, hopefully, each day is better.

It took a couple of days for what happened that night at the sweat to sink in. I was so fresh out of jail and just trying to get used to the pace of being outside. But it made me think that I had something to offer and that if I didn't continue working with youth, everything in my life was going to be for naught. I don't want to just piss away twenty-five years of my life, which I will if I don't take the opportunity to help other people. That night pushed me to where I am now, wanting to work with youth at risk. I hope to plant a seed in some kid's head. That's why I am doing this book too. Maybe I can help someone.

WHY WAS I SO SUCCESSFUL in organized crime? Well...I was always good at multitasking. I could have ten or twelve things on the go, plus a day job, and not even blink an eye. I think that's my ADD. Then there was my character that was formed from all the sports I played. I could deal with whatever came my way. And if something did knock me down, I'd get back up real quick and chalk it up to a lesson learned. I am mentally tough and resilient.

I was also really good at crime because I put a lot of time and effort into studying how the police acted. When you have a club patch, you are automatically under investigation by the cops. I had a buddy who was suing the RCMP over an incident and he got their parameters (the paper work) on how they had to conduct themselves. I took that and studied it and studied it. I would create a structure and routine in my day and I'd make minute changes to set a trap, to see if things around me weren't quite right, if there were cars or people that seemed out of place. Then I'd know I was being watched.

I was also very careful with what phone I talked on. I could figure out if my phone was being tapped because I'd give a few details and see if the cops acted on them. When I wanted a private phone, I'd use a burner phone. (In layman's terms, that's a pay-as-you-go phone.) We used to be able to buy one and register the phone to a fake name and address. I was always a step ahead. That's why it took the cops almost a decade to catch me.

I am also really good at reading people and I can do it real quick. I get a gut feeling around people I shouldn't be with. I also used to rely on my dogs because they could tell me straight out if I should trust someone or not. If my terrier mix, Badger, put his nose up and wouldn't go near a person, I'd know that person was no good. I trust dogs more than I trust people.

When it comes to certain things, I excel really quick, faster that the average person. I look at life scenarios, take the whole 360-degree perspective and start to pick it apart. I can see the parts and the whole. Plus, I can anticipate bad stuff coming that other people don't expect. It's from all the years I had to protect myself on a daily basis.

When I was a kid, I had a complex that I didn't measure up in school. I got degraded a bit by my parents—it was the way they came at me. Like with math, I had to do flash cards every night with my dad standing over top of me like a jail instructor trying to plow the schoolwork into me. I used to ask myself, *Why can't I learn at the rate the other kids are learning?* I put that stigma on myself. But now, if you ask me, *Do you think you're smart?* I'd say, *Yes.* If I could give advice to my ten-year-old self then, I'd say, *Everything takes time.* But I'm still not good at giving myself time to go through things. I am impatient and hard on myself. A lot of people look at me and shake their heads and say, "If you would've taken all that effort and knowledge that you have and used it for something good…" Yeah, but who knows?

MY DAD HASN'T TALKED TO ME since I got arrested in 2012. But in January of that year, just before I got arrested, my mom and

I rekindled our relationship. We had not spoken in thirteen years. We've been tight ever since. She came to visit me in Stony and Rockwood every weekend until I got released.

I was married from 2003 until 2009, when my wife started liking the cocaine a bit too much and became a liability. Then she fucked up and showed me she didn't have my back, so I put the club before her and told her the marriage was done. We never had any kids because of the lifestyle I was leading. I didn't want to worry about leaving kids behind if I had to cut and run. And I didn't want kids growing up with me, figuring that my lifestyle would be all right, because I wouldn't want to wish it on anybody. I would've been bringing a defenceless person into the world that I couldn't be sure I could care for.

Now, I have a new wife. We got married in 2017. Mitch was in my wedding party. I knew her back in 2008 because she trained at the same martial arts dojo as me. Then later, her son was at Rockwood with me and when she was visiting him, we saw each other. She asked her son to ask me if she could write me letters while I was in prison. She's got two girls and three boys. Two of her kids live with us today. And I have two dogs: an

KEITH LEVIT

eight-year-old Staffordshire terrier (aka a Pitbull) and I've still got that husky. Justice and Tango: those are my kids.

My wife is very humble, forthcoming, loving, and caring. She doesn't get fazed easily. I am in awe of her, and she inspires me. She is the way I strive to be, but I've still got this hard core inside of me. I'm upfront and I tell it the way it is. People around me know to expect it. That's the type of person I am. My wife will look at me, smile, shake her head, and say, "You are such an asshole sometimes." But my friend, Brian, says that my straight talk is a gift and that some people need to hear it.

I do wear my heart on my sleeve. I've always wanted to help people in need— even when I was in the club. Back then, I might have looked like I was weak, but nobody had the balls to step up and say anything. Today, my emotions are all out. Everything. Some days it's hell because I have to learn how to deal with them. When my emotions first started opening up, I cried a lot. Shit, the first few months after I started dating my wife, my faucets were running and I was crying two or three times a week. It was all the years I had suppressed my emotions and memories. I had to learn to settle down and just focus on one memory or feeling at a time. I still deal with this today, but it's manageable.

But if somebody thinks I'm soft, they are wrong. There is nothing soft about me. If I ever had to defend my family, I'd put my life on the line. I will do that for anybody I love. Now I'm not being soft, I'm just being what a man is supposed to be. I used to have a grand delusion of what that was, but it was a false sense back then because of the lifestyle I led. I was portraying what I *thought* a man was

supposed to be. Now, I know I don't need to suck it up and it's okay to cry. You can only pack so much shit away before you need to release it through your emotions. I think it's better to take ten minutes of crying to process something, so it doesn't cloud my thinking. I don't give a shit what people think about me, except the people I love and who love me back.

One of my hopes for the future is that my old ways of thinking become more and more distant. I want to be a happier person. Sometimes when I am around happy people, I get pissed off because I want a little more of that too. I think I'll be happier if I have a little more humility and humbleness in my life. I've just got to keep working on myself every day. I'm so used to being in control. It came with the lifestyle because I *had* to control things. It's hard giving up the control factor and just blending back into society. Now, I have to leave things to fate more, to accept that I can't really control a lot in life. It's a daily challenge for me. Also, I am used to looking for the worst in a situation. If I can change my thinking to look for the good that could happen, life will get easier. I know that with time, more happiness will eventually come my way.

But I will never forget where I've come from or what I've done because that is what makes me who I am.

I looked into doing my social work degree, but at my age and with the bills I've got to pay, a four- or six-year course is too long. I really wanted to open my own consulting firm and help youth at risk. Mitch says that if I could turn my life experience into a degree, I'd have a doctorate in ten seconds. But it's hard to get started and I needed income, so I've had a few different jobs, mostly driving trucks. It is really important to me to give my wife and her kids a good life.

FAMILIES ARE FACING SO MUCH and kids face shitty situations every day. Life is so fucking messed up. There's a lot of stress out there. People are losing their jobs, money doesn't go as far as it used to, there's poverty and addiction. If families can get the help they need, they can start loving their kids. A lot of kids can get turned around onto the right path or into the right people if they've got love and support at home. If it wasn't for my grandparents, I would have missed having that love too. The main thing is loving and caring about your family.

Jamie is a regular at NA (Narcotics Anonymous) and even chairs some meetings. He says this about addiction: "It's an everyday struggle. No matter how many years you are away from it. If you don't have the proper tools or supports, it can creep back into your life. Nowadays, there are so many struggles and stresses in life. I need to be around people who suffer with the same type of stuff. It took a lot of strength and courage to walk through the doors of NA, but I am so grateful that I did."

Jamie says he knows himself well. I found him to be insightful, self-aware, and highly emotionally intelligent.

In June of 2017, Jamie's trusted canine companion, Justice, passed away. Jamie says he misses him every day and that Justice taught him so much about life. Jamie says, "I will eventually get another dog, but nothing could replace Justice in my heart."

Acknowledgements

THERE WOULD BE NOTHING HERE TO READ if not for the courageous and trusting participants of this book. Thank you for sharing your lives with me, sometimes in very intimate ways. Your strength, and the strength of those who love you, inspires me. Thank you Keith Levit, for your beautiful portraits and volunteering your time so generously. And thank you Andrew Mahon, for the evocative cover photograph of the Arlington Street Train Bridge, which is located in the heart of Winnipeg's gang turf. Thank you Father Greg Boyle, for your beautiful book *Tattoos on the Heart*, which started this whole adventure, for your thoughtful foreword, and for your support, wisdom, and tremendous kindness. Thank you to my dear friend and first-draft editor, Marjorie Anderson, for *getting it*. Thank you to Mitch Bourbonniere, a loyal friend to many and the first champion of this book. Thank you to all the generous people who took the time to speak with me during my research phase and especially those who introduced me to possible participants: Shaun Loney, Abdi Ahmed, Matt Fast, Mitch Bourbonniere, Cora Morgan, Ervin Chartrand, Jamil Mahmood, Wally Swain, and Dave Christmas. Thank you to the places that allowed us to use space for interviews: Magnus Eliason Recreation Centre, Spence Neighbourhood Association, St. Timothy's Church, and especially Onashowewin. Thank you to the first-draft readers for your time, attention to detail, and helpful comments: Joe McClellan, Cathy

Finnbogason, Catherine Shields, Paula Isaak, Renate Schulz, Mitch Bourbonniere, Dave Christmas, and Tim Byrne. Thank you to all those at Great Plains Publications and Relish Design, and especially to my editor, Ingeborg Boyens, for your dedication to making this book as strong as possible. Special thank yous to Clayton Sandy for enabling my first sweat lodge, S. Laurette Doiron, and Emily Brownell. Thank you to the Winnipeg Foundation for your generous grant that will distribute 400 copies of this book throughout Manitoba. Also, my thanks to the Manitoba Library Association (and Alix-Rae Stefanko) and the John Howard Society of Manitoba (and Executive Director John Hutton) for your invaluable support. Finally, I thank my mom, Donna Thain, for always being a good listener, and my family: Paul, Kendra, Mark, and Andrew, for trusting me and loving me no matter what.

AMDG

Some Great Books

Bernardo, Sabrina, *Inner City Girl Like Me*, Harper Trophy, Canada, 2009.

Boyle, Gregory, *Tattoos on the Heart: The Power of Boundless Compassion*, Free Press a Division of Simon Schuster, New York NY, 2010.

Chettleburgh, Michael, *Young Thugs: Inside the Dangerous World of Canadian Street Gangs*, Harper Collins, Canada, 2008.

Comack, Elizabeth, Deane, Lawrence, Morrissette, Larry, and Silver, Jim, *Indians Wear Red: Colonialism, Resistance and Aboriginal Street Gangs*, Fernwood Publishing, Winnipeg, 2013.

Fast, Matt, *Finding Their Way Again:The Experiences of Gang Affected Refugees,* Fernwood Publishing, Winnipeg, 2017.

Fremon, Celeste, *G-Dog and the Homeboys: Father Greg Boyle and The Gangs of East Los Angeles*, University of New Mexico Press, United States of America, 1995.

Friesen, Joe, *The Ballad of Danny Wolfe: Life of a Modern Outlaw*, Signal, a Division of McClelland and Stewart, Canada, 2016.

Henry, Robert, *Brighter Days Ahead*, Hear My Heart Books Inc., Saskatoon SK, 2013.

John Howard Society, Saskatoon Branch, *STR8UP and Gangs: The Untold Story*, Hear My Heart Books, Saskatoon SK, 2012.

Leap, Jorja, *Jumped In: What Gangs Taught me about Violence, Drugs, Love, and Redemption*, Beacon Press, Boston, 2012.

Masters, Jarvis Jay, *Finding Freedom: Writings from Death Row*, Padma Publishing, Junction City CA, 1997.

Stevenson, Bryan, *Just Mercy: A Story of Justice and Redemption*, Spiegel and Grau an imprint of Random House, United States, 2015.

Totten, Mark, *Gang Life: 10 of The Toughest tell their Stories*, James Lorimer and Co. Publishers, Toronto ON, 2014.

Totten, Mark, *Nasty, Brutish and Short: The Lives of Gang Members in Canada*, James Lorimer and Co. Publishers, Toronto ON, 2012.

Venkatesh, Sudhir, *Gang Leader For A Day: A Rogue Sociologist Takes To The Streets*, Penguin Books, USA, 2008.

Discussion Questions

What were your expectations before reading this book? How were the stories similar or different to those expectations?

Were there specific stories that challenged you? Surprised you? Which ones and why?

Do you know anyone who has been in a gang, incarcerated, or drug addicted?

How do the stories in this book differ from the stories we see in the media about criminals and gang members?

What attributes helped the participants in the book to get out of gangs? Stay out?

What role does faith in a higher power play in these personal stories?

Is joining a gang a choice? What role does survival play in joining a gang? Discuss these concepts in the context of the stories in the book.

Almost all the participants in the book were quite successful in their gangs (founding members, officers). Why do you think this was the case?

What stories inspired you?

Anonymous tells of being close to deportation. Do you feel the judge should have deported him or was wise to give him a chance?

Did you react to Regina's story any differently than to the men's stories in the book? Why?

What contributes to people joining gangs? What contributes to them leaving successfully?

How do gender, class, race, poverty, and culture affect the participants in this book?

Winnipeg has been called "Canada's Aboriginal street-gang capital." Do you feel colonization and residential schools have any role in the prevalence of Indigenous gangs in the city? Explain.

Do you believe people can change?

Compare and contrast the story of *Anonymous*, who was a refugee, with the stories of the Indigenous participants (Ian, Chris, Regina, Ervin, Jamie). How were their circumstances similar? Different?

Participants seemed to be affected by witnessing violence early in their lives through either their home or community. Can cycles of violence be broken? If so, how?

Were you surprised at how participants articulated concepts of goodness and virtue in their stories? Why?

Jamie contrasts his old view of how a man was supposed to act with his current view today. How did suppressing emotions affect the participants in this book? How does this affect men today?

What role does opportunity and hope play in exiting a gang? What forms does this take in the book?

Index